ORIENTALIST POETICS

To
Philip and Robby
and to the memory of
George

Orientalist Poetics
The Islamic Middle East in nineteenth-century English and French poetry

EMILY A. HADDAD

Ashgate

Aldershot • Burlington USA • Singapore • Sydney

© Emily A. Haddad 2002

All rights reserved. No part of this publication may be reproduced, stored in a retrieval system, or transmitted in any form or by any means, electronic, mechanical, photocopying, recording or otherwise without the prior permission of the publisher.

Emily A. Haddad has asserted her moral right under the Copyright, Designs and Patents Act, 1988, to be identified as the author of this work.

Published by
Ashgate Publishing Limited
Gower House
Croft Road
Aldershot
Hants GU11 3HR
England

Ashgate Publishing Company
131 Main Street
Burlington, VT 05401-5600 USA

Ashgate website: http://www.ashgate.com

British Library Cataloguing in Publication Data
Haddad, Emily A.
   Orientalist poetics : the Islamic Middle East in
nineteenth-century English and French poetry. - (Nineteenth
century series)
   1. English poetry - 19th century - History and criticism
   2. French poetry - 19th century - History and criticism
   3. Middle East - In literature
   I. Title
   821.8'09956

Library of Congress Cataloging-in-Publication Data
Haddad, Emily A.
   Orientalist poetics : the Islamic Middle East in nineteenth-century English and French poetry/ Emily A. Haddad.
      p. cm. -- (The nineteenth century series)
   Includes bibliographical references (p.   ) and index.
   ISBN 0-7546-0304-0 (alk. paper)
   1. English poetry--Oriental influences. 2. Middle East--In literature. 3. English poetry--19th century--History and criticism. 4. French poetry--19th century--History and criticism. 5. Civilization, Islamic, in literature. 6. French poetry--Oriental influences. 7. Islam in literature. 8. Orientalism. I. Title. II. Nineteenth century (Aldershot, England)

PR129.M54 H33 2001
821'.8093256--dc21   2001046047

Printed and bound in Great Britain by MPG Books Ltd, Bodmin, Cornwall

ISBN 0 7546 0304 0

experimentation. Nineteenth-century orientalism's Orient functions as an alternative aesthetic space in which poems play out a variety of responses to both contemporary and past trends in poetry. Orientalist poetics does not yield a single, unified approach; rather, it provides a medium for the cultivation and refinement of a broad range of poetic positions. Thus Wordsworth's devotion to nature, Hugo's to poets' autonomy, Shelley's to liberal political morality, Robert Southey's to poetry as information, Gautier's to art for art's sake, Tennyson's to the social context of art, and Oscar Wilde's to art's freedom from what he calls "the prison-house of realism"[6] are all asserted and confirmed through the mediation of orientalism.

Given orientalism's infiltration of the nineteenth century's poetic oeuvre, it should come as no surprise that orientalism has had an extensive and important impact on the large developments of nineteenth-century British and French poetics and poetry. However, that impact has not been fully addressed by critics. From M.H. Abrams's *The Mirror and the Lamp* (1953) to Isobel Armstrong's *Victorian Poetry* (1993), overviews of poetics are relatively disinterested in orientalism. Since the appearance of Edward Said's *Orientalism* (1978), a number of critics have undertaken serious studies of literary orientalism, but like Said they do not pursue in depth the interaction between orientalism and nineteenth-century poetics in general. This book bridges the gap between the analysis of poetics and the analysis of orientalism; its aim is to demonstrate orientalism's centrality to the evolution of poetry and poetics in France and Britain during this period. Specifically, it will show how orientalism functions as a diffuse avant-garde, a matrix for the reexamination of both preexisting conventions and contemporary expectations in poetry and poetics. In suggesting that major poetic developments have roots in orientalism, this book offers a revisionist view of the literary history of the nineteenth century.

The notion of the Orient that underlies this version of orientalism is more narrowly defined than the nineteenth century's grand idea of the oriental. Nineteenth-century poets and readers could perceive the oriental virtually anywhere between Greece and the Pacific Ocean. At times, orientalism's Orient appears as a monolith, its constituents undifferentiated, occasionally to the point that "oriental" stands simply for "exotic" or "other" rather than for any identifiable region. At other times, the Orient is represented with clearly drawn features that indicate a specific geographic location. But among the nineteenth century's several oriental "others," the Islamic Middle East is primary; as Raymond Schwab argues, "The Islamic Orient [...] is the Orient most acclimated in our literary traditions, which have, in every case, abandoned other orients whenever there has been a massive return of the

---

[6] Wilde, "The Decay of Lying," *The Complete Works of Oscar Wilde*, ed. J.B. Foreman. (London: Collins, 1983) 981.

Introduction

Throughout the nineteenth century, British and French poets wrote widely and often on oriental topics. Even William Wordsworth, who was never an enthusiastic orientalist, participated, sketching the Orient as a place of risk and fantasy,

> Stocked with Pachas, Seraskiers,
> Slaves, and turbaned Buccaneers;
> Sensual Mussulmen atrocious,
> Renegados, more ferocious![1]

Percy Bysshe Shelley saw instead a languid woman lying "in the paradise of Lebanon / Under a heaven of cedar boughs."[2] Victor Hugo found a city of crescents, blue domes, and great harems in which sultanas danced on silk carpets to the sound of drums.[3] Théophile Gautier observed Muslim pilgrims who counted amber rosaries and an Egyptian peasant woman who, in the guise of a sphinx, "propose[d] a riddle to desire."[4] For Alfred Tennyson, on the other hand, the East was a "Land of bright eye and lofty brow! / Whose every gale is balmy breath / Of incense from some sunny flower."[5]

The striking diversity of these visions of the East reflects the fertility of the Islamic Orient as a poetic source. The Orient's appeal to poets was formidable throughout the nineteenth century, more obviously in the early decades, but in increasingly complex and aesthetically significant ways later on. A comprehensive anthology of nineteenth-century orientalist poetry would include poems by almost every British or French poet of the time; poets made reputations and even a living from writing poems on oriental topics. These poets were united in a sense of the Orient as an arena for poetic

---

[1] William Wordsworth, *Poems*, ed. John O. Hayden, vol. 2 (London: Penguin, 1977) 309; the citation is from "Mary Barker's Lines Addressed to a Noble Lord," written 1814.

[2] Percy Bysshe Shelley, *The Complete Poetical Works of Percy Bysshe Shelley*, ed. Thomas Hutchinson (New York: Oxford UP, 1933) 660; the lines are from an 1821 fragment, "The Lady of the South."

[3] Victor Hugo, *Odes et ballades, Les Orientales*, ed. Jean Gaudon (Paris: Flammarion, 1968) 340; the poem is "Les Têtes du sérail" ["The Heads of the Seraglio"], published 1829.

[4] Théophile Gautier, *Poésies Complètes de Théophile Gautier*, ed. René Jasinski, vol. 3 (Paris: Nizet, 1970) 94, 112; the poems are "Ce que disent les hirondelles" ["What the Swallows Say"] and "La Fellah" ["The Fellah"], written 1859 and 1861, respectively. The cited line is "Propose une énigme au désir," from "La Fellah."

[5] Alfred Tennyson, *The Poems of Tennyson*, ed. Christopher Ricks, vol. 1 (Berkeley: U of California P, 1987) 114; these are the opening lines of "Persia," published 1827.

nineteenth-century Europe remained the *Thousand and One Nights*. Antoine Galland's French translation appeared beginning in 1704, with the first English version recorded in 1706; there were four English editions by 1713.[10] Three major new English translations of the *1001 Nights* from Arabic sources were published in the course of the nineteenth century.[11]

The *1001 Nights* exercised a uniquely powerful hold on nineteenth-century European imaginations and played an important role in the implicit designation of the Islamic East as an amimetic space. As Frances Mannsåker points out, the *1001 Nights* "largely pre-dates the scholarly and the experienced discoveries" of the Orient; as a result, it is able to establish the terms for Europe's interpretation of the East.[12] It is understood to represent with exciting accuracy the places it portrays; as Galland proclaims in the foreword to his translation of the *1001 Nights*,

> Tous les Orientaux, Persans, Tartares et Indiens, s'y font distinguer, et paraissent tels qu'ils sont, depuis les Souverains jusqu'aux personnes de la plus basse condition. Ainsi, sans avoir essuyé la fatigue d'aller chercher ces Peuples dans leur Pays, le Lecteur aura ici le plaisir de les voir agir, et de les entendre parler.[13]

Construction of the European Image of the Orient: A Bicentenary Reappraisal of Sir William Jones as Poet and Translator," *Comparative Criticism* 8 (1986): 167–88.

[10] The *1001 Nights*' publication and reception in England has been studied extensively. Useful sources include Leila Ahmed, *Edward W. Lane* (London: Longman, 1978) chs. 6–8; Muhsin Jassim Ali, *Scheherazade in England: A Study of Nineteenth-Century English Criticism of the Arabian Nights* (Washington: Three Continents Press, 1981); Peter L. Caracciolo, ed., *The Arabian Nights in English Literature: Studies in the Reception of The Thousand and One Nights into British Culture* (London: Macmillan, 1988); Husain Haddawy, introduction, *The Arabian Nights* (New York: W.W. Norton, 1990); Robert Irwin, *The Arabian Nights: A Companion* (London: Allen Lane, 1994); and Sari J. Nasir, *The Arabs and the English* (London: Longman, 1979) ch. 3.

[11] These translations are by Edward Lane (1838–41), John Payne (1882–84), and Richard Burton (1885–88).

[12] Frances Mannsåker, "Elegancy and Wildness: Reflections of the East in the Eighteenth-Century Imagination," *Exoticism in the Enlightenment*, ed. G.S. Rousseau and Roy Porter (Manchester: Manchester UP, 1990) 175.

[13] Antoine Galland, foreword, *Les Mille et une nuits: contes arabes traduits par Galland*, vol. 1. (Paris: Garnier, 1960) xxxii. The astonishing persistence of the belief in the *Nights*' truthfulness is revealed in Marie E. de Meester's unselfconscious assertion — in a supposedly scholarly book in 1915 — that "The *Arabian Nights* [...] have imprinted on our minds many scenes of oriental life. This last point is among the greatest merits of the *Thousand and One Nights*: they give such a faithful picture of the Orient, its life and customs, that many people who afterwards happen to visit those countries seem to be quite familiar with them already. The best authorities on oriental conditions and manners have attested the veracity of the scenes described in the Nights [sic]" (de Meester, *Oriental Influences in the English Literature of the Nineteenth Century* [Heidelberg: Carl Winters, 1915] 13). For further discussion of this phenomenon, see Ali, *Scheherazade in England* 91–2; and Haddawy, *The Arabian Nights* xxi.

picturesque Mussulman whose charm recaptures poets and storytellers through the glamour of the *Thousand and One Nights*."[7]

Thus although in some respects the Islamic Middle East can be seen simply as one exotic locale among many, the specificity of both Islam and the Middle East is significant. Nineteenth-century aesthetics constitutes the Islamic Orient in particular as a fundamentally amimetic site. Because the problem of poetry's relationship with mimetic representation underlies the various troublesome issues of nineteenth-century poetics, the Islamic East thus becomes an obvious milieu for the exploration of essential questions such as: What is the purpose of poetry? Does (or should) poetry represent the empirical world? Does (or should) nature serve as a basis for poetic representation, and if so, how? What is the relationship between nature (however construed) and art (in general as well as specifically in poetry)? So despite the current critical emphasis on orientalist poetry as a cultural artifact manifesting European attitudes towards the Orient and imperialism, it is clear that we must also consider orientalist poems from the point of view of aesthetics, taking into account their participation in the nineteenth century's negotiation of major poetic concepts and problems.

The Islamic Orient's usefulness in this regard derives from a number of European assumptions about mimetic representation as it is practiced in both oriental and orientalist discourses. First of all, because of Islamic cultures' well-known disapproval of depictions of the human figure, and because of the predominance of geometric motifs and of calligraphy in certain forms of Middle Eastern visual art, Europeans often assumed that oriental art was not representational.[8] This position was confirmed by the Middle Eastern literature available in translation at the time. Some small range of texts had been published in English or French by the beginning of the century; many were translated by William Jones (1746–1794), a prolific polymath who is often cited as the founder of orientalism. Jones's work as a translator, poet, critic, and linguist with expertise in Arabic, Persian, and Sanskrit had great impact on European poets and intellectuals around the turn of the century and into the 1800s.[9] Nonetheless, the most influential work of Middle Eastern literature in

---

[7] Raymond Schwab, *The Oriental Renaissance: Europe's Rediscovery of India and the East, 1680–1880*, 1950, trans. Gene Patterson-Black and Victor Reinking (New York: Columbia UP, 1984) 5.

[8] Europeans were of course also familiar with clearly referential forms of Middle Eastern art such as Persian miniature illustration. However, the intense stylization of such pictures, their failure to acknowledge the rules of perspective, and the divergence between their subject matter and the world as perceived by Europeans, combined to prevent these pictures from countering the assumption that oriental art was not representational.

[9] For comprehensive assessment of Jones's influence, see Garland Cannon, "Sir William Jones and Literary Orientalism," *Oriental Prospects: Western Literature and the Lure of the East*, ed. C.C. Barfoot and Theo D'haen (Amsterdam: Rodopi, 1998) 27–41; and "The

Acknowledgments

A poem may be the product of a single mind and heart, but a work of criticism usually is not. I have many people to thank for their help. First always are my husband, John Erikson, and my sons, Philip and Robby. I am grateful to my mother, Helen R. Haddad, for caring for my children so that I could complete my dissertation (the basis for this book), and to my father, Robert M. Haddad, for being the model of a committed and honest scholar. My sister Josette Haddad edited this book with more attention than it deserves. Leila Borowsky, George Haddad, Josette Generale, and Jean Rogerson provided cheering support at difficult moments.

The shape of this book owes much to Barbara Johnson, who directed my dissertation with sensitivity and brilliance, and to Sandra Naddaff, who introduced me to orientalism and whose clear perspective and warm friendship have been important to me for nearly twenty years. Stephen Owen and James Engell provided invaluable help with early drafts. Linda Simon has been a source of calm and good advice throughout. My thanks are due as well to Wheeler Thackston for comments on part of chapter 4, and to Amber Vogel for suggestions on the portion of chapter 3 published in modified form by the *Journal of African Travel-Writing*. Since receiving my doctorate from Harvard University and taking a position in the English Department at the University of South Dakota, I have been especially grateful to Susan Wolfe for her confidence in my work and for making sure that I had the time I needed to finish writing this book. I must also thank Sasha Erickson for assistance with research and Christelle Gonthier for checking my translations of French texts.

I would not have been in a position to undertake this project without the financial support of several institutions. Grants from the Fulbright Foundation and the Center for Arabic Study Abroad enabled me to study in Cairo for almost two years. A Jacob Javits Fellowship supported much of my graduate education. I completed my dissertation with the help of a fellowship from the Whiting Foundation. Support for additional research was provided by a faculty development grant from the University of South Dakota.

I acknowledge with thanks permission to quote copyrighted material from Oxford University Press and from Société d'édition "Les Belles Lettres."

This book was expertly guided through the publication process by Erika Gaffney of Ashgate Publishing. I am grateful also to Claire Annals, Alec McAuley, and Ruth Peters for additional help at various stages of that process.

[All the Orientals, Persians, Tartars, and Indians become distinct and appear such as they are, from the sovereigns to persons of the lowest condition. Thus, without having to endure the fatigue of going to seek out these peoples in their country, the reader will have here the pleasure of seeing their behavior and of hearing them speak.]

Paradoxically, the same *1001 Nights* that has such documentary value is also presumed to depict a world in which the possible and the impossible mingle uninhibited. In other words, the universe of the *1001 Nights* is one for which there is no correlate in nineteenth-century European experience; as orientalist Guillaume Pauthier said in 1840, it is "un de ces mondes fantastiques [...] qui ne présente pas même l'ombre de la réalité" [one of those fantastic worlds ... which does not present even the shadow of reality].[14] As European readers' foremost source on eighth-century Baghdad, the *1001 Nights*' accuracy is fundamentally unverifiable. So the text provides the effect of mimesis, but without entailing any obligation to an empirical reality. The constituent parts of that reality are, moreover, not even bound by the usual rules of verisimilitude; after all, who is to say what a genie can or cannot do?[15]

Of even greater importance than the *1001 Nights* and other oriental art is the growing body of European orientalism.[16] This material includes travel narratives, "translations" and imitations, and scholarly philology and ethnography. While some nineteenth-century poets consume orientalist texts more avidly than others, all rely upon them to some extent, whether as a source for information about the Islamic East or as a model for their own efforts. Like the *1001 Nights*, orientalist art and scholarship stand in a paradoxical relationship to reality and to the representation of reality. Because of orientalism's dependence upon its own past, texts often reveal their roots in preceding texts rather than in the Middle East as it might be experienced in the flesh.[17] As poets in turn ground their work in this already textually determined orientalist tradition, the empirical East tends to recede still further, becoming less a point of origin than one of oblique allusion. Thus whether poems follow oriental or orientalist models, they gain a double benefit from their oriental subject matter. On the one hand, they can plausibly claim to represent the truth

---

[14] Cited in Jean Bruneau, *Le "Conte oriental" de Flaubert* (Paris: Denoël, 1973) 16. Unlike many in his time, Pauthier also recognized the geographical East as distinct from that of the *1001 Nights*.

[15] One might compare the inclusion of figures from Greco-Roman mythology as supernatural elements in Western European poetry. A poem that includes a wood nymph must accommodate long-standing expectations about the character and behavior of wood nymphs, whereas one that includes a genie is much less constrained.

[16] Chapter 4 includes a discussion of the *Nights* with reference to poems by Felicia Hemans and Alfred Tennyson.

[17] Said emphasizes this point throughout his *Orientalism* (New York: Random House, 1978); see esp. 23, 305.

of the Orient. On the other hand, because of European readers' inability to verify poems' portrayals of the Orient, poets can manipulate their depictions unchecked. Through this paradoxical relationship with authenticity, orientalism offers an ideal point of entry for the destabilization of mimesis and of the other conventions of literary art that depend upon it.

Of the poems that are studied in this book, some, such as Robert Southey's *Thalaba the Destroyer* and Charles Leconte de Lisle's "L'Orient" are thoroughly orientalist, with Middle Eastern settings, Arab personae, and arabesque motifs. Others make more limited contact with the Orient. Such poems range from Felicia Hemans's "An Hour of Romance" and Victor Hugo's "Novembre," each built around an elaborate contrast between Europe and the Middle East; to William Wordsworth's "Septimi Gades," in which the Middle East offers a supplementary perspective on a principally European situation; to Thomas Moore's "Beauty and Song" and Théophile Gautier's "L'Art," in which the Middle East is merely implicit. These poems and the others analyzed in this book are representative of the varying degrees to which poetry of this period engages with the Orient. As a group, they reveal orientalism's progressive assimilation into nineteenth-century poetics.

Above all, these poems suggest that regardless of its level of conspicuous involvement in a poem, the Islamic Middle East is a consistently significant player in nineteenth-century poetics. Unlike early-twentieth-century avant-gardes, literary orientalism does not constitute an organized movement. Rather, it maintains a pervasive and flexible presence both within a range of movements, from romanticism to Parnassianism and aestheticism, and at the margins of these movements. In each case, orientalism emerges as a means towards alternatives to the literary status quo; those alternatives are as varied as the oriental imagery in which they are figured. At the same time, for instance, that Wordsworth can use orientalist imagery to establish the position of nature in his poetics, his contemporary Walter Savage Landor can use it to propose a view of the relationship between nature and poetic art that diverges sharply from the one advocated in Wordsworthian romanticism. Similarly, both Tennyson and Wilde call upon orientalism as they articulate views of art for art's sake, yet Tennyson is skeptical where Wilde is enthusiastic. Hugo's qualified acceptance of mimesis is figured through his orientalism, but so is Musset's dismissal of mimesis.

Like all other interpretations of orientalism since 1978, this book relies in certain respects upon the work of Edward Said. Although Said's analysis arises in part from those of other scholars, including Raymond Schwab, Norman Daniel, and Michel Foucault, his argument opens orientalism (and literary colonialism generally) to a largely new reading.[18] In brief, Said argues that the

---

[18] Earlier major works on orientalism and the literary and cultural relations between Europe and the East include Norman Daniel, *Islam and the West: The Making of an Image*

discourse of orientalism enables "European culture [...] to manage — and even produce — the Orient politically, sociologically, militarily, ideologically, scientifically, and imaginatively during the post-Enlightenment period," and further that "European culture gained in strength and identity by setting itself off against the Orient as a sort of surrogate and even underground self."[19] While Said's wide-ranging and polemical argument about orientalism is concerned with prose texts of many kinds, it gives only incidental attention to poetry, and none to how orientalism intersects with problems in poetics. Although my reading of orientalism by no means excludes the political, it diverges from Said's in holding its focus firmly on poetry and poetics.

Said's *Orientalism* has given rise to several trends in criticism of the cultural and literary relations between the Middle East and the West. Some critics, such as John MacKenzie, Maxime Rodinson, and Bryan S. Turner, cover much the same ground as Said, but with attitudes ranging from disinterest to skepticism to hostility towards his line of argument.[20] Said's impact on fields outside literature can be felt in the work of Zeynep Çelik in architecture, Timothy Mitchell in history, and Meyda Yegenoglu in gender studies, as well as more generally in the emergence of postcolonial studies as a full-fledged disciplinary category.[21] Chris Bongie and Patrick Brantlinger

---

(Edinburgh: Edinburgh UP, 1960); Daniel, *Islam, Europe and Empire* (Edinburgh: Edinburgh UP, 1966); and Raymond Schwab, *The Oriental Renaissance*. More specialized pre-Said treatments include Martha Pike Conant, *The Oriental Tale in England in the Eighteenth Century* (New York: Columbia UP, 1908); de Meester, *Oriental Influences in the English Literature of the Nineteenth Century*; Hichem Djaït, *L'Europe et l'Islam* (Paris: Éditions du seuil, 1978); Hassan El Nouty, *Le Proche-Orient dans la littérature française, de Nerval à Barrès* (Paris: Nizet, 1958); Albert Hourani, *Europe and the Middle East* (Berkeley: U of California P, 1980); Pierre Jourda, *L'Exotisme dans la littérature depuis Chateaubriand*, 2 vols. (Paris: Boivin, 1938, 1956); Dorothee Metlitzki, *The Matter of Araby in Medieval England* (New Haven: Yale UP, 1977); Sari J. Nasir, *The Arabs and the English*; Edna Osborne, *Oriental Diction and Theme in English Verse, 1740–1840* (Bulletin of the University of Kansas Humanistic Studies 2.1 [1916]); Byron Porter Smith, *Islam in English Literature* (Delmar, NY: Caravan Books, 1939; 2nd ed. 1977); R.W. Southern, *Western Views of Islam in the Middle Ages* (Cambridge: Harvard UP, 1962); and Jean-Jacques Waardenburg, *L'Islam dans le miroir de l'occident* (Paris: Mouton, 1963).

[19] Said, *Orientalism* 3. Of the many reviews of Said's book, Dennis Porter's is an especially useful one; see "*Orientalism* and Its Problems," *The Politics of Theory*, ed. Francis Barker et al. (Colchester, UK: University of Essex, 1983).

[20] John MacKenzie, *Orientalism: History, Theory and the Arts* (Manchester: Manchester UP, 1995); Maxime Rodinson, *Europe and the Mystique of Islam*, 1980, trans. Roger Veinus (Seattle: U of Washington P, 1991); and Bryan S. Turner, *Orientalism, Postmodernism and Globalism* (London: Routledge, 1994). See also Kathryn Tidrick, *Heart-beguiling Araby: The English Romance with Arabia* (Cambridge: Cambridge UP, 1981; rev. ed. 1989).

[21] Zeynep Çelik, *Displaying the Orient: Architecture of Islam at Nineteenth-Century World's Fairs* (Berkeley: U of California P, 1992); Timothy Mitchell, *Colonising Egypt* (Cambridge: Cambridge UP, 1988); and Meyda Yegenoglu, *Colonial Fantasies: Towards a Feminist Reading of Orientalism* (Cambridge: Cambridge UP, 1998). Other interdisciplinary analyses influenced by Said include Malek Alloula's study of French postcards of Algerian women, *The Colonial Harem*, 1981, trans. Myrna Godzich and Wlad Godzich (Minneapolis: U

represent those whose study of literature owes a debt to Said, but who seldom contend directly with his thesis or the material he analyzes.[22]

The approach most closely allied with my own is that exemplified by Ali Behdad, Nigel Leask, Lisa Lowe, Saree Makdisi, and Mohammed Sharafuddin. Each accepts Said's work as a foundation, but argues against a totalizing interpretation of orientalism and instead emphasizes its heterogeneity, both synchronically and diachronically.[23] Neither Behdad nor Lowe is concerned with the presence and implications of orientalism in poetry, although both critics offer valuable interpretations of prose texts. Poetry is Leask's focus; his interesting argument emphasizes imperialist politics and their self-destructive effects as manifested in poetry. Less persuasively, Sharafuddin proposes to rehabilitate orientalism in the course of analyzing a number of major romantic narrative poems. Like Leask, he does not contend with orientalist poetics as the important aesthetic problem it is. Makdisi does address that issue, arguing that the Orient, like nature, operates as a "pre- or anti-modern" space from which British romantic poets engage in a "critique of modernization."[24] However, Makdisi's otherwise compelling analysis does not account for certain essential distinctions between nature's role and the Islamic Orient's; while the Orient undoubtedly joins nature in standing at a great distance from modernity and the forces of modernization, its function in poetry is both more avant-garde than nature's and indeed often juxtaposed to nature's.

---

of Minnesota P, 1986); and the collection of essays in cultural studies edited by Mahmut Mutman and Meyda Yegenoglu, *Orientalism and Cultural Differences*, Inscriptions 6 (Santa Cruz: Center for Cultural Studies, University of California at Santa Cruz, 1992).

[22] Bongie, *Exotic Memories: Literature, Colonialism, and the Fin de Siècle* (Stanford: Stanford UP, 1991); and Patrick Brantlinger, *Rule of Darkness: British Literature and Imperialism, 1830–1914* (Ithaca: Cornell UP, 1988). For other studies taking a comparable approach, see Jonathan Arac and Harriet Ritvo, eds., *Macropolitics of Nineteenth-Century Literature: Nationalism, Exoticism, Imperialism* (Philadelphia: U of Pennsylvania P, 1991); Claudine Grossir, *L'Islam des Romantiques*, vol. 1 (Paris: Maisonneuve et Larose, 1984); Rana Kabbani, *Imperial Fictions: Europe's Myths of Orient* (London: Pandora, 1994); Véronique Magri, *Le Discours sur l'autre: à travers quatre récits de voyage en Orient* (Paris: Honoré Champion, 1995); G.S. Rousseau and Roy Porter, ed., *Exoticism in the Enlightenment*; Barry Milligan, *Pleasures and Pains: Opium and the Orient in Nineteenth-Century British Culture* (Charlottesville: UP of Virginia, 1995); and Jyotsna G. Singh, *Colonial Narratives/Cultural Dialogues: "Discoveries" of India in the Language of Colonialism* (London: Routledge, 1996).

[23] Ali Behdad, *Belated Travelers: Orientalism in the Age of Colonial Dissolution* (Durham: Duke UP, 1994); Nigel Leask, *British Romantic Writers and the East: Anxieties of Empire* (Cambridge: Cambridge UP, 1992); Lisa Lowe, *Critical Terrains: French and British Orientalisms* (Ithaca: Cornell UP, 1991); Saree Makdisi, *Romantic Imperialism: Universal Empire and the Culture of Modernity* (Cambridge: Cambridge UP, 1998); and Mohammed Sharafuddin, *Islam and Romantic Orientalism: Literary Encounters with the Orient* (London: I.B. Tauris, 1994). Related analyses include Alain Buisine, *L'Orient voilé* (Paris: Zulma, 1993); Thierry Hentsch, *Imagining the Middle East*, trans. Fred A. Reed (Montreal: Black Rose Books, 1992); and Dennis Porter, *Haunted Journeys: Desire and Transgression in European Travel Writing* (Princeton: Princeton UP, 1991).

[24] Makdisi, *Romantic Imperialism* 10.

That orientalism serves as an unacknowledged avant-garde is a premise of all four chapters of this book. Any new literary movement must develop a position on the conventions it inherits from its antecedents. For instance, when Wordsworth asserts that "[p]oetry is the image of man and nature,"[25] he is reacting against the perceived artificiality and mannerism of his neoclassical contemporaries and predecessors. Yet of course no such reaction is ever really so simple. Chapter 1 discusses a case in point, that of the traditional notion that poetry should both entertain and educate. Neither Percy Shelley nor Robert Southey is willing to abandon this notion, but neither can accept it unquestioned. In introducing *The Revolt of Islam*, Shelley explicitly denies any didactic motive, yet the poem itself offers direct moral instruction that competes with, rather than complements, its effort to entertain. Southey's *Thalaba the Destroyer* informs rather than moralizes, but the vaunted amusement value of the poem is equally threatened. Thus while both poems appear to follow the letter of the classical law, they vigorously attack its spirit of balance and complementarity. In each case, the resistant implementation of that law is structured in multiple ways by the poem's orientalism.

Even more ancient and formidable than the idea that poetry should amuse and instruct is the assumption that it should be mimetic, that it should represent an experientially accessible world. Chapter 2 shows how Victor Hugo's collection *Les Orientales* juxtaposes the Islamic Middle East to Europe so as to explore the possibility of a poetry that is not strictly representational; while Hugo's poems remain referential, they do not rely on a secure relationship with empirical reality. When Alfred de Musset parodies both *Les Orientales* and George Gordon Byron's *Don Juan* in his long poem "Namouna," he assumes that the Orient offers nonmimetic options, and then proceeds to question the notion that poetry can be genuinely representational at all. "Namouna" exposes orientalism's Orient as the projection of European fantasy while using that Orient to explore a specific aesthetic fantasy, that of a poem which lacks any intimate connection with its purported subject matter.

Since the classical definition of mimesis entails the representation of nature, orientalism's antimimetic tendencies must also be examined in terms of orientalist poems' representations of nature, variously defined. As chapter 3 explains through readings of poems by William Wordsworth, Felicia Hemans, Matthew Arnold, Alfred Tennyson, George Gordon Byron, Charles Leconte de Lisle, and Théophile Gautier, orientalist convention construes the Islamic Middle East as ontologically unnatural. The Orient portrayed in nineteenth-century poems satisfies none of the usual European criteria of the natural. Its quintessential rural landscape, the desert, is typically hostile rather than comforting or inspirational; its cities are disordered blends of man-made and natural elements; and its inhabitants are at worst morally deformed, at best

---

[25] William Wordsworth, preface, *Lyrical Ballads* (1802), *Poems* 1: 879.

well-meaning but ineffectual. This unnaturalness — environmental, moral, and spiritual — in turn situates the region as an ideal locus from which to challenge nature as poetry's primary subject. Thus instead of depicting nature as it has been traditionally understood, poems on oriental subjects displace nature in favor of the Orient. The implications of this experimental substitution are important both because of the historical dependence of mimesis on the concept of nature and because of the centrality of nature in nineteenth-century poetics.

By midcentury, the Islamic Middle East had been for decades a monumental poetic source yielding not only settings, motifs, themes, plots, and characters but also the means to envisage and implement alternative aesthetic priorities for poetry. Chapter 4 shows how the Orient's aesthetic potential is grounded in its presumed linkage with art to the exclusion of nature, a linkage fully evident in poems by William Wordsworth, Felicia Hemans, Walter Savage Landor, Thomas Moore, Alfred Tennyson, Oscar Wilde, Charles Leconte de Lisle, and Théophile Gautier. Nineteenth-century poetics' evolution towards a stance of art for art's sake owes both its origin and its progression in large part to this essential aspect of orientalism, for the Orient's supposedly inherent artfulness is the root of the orientalist poetics that points the way towards art for its own sake. Poets affiliated with this movement — best represented in France by Théophile Gautier and in England by Oscar Wilde — begin to dispense with the oriental aspect of orientalist poetics. They retain orientalism's alternative ways of thinking about and writing poetry, but they no longer depend upon the Orient as a prop. The resulting aesthetic coalesces as art for art's sake.

Nineteenth-century poets discovered in orientalism an imaginative landscape that they deployed as a venue for experimentation with alternatives to poetic conventions, whether contemporary or traditional. Because of its distinctive relationships with art and nature, the Islamic Orient assumes a central role in poetry's interactions with both of these essential concepts. Orientalism is thus a major contributor to the literary history of the nineteenth century, one whose engagement with poetry must be taken into account if we are to understand the genesis and the trajectory of poetic developments.

Chapter 1

To instruct without displeasing: Percy Shelley's *The Revolt of Islam* and Robert Southey's *Thalaba the Destroyer*

The notion that poetry's goal is to amuse and instruct the reader is a venerable one in Western aesthetics. In his *Poetics*, Aristotle links "the art of poetry" to both "pleasure" and "learning."[1] Horace explains that:

> The aim of the poet is to inform or delight, or to combine together, in what he says, both pleasure and applicability to life. [...] He who combines the useful and the pleasing wins out by both instructing and delighting the reader. That is the sort of book that will make money for the publisher, cross the seas, and extend the fame of the author.[2]

From the outset, canonical English critics adopt Horace's stance as their own, though with varying degrees of emphasis and usually without such blunt acknowledgment of poets' financial motives. Philip Sidney's *An Apology for Poetry* (1595), for instance, describes poetry's "end" as "to teach and delight," and goes on to "affirm, that no learning is so good as that which teacheth and moveth to virtue, and that none can both teach and move thereto so much as Poetry."[3] A century and a half later, Samuel Johnson concurs succinctly: "The end of writing is to instruct; the end of poetry is to instruct by pleasing."[4]

As the turn of the nineteenth century approaches, this formulation remains basic, but its articulation becomes more complex. In 1786 Joshua Reynolds proposes that "the true test of all the arts is [whether] the production [...]

---

[1] Aristotle, *Poetics*, trans. Leon Golden (Tallahassee: UP of Florida, 1981) 7.
[2] Horace, *Art of Poetry*, trans. W.J. Bate, *Criticism: The Major Texts*, ed. W.J. Bate (New York: Harcourt Brace Jovanovich, 1970) 56.
[3] Sidney, *An Apology for Poetry*, *Criticism: The Major Texts*, ed. W.J. Bate 86, 97.
[4] Johnson, *Preface to Shakespeare* (1765), *Criticism: The Major Texts*, ed. W.J. Bate 210.

answers the end of art, which is to produce a pleasing effect upon the mind."[5] Horace's dictum is clearly in view here, but Reynolds departs from it in decisively emphasizing pleasure rather than instruction. William Hazlitt follows Reynolds's lead, proclaiming that "Poetry [...] relates to whatever gives immediate pleasure or pain to the human mind." Although Hazlitt does not discount poetry's ability to improve the human mind, his terms are much less pedagogical than Sidney's or Johnson's: "Poetry," he says, "is that fine particle within us, that expands, rarefies, refines, raises our whole being."[6] Percy Bysshe Shelley's analysis of poetry's function in *A Defence of Poetry* (1821) avoids the pedagogical as well. Shelley declares first that "Poetry is ever accompanied with pleasure." Poetry's ability "to produce the moral improvement of man," on the other hand, depends not upon "schemes," "examples," or "doctrines," but rather upon poetry's capacity to "awaken and enlarge the mind itself by rendering it the receptacle of a thousand unapprehended combinations of thought."[7] These general directives apply equally to orientalist poetry in the early nineteenth century; for example, Walter Scott's review of Southey's *The Curse of Kehama* evaluates that poem according to the same customary criteria of "pleasure" and "edification."[8]

As we turn now to Shelley's long poem *The Revolt of Islam* (1817), and later to Robert Southey's *Thalaba the Destroyer* (1801), we should carry away two points from the preceding discussion. First, as the comments of both Hazlitt and Shelley reveal, there is at this time a certain prejudice against explicitly didactic poetry; if a poem instructs, it should do so by simply representing beauty so as to enlarge the mind.[9] Second, no critic or poet during the early nineteenth century can raise the issue of poetry's function without making reference to the traditional perception of poetry as a vehicle for the delight and instruction of the reader. Given that this idea is a fundamental tenet of early nineteenth-century poetics, any comprehensive view of orientalist poetics during this time must take into account orientalist poetry's engagement with it. This chapter will show how *The Revolt of Islam* and *Thalaba the Destroyer* polarize the classical terms, exaggerating both instruction and

---

[5] Reynolds, *Discourse XIII*, *Criticism: The Major Texts*, ed. W.J. Bate 263. John Boyd includes Reynolds in his useful analysis of pleasure and instruction; see *The Function of Mimesis and Its Decline* (Cambridge: Harvard UP, 1968) esp. 267.
[6] Hazlitt, *On Poetry in General* (1818), *Criticism: The Major Texts*, ed. W.J. Bate 303, 304.
[7] Shelley, *A Defence of Poetry*, *Criticism: The Major Texts*, ed. W.J. Bate 431, 432.
[8] [Scott], Review of *The Curse of Kehama*, *Quarterly Review* 9 [Feb. 1811]: 55, 41.
[9] Although dominant, the emphasis on pleasure was not, of course, universal. An 1814 review of a collection entitled *The Works of the English Poets, from Chaucer to Cowper*, for instance, praises critic John Dennis (1657–1734) because "he knew what poetry ought to be, and did not define it, like some others, to be the Art of Pleasing. 'It is an art,' he says, '[that] has two ends, a subordinate and a final one; the subordinate one is pleasure, and the final one is instruction'" (*Quarterly Review* 23 [Oct. 1814]: 89). However, this reviewer clearly feels himself in the minority on what he recognizes to be a fundamental aesthetic question of his age.

amusement in such a way as to undermine the classical doctrine while appearing to support it. Moreover, whereas entertainment and edification are both conventionally linked with the central notion of mimesis, these poems also begin to question the primacy of mimesis. In each case, the poem's orientalism is essential to its experimental aesthetic stance.

Instruction in *The Revolt of Islam*

Despite its oriental setting, Shelley's *The Revolt of Islam* is meant, according to Shelley's preface to it, to communicate the lessons of the French Revolution. The poem proved to be unpopular, although its pedagogical impulses were probably less to blame than the poem's (and the poet's) unconventional morality; reviewers tended to criticize the poem on the basis of the sexual improprieties of Shelley's life.[10] Nonetheless, the preface reveals, with characteristic defensiveness, a certain anxiety about the poem's substantial didactic component. Shelley insists that the poem is "narrative, not didactic," even while admitting that it is composed "in the cause of a liberal and comprehensive morality."[11] It cannot be didactic, he says, because

> I have made no attempt to recommend the motives which I would substitute for those at present governing mankind, by methodical and systematic argument. I would only awaken the feelings, so that the reader should see the beauty of true virtue, and be incited to those inquiries which have led to my moral and political creed, and that of some of the sublimest intellects in the world.[12]

Even if a poem's aim is the moral improvement of its readers, Shelley claims, the poem is not didactic unless it contains a "methodical and systematic argument." Given the absence of such an argument in *The Revolt of Islam*, the poem's chief structural feature — its narrativeness — becomes supposedly the defining one, with narrative and argumentative/didactic presumed to be mutually exclusive.[13]

---

[10] For analysis of critical response to *The Revolt of Islam* and of Shelley's reactions to his reviewers, see Michael Laplace-Sinatra, "'I *Will* Live Beyond This Life': Shelley, Prefaces and Reviewers," *Keats-Shelley Review* 13 (1999) 90–4.

[11] Shelley, *The Complete Poetical Works of Percy Bysshe Shelley*, ed. Neville Rogers, vol. 2 (Oxford: Oxford UP, 1975) 99–100.

[12] Shelley, *Complete Poetical Works*, ed. Rogers 2: 100.

[13] Both Shelley's choice of terminology ("narrative," "didactic," "argument") and the concepts that underlie it are rather too broad to be of general use. Harold Orel and Stuart Sperry are among the critics to question Shelley's formulation; see Orel, "Shelley's *The Revolt of Islam*: The Last Great Poem of the English Enlightenment?" *Studies on Voltaire and the Eighteenth Century* 89 (1972): 1190; and Sperry, "The Sexual Theme in Shelley's *The Revolt of Islam*," *Journal of English and Germanic Philology* 82.1 (1983): 32.

Although Shelley goes on to discuss in greater detail the lessons of the French Revolution that he plans to convey, he does not explain why he has selected an oriental setting for this purpose. On the contrary, he specifies that he has "chosen a story of human passion in its most universal character [...] appealing [...] to the common sympathies of every human breast."[14] In the context of such universal moral aims, the poem's Middle Eastern characters and its siting in Turkey appear without consequence, as Shelley states explicitly in a letter written at the time. He asserts first that he has "attempted [...] to speak to the common elementary emotions of the human heart," and then firmly denies any significance to his setting's oriental identity:

> The scene is supposed to be laid in Constantinople and modern Greece, but without much attempt at minute delineation of Mahometan manners. It is in fact a tale illustrative of such a Revolution as might be supposed to take place in a European nation [...] It is a revolution of this kind that is the *beau ideal*, as it were, of the French Revolution.[15]

Indeed, it is almost as if the choice of an oriental setting serves paradoxically to guarantee the universality of the story by freeing the idealized revolution from the specificity of France, the site of its failure.

The emphasis on the story's universality is consistent throughout *The Revolt of Islam*. Briefly, the poem traces the following course: after a largely allegorical first canto, the speaker encounters the three main characters. These are the poet Laon, Cythna (also known as Laone), who is Laon's wife and fellow social reformer, and the tyrant Othman. Other figures include the Hermit, who provides spiritual guidance to Laon, and Cythna's daughter, who is the result of Othman's rape of Cythna, but who is identified as Laon's child in spirit. Troubled by many setbacks, Laon and Cythna attempt the reform and

---

For further discussion of this portion of the preface, see Stephen C. Behrendt, *Shelley and His Audiences* (Lincoln: U of Nebraska P, 1989) 23; and Hermann Fischer, *Romantic Verse Narrative: The History of a Genre*, 1964, trans. Sue Bollans (Cambridge: Cambridge UP, 1991) 188–9.

[14] Shelley, *Complete Poetical Works*, ed. Rogers 2: 100.

[15] Shelley, "To a Publisher," Oct. 13, 1817, letter 266 of *The Letters of Percy Bysshe Shelley*, ed. Roger Ingpen, vol. 2 (London: Sir Isaac Pitman & Sons, 1909) 559. There is no indication that the addressee is Charles Ollier, who eventually published the poem. For additional information, see Behrendt, *Shelley and His Audiences* 23, 26; Donald H. Reiman, ed., *Shelley and His Circle, 1773–1822*, vol. 5 (Cambridge: Harvard UP, 1973) 154; and Charles E. Robinson, "Percy Bysshe Shelley, Charles Ollier, and William Blackwood: The Contexts of Early Nineteenth-Century Publishing," *Shelley Revalued: Essays from the Gregynog Conference*, ed. Kelvin Everest (Leicester: Leicester UP, 1983) 191.

"Beau idéal" normally means "ideal beauty." However, Shelley evidently uses the phrase to mean "beautiful ideal," ungrammatically reversing the positions of noun and adjective.

liberation of the Golden City (Constantinople).[16] Their peaceful revolution, based on the principle of love, succeeds in deposing Othman. However, Othman quickly and violently regains his throne, and Laon and Cythna are put to death, achieving joy only in the afterlife. The outcome of this revolution is not much happier than that of the French original. The main difference is the attitude taken by Laon and Cythna, who reject the idea of revenge for past or present wrongs and who are committed to achieving their aims without bloodshed. It is chiefly in this respect, and in the exalted role given to Laon as a poet, that *The Revolt of Islam* becomes the "beau ideal" of the French Revolution.[17]

Shelley's emphasis both on the universality of the story and on its derivation from the French Revolution raises once again the obvious question: why is this poem set in the Orient? There are several answers. First, although the French Revolution is Shelley's point of reference, it is ultimately only the most immediate example of what he sees as a phenomenon of human history; as Marilyn Butler says, he is interested in "the generic structure of revolutions."[18] His thought experiment in political philosophy here need not then be compromised by being limited to the particulars of a single nation's experience. Moreover, given that he wishes his poem to help dissipate the "infectious gloom" that followed the failure of the French Revolution,[19] he would scarcely choose to reproduce the same flawed course of events. He needs a different revolutionary path; obviously, this would be easier to construct if he did not locate his revolution in France. Finally, by selecting an entirely different setting and a revolt with no apparent correlate to any actual event in history, Shelley is liberated from any need for historical correctness, which might have both required burdensome additional research and inhibited his development of the story.[20]

---

[16] On the idea of the Golden City, see Douglas Thorpe, "Shelley's Golden Verbal City," *Journal of English and Germanic Philology* 86.2 (1987): 215–27.

[17] As I will explain shortly, *The Revolt of Islam* was first printed, although not distributed, as *Laon and Cythna*. The poem's plot was not substantially affected by the revisions implemented before distribution; preface was unchanged but for the suppression of its final paragraph. For a more complete discussion of the structure, characters, and political significance of *The Revolt of Islam*, see James Lynn Ruff, *Shelley's* The Revolt of Islam (Salzburg: Institut für Englische Sprache und Literatur, Universität Salzburg, 1972). Other general studies of the poem include Deborah A. Gutschera, "The Drama of Reenactment in Shelley's *The Revolt of Islam*," *Keats-Shelley Journal* 35 (1986): 111–25; Richard H. Haswell, "Shelley's *The Revolt of Islam*: 'The Connexion of Its Parts,'" *Keats-Shelley Journal* 25 (1976): 81–102; Gerald McNiece, *Shelley and the Revolutionary Idea* (Cambridge: Harvard UP, 1969) ch. 10; Orel, "Shelley's *The Revolt of Islam*"; and Sperry, *Shelley's Major Verse: The Narrative and Dramatic Poetry* (Cambridge: Harvard UP, 1988) ch. 3.

[18] Marilyn Butler, "Byron and the Empire in the East," *Byron: Augustan and Romantic*," ed. Andrew Rutherford (London: Macmillan, 1990) 68.

[19] Shelley, *Complete Poetical Works*, ed. Rogers 2: 102.

[20] It is no doubt in keeping with his professed disinclination towards "minute delineation of Mahometan manners" that Shelley tends to rely on vaguely defined precedents from

16   ORIENTALIST POETICS

These rationales for choosing a setting other than France would be equally valid for any setting, oriental or not. An oriental setting offers several advantages, however. First, the situation of the Ottoman Turkish empire at this time offered a partial parallel to that of late-eighteenth-century France. Butler, for instance, situates *The Revolt of Islam* as one in

> a whole series of poems by well-connected liberal poets welcoming the prospect of revolution in the Middle East. [These poems] describe revolutions, or failed revolutions, directed against an Asiatic old regime that has the same characteristics as European old regimes. In this period of Napoleon's decline and fall, when European old regimes were being reinstated, it was widely expected that the Ottoman empire would soon break up: it appealed to radicals, then, as the likeliest site for a hoped-for replay of the French Revolution.[21]

But if the Middle East's historical particularity makes it useful as a revolutionary location, its lack thereof does so as well. As Edward Said and other scholars have pointed out, the Orient is stereotypically an unchanging place, neither subject to the passage of historical time nor extant in any historical present.[22] Azade Seyhan elaborates:

> In the final analysis, one can argue that Romanticism's exotic Orient remained just that, a faraway time and place whose traditions and symbolic wealth the Romantics excavated, carried off, and converted to their own currency without attempting to understand its historical present. Furthermore, escape into another time before time assured the subject a kind of theoretical innocence by sublating the ideological bonds of one's own history.[23]

The Orient, then, offers a venue for the poet's disentanglement from the complications of history. As Seyhan remarks, "the exotic, perceived as

---

orientalist literary convention rather than researching oriental(ist) sources, as many other nineteenth-century writers of orientalist poems do. During a brief period in 1820, he did express a desire to learn Arabic and to go to India, but this is long after the composition of *The Revolt of Islam*; see Michael Rossington, "Shelley and the Orient," *The Keats-Shelley Review* 6 (1991): 26–7. For *The Revolt of Islam* itself, Shelley seems to have had relatively few historical sources. For further discussion, see Kenneth N. Cameron, "A Major Source of *The Revolt of Islam*," *PMLA* 56 (1941): 175–206; Leask, *British Romantic Writers and the East* 114–20; McNiece, *Shelley and the Revolutionary Idea* esp. chs. 2, 10; Rossington, "Shelley and the Orient" 18–36; and Schwab, *The Oriental Renaissance* 195.

[21] Butler, "Byron and the Empire in the East" 68.

[22] Said, *Orientalism* esp. 96, 167, 240. See also Leask, *British Romantic Writers and the East* 108–9 and MacKenzie, *Orientalism* 58–9. The stereotype of timelessness will be discussed further in chapter 2.

[23] Seyhan, *Representation and Its Discontents: The Critical Legacy of German Romanticism* (Berkeley: U of California P, 1992) 79.

distance in time and space, provides access to the absent"[24] — or in this case, to that never-was, the universalized "beau ideal." In the words of Nigel Leask, Shelley appropriates the East "as an uncluttered site for the fulfillment of frustrated dreams of liberty."[25] The Orient's otherness is important in this context not because it supplies any specific features but precisely for its lack of historical specificity, which allows Shelley to inscribe onto it a universalizing revision of European history.[26] However, it is not really that he "translate[s] British imperialism into a displaced form of revolutionary politics which, in the name of universal enlightenment, alchemize[s] the Other into the Same," as Leask argues.[27] Rather, from the material of recent European history and a conventional, ahistorical Orient, Shelley creates a universalized entity both other and same, both oriental and European.

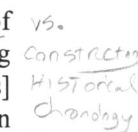

Tyranny: the Orient's chief export

The Revolt of Islam retains its otherness most distinctly in its reliance on the Islamic Middle East's conventional association with tyranny and slavery.[28] Shelley's professed hatred of tyranny and slavery is of course not limited to their oriental manifestations, but his poems consistently associate these horrors with the Middle East. His famous sonnet "Ozymandias" (1817) profiles a pharaonic, rather than an Islamic, tyrant, but the setting is unmistakably Middle Eastern. Indeed, when read with Shelley's contemporaneous poems

---

[24] Seyhan, *Representation and Its Discontents* 66.
[25] Leask, *British Romantic Writers and the East* 10. Sharafuddin's argument resembles Leask's; see *Islam and Romantic Orientalism* 200.
[26] Compare Makdisi's argument that Shelley's *Alastor* (1816) "produces a version of the Orient in which otherness has been all but obliterated [...] and in which a search can take place for images and reflections of Europe; this new Orient is thus no longer a refuge offering and containing the other, it is a cleaned-out slate ready for European colonization and inscription" (Makdisi, *Romantic Imperialism* 152).
[27] Leask, *British Romantic Writers and the East* 6.
[28] Many critics have noted this association. See especially Talal Asad, "Two European Images of Non-European Rule," *Anthropology and the Colonial Encounter*, ed. Talal Asad (London: Ithaca P, 1973) 103–18; and Claudine Grossir, *L'Islam des Romantiques* ch. 2. See also Schwab, *The Oriental Renaissance* 106; and Sharafuddin, *Islam and Romantic Orientalism* xxi–xxiii. Sharafuddin rightly observes the Islamic Orient's connection with tyranny in Walter Savage Landor's influential poem *Gebir* (*Islam and Romantic Orientalism* 19) but muddies his argument by claiming that "the Romantic movement['s] resistance to massive despotism" contributes to the development of "a genuine interest in other countries and cultures," including the Islamic Middle East (xvii), and that Islam "offered an alternative to the compromised or corrupted political and social systems of Europe" (xxi). This view seems unrealistic; there is undoubtedly a genuine interest in the Orient at this time, but when poets use the Orient as an opportunity to rail against tyranny, the Orient's affiliation with tyranny overshadows the other features of the region in which a genuine interest might otherwise evolve. As *The Revolt of Islam* shows, European poets evince attraction to Islamic Middle Eastern political or social alternatives only in very limited respects.

featuring Islamic tyrants, "Ozymandias" gives the impression of a genealogy of Middle Eastern tyranny reaching back to Ozymandias (Ramses II) in the thirteenth century BCE.[29] *Hellas* (1822), Shelley's only other predominantly orientalist longer poem, is, like *The Revolt of Islam*, set in Constantinople and concerned with a political conflict; *Hellas* treats the struggle between Turkey and Greece. Shelley's sympathies lie clearly with the Greeks, and his portrayal of Islam in this poem is more hostile than in *The Revolt of Islam*. However, his linkage of Islam with tyranny and violence is equally firm in the two poems.[30]

Although the association of the Orient with tyranny and slavery would have been commonly assumed by Shelley's readers, the poet is still careful to confirm it in his preface to *The Revolt of Islam*. As he somewhat arrogantly justifies his disregard for his critics' opinions, Shelley describes the unconcerned attitude that he supposes Lucretius to have had towards his own critics "when he meditated that poem whose doctrines are yet the basis of our metaphysical knowledge, and whose eloquence has been the wonder of mankind."[31] Although Shelley identifies Lucretius's critics as "the hired sophists of the impure and superstitious noblemen of Rome,"[32] the origin of these "sophists" is not Rome but farther east:

> It was at the period when Greece was held captive, and Asia made tributary to the Republic, fast verging itself to slavery and ruin, that a multitude of Syrian captives, bigotted to the worship of their obscene Ashtaroth, and the unworthy successors of Socrates and Zeno, found there a precarious subsistence by administering, under the name of freedmen, to the vices and vanities of the great. These

---

[29] Further evidence of this can be found in Shelley's "Ode to Liberty" (1820), which links Islamic and pharaonic symbols ("palace and pyramid") in an orientalized depiction of tyranny and its "sister-pest," slavery. Shelley's other orientalist poems include "Zeinab and Kathema" (1811), "To the Nile" (1818), "The Indian Serenade" (1819), and "From the Arabic: An Imitation" (1821). Michael Rossington reads "Ozymandias" with "To the Nile," emphasizing the relationship between art and political tyranny, and also offers a useful analysis of the orientalism of "Alastor" (1815) and "The Witch of Atlas" (1820); see "Shelley and the Orient" 25-6, 29-36.

[30] The stereotypical association between tyranny and the Islamic Middle East has continued throughout the twentieth century. In a 1992 *Time* profile of Edward Said, for instance, tyranny is mentioned as an identifying characteristic of the Middle East five times. Democracy now substitutes for Shelley's "liberty," and terrorism (mentioned four times) for slavery as tyranny's sidekick, but the basic construct appears unchanged (Robert Hughes, "Envoy to Two Cultures," *Time* [21 June 1992]: 60-2). The interrelationships among Islam, tyranny (especially in opposition to intellectual freedom), and terrorism are similarly fundamental to the argument of Jeffrey Goldberg's recent anti-Muslim exposé of Pakistan's Haqqania madrasa, which he terms "a jihad factory" and whose students he calls "perfect jihad machines" (Goldberg, "The Education of a Holy Warrior," *New York Times Magazine* [25 June 2000] 34, 71).

[31] Shelley, *Complete Poetical Works*, ed. Rogers 2: 105. Lucretius (c. 99 BCE–c. 55 BCE) wrote his *On the Nature of Things* in hexameter.

[32] Shelley, *Complete Poetical Works*, ed. Rogers 2: 105.

wretched men were skilled to plead, with a superficial but plausible set of sophisms, in favour of that contempt for virtue which is the portion of slaves, and that faith in portents, the most fatal substitute for benevolence in the imaginations of men, which, arising from the enslaved communities of the East, then first began to overwhelm the western nations in its stream.[33]

What Shelley holds against these pre-Islamic Syrians is not their easternness per se but rather their overdetermined affiliation with tyranny and slavery. On the other hand, their easternness is defined largely in terms of that affiliation. In this brief passage, for instance, words relating directly to slavery occur six times, all but once in connection with "the East."[34] Tyranny is implicit in the references to "the vices and vanities of the great," and to the threat of eastern moral decadence beginning "to overwhelm the western nations in its stream." Indeed, Shelley draws the reader's particular attention to this threat by ending his expostulation with it. By implication, then, the worst thing about tyranny (with its accompanying evils) in "the East" is that it might "overwhelm the western nations." As the East is identified by its tyranny, the victory of tyranny in the West would constitute a victory of the East itself over the West.[35]

Having thus informed the reader in the preface that tyranny and the East are closely (and alarmingly) linked, Shelley seldom introduces this question in the poem itself, focusing instead on tyranny per se. Where he does return to the Orient's connection with tyranny, though, he reaffirms it emphatically. The figure of the tyrant Othman is central here, for his orientalness (both of person and of surroundings) is stressed as no one else's. He is the only figure given an

---

[33] Shelley, *Complete Poetical Works*, ed. Rogers 2: 105. Another editor of *The Revolt of Islam* gives as an alternative: "Asia was first made tributary, Greece was enslaved to the Republic, fast verging itself to slavery and ruin, and a multitude of Syrian captives bigoted to the worship of their obscene Ashtaroth, and the unworthy successors of Socrates and Zeno, found a precarious subsistence by administering," etc. (H. Buxton Forman, cited in *The Complete Works of Percy Bysshe Shelley*, ed. Roger Ingpen and Walter E. Peck, vol. 1 (New York: Charles Scribner's Sons, 1927) 424. The elements relevant to my argument are unaltered, however.

[34] For analysis of Shelley's use of the term "slave," see Kyle Grimes, "Censorship, Violence, and Political Rhetoric: *The Revolt of Islam* in Its Time," *Keats-Shelley Journal* 43 (1994): 104–5. Lowe's comments on slavery and orientalism are also relevant; see *Critical Terrains* 60–2.

[35] Four years later, Shelley expresses similar concerns in the preface to *Hellas* as he defends Greece against Turkish domination. His argument is based on the view that "We are all Greeks," that western European civilization is defined by its Greek heritage (*The Complete Poetical Works of Percy Bysshe Shelley*, ed. Thomas Hutchinson 447). The idea of an alliance between Britain and Turkey is therefore abhorrent to him, as the poem itself also makes clear. Underlying Shelley's attitude is very probably the fear of Ottoman Turkish expansion towards western Europe, although the Ottoman threat had been weakening for decades; see Hourani, *Islam in European Thought* (Cambridge: Cambridge UP, 1991) 10. For further discussion, see Leask, *British Romantic Writers and the East* 72–3; and Makdisi, *Romantic Imperialism* 148–50.

Arabic name; Laon and Cythna/Laone both have more or less Greek names, and the other characters are generally given a type ("the Hermit," etc.) rather than a name.[36] While the use of Greek names suggests an association, however vague, with supposedly universal humanist values, the Arabic name has a much more particular, as well as more negative, connotation. It cannot be a coincidence that Shelley chooses the same well-known name, "Othman," to symbolize Turkish military power in *Hellas*, or that the term "Ottoman" and the name "Othman" are etymologically related. Moreover, by naming only these three characters in *The Revolt of Islam*, divided as they are into two opposing camps along a binary cultural axis, Shelley reaffirms and specifies the element of threat introduced in his preface. In the preface, classical Rome and "the western nations" were opposed by a morally and politically corrupt "East;" now in the poem itself, the Greek world, with its classical and humanist associations, stands against the Islamic Middle East, represented by a tyrant who deceives, kidnaps, imprisons, rapes, and kills.

It is to be expected, then, that when Othman is at his cruelest he is also at his most explicitly oriental. The scene that describes his plan to imprison Cythna provides an example:

> The King felt pale upon his noonday throne:
> At night two slaves he to her chamber sent,
> One was a green and wrinkled eunuch, grown
> From human shape into an instrument
> Of all things ill — distorted, bowed and bent.
> The other was a wretch from infancy
> Made dumb by poison; who nought knew or meant
> But to obey: from the fire-isles came he,
> A diver lean and strong, of Oman's coral sea. (7.64–72)[37]

The power of the King — his tyranny — is carefully emphasized in the first line by the prominent (and otherwise irrelevant) mention of the throne. He exercises this power by dispatching the two slaves; tyranny and slavery are, as usual, conjoined. Only when the characteristics of these slaves are specified in the third line, though, does the orientalization begin. The first slave is a "green and wrinkled eunuch." The fact of his castration makes an immediate reference to (unnatural) oriental practice; so too do his color and texture. Not only does his greenness allude to the pallor of the tyrant, mentioned in the first line,

---

[36] On the names of Laon and Cythna, see Ruff, *Shelley's* The Revolt of Islam 60–2. It is remotely possible that Shelley had in mind Othman II (1603–1622), the unpopular sixteenth sultan of the Ottoman Empire, as a prototype for his Othman. Of the major Othmans of history, he is the only one to have been involved in a rebellion, but unlike Shelley's Othman, he was put to death after being overthrown (see *The Encyclopedia of Islam*, 1st ed., vol. 6 [Leiden: E.J. Brill, 1913–36; rpt. 1987] 1007).

[37] My source for *The Revolt of Islam* is Shelley's *Complete Poetical Works*, edited by Roger Ingpen and Walter E. Peck.

thereby once again conflating slavery and tyranny, but the bizarre appearance of this person refers directly, if implicitly, to the unnaturalness that typifies the Orient. Moreover, the human status of this oriental eunuch is characteristically unclear.[38] Not only is the eunuch a slave, and therefore in the legal category of property rather than person, but he is also outside both of the two basic categories of human being, male and female. And were this not enough, he is also morally inhuman: "grown / From human shape into an instrument / Of all things ill."[39]

The second slave's position is similar; he is deprived of his voice rather than his testes, but since both are instruments of power, the result is much the same. This second slave, like the first, lacks both human agency and moral independence, relying instead upon the tyrant's initiative (he "nought knew or meant / But to obey"). While his artificial muteness, like the first slave's castration, makes implicit reference to the Orient, his Middle Eastern identity is even more clearly specified: "from the fire-isles came he, / A diver lean and strong, of Oman's coral sea." Although this description's immediate purpose is to identify the slave's origin, it also confirms the oriental quality of the entire scene. The virtually unlimited play the scene gives both tyranny and slavery on the one hand and the scene's heightened orientalism on the other hand enable and reinforce each other to such a degree that the oriental and the tyrannical become fundamentally indivisible. The Islamic Middle East, then, is defined in this poem as a place desperately in need of revolution; as such, it is an especially productive site for the revolution of liberty and love that Shelley proposes for the inspiration of his readers.

Tyranny's comrades: religion and sexism

The lessons of *The Revolt of Islam* extend from the political to the moral, however, and there again, the Turkish setting proves valuable. As Shelley criticizes both religion and sexism, he calls upon the Islamic Orient's association with this pair of moral ills. Religion and sexism function both as allies of tyranny and as forms of tyranny in their own right. Religion's alliance with tyranny is exposed most plainly towards the end of the poem (especially the tenth canto), where "kings and priests" (10.60) are joined in defense of the status quo and against the revolt on behalf of liberty. In the end, it is a priest who instigates the execution of revolutionary leaders Laon and Cythna (10.344). "Faith" and "tyranny" are presented as twin evils, to be "trampled

---

[38] The issues of human status and of the Orient's relationship with nature will be discussed in detail in chapter 3.

[39] See for comparison Lowe's discussion of eunuch slaves and orientalism in Montesquieu's *Lettres persanes* (*Critical Terrains* 60–9).

down" together (10.294). The notion of religion as a form of tyranny is also established firmly in this stanza of the poem. The priests praise God in virtually the same terms that are used elsewhere to censure the tyrant (10.244–6), in effect positioning God as the ultimate tyrant, whose priests — themselves petty spiritual tyrants — are as disinterested in freedom as their political allies are.

Although the poem's censure of religion in general is unmistakable, its view of the individual creeds, and especially of Islam, is harder at first to discern.[40] On the one hand, all religious denominations, including Islam, are grouped together. When the speaker relates the priests' various appeals in time of plague, for instance, he describes how

> Oromaze, and Christ, and Mahomet,
> Moses, and Buddh, Zerdusht, and Brahm, and Foh,
> A tumult of strange names, which never met
> Before, as watchwords of a single woe,
> Arose (10.271–5)[41]

The point of these lines is clearly the unity of faiths, but this unity evaporates in the remainder of the stanza:

> each raging votary 'gan to throw
> Aloft his armed hands, and each did howl
> "Our God alone is God!" and slaughter now
> Would have gone forth (10.275–8)

Although all denominations appear to be equally condemned, the phrase "Our God alone is God!" refers to part of the Muslim declaration of faith. The choice of these words to symbolize the evil of denominational religion thus lays blame more forcefully upon Muslims than upon the Zoroastrians,

---

[40] For discussion of nineteenth-century attitudes towards Islam in general, see esp. Grossir, *L'Islam des Romantiques* ch. 4; and Hourani, *Islam in European Thought* ch. 1.

[41] This citation is from the *Laon and Cythna* version of the poem. Neville Rogers notes that "'Oromaze' is Ormuzd, the Principle of Good among the Zoroastrians. 'Zerdusht', in the next line, is Zoroaster" (Shelley, *Complete Poetical Works*, ed. Rogers 2: 393). "Foh" is probably Fu Hsi (also spelled Fo-Hi), a Chinese "god emperor," c. 3000 BCE, to whom "is attributed the development of the philosophical framework of Chinese medicine" (*The Encyclopedia of Religion* [New York: Macmillan, 1987] 313). Shelley's list here can be compared to a shorter one in the Prologue to *Hellas*: "Satan, Christ, and Mahomet" (76).

This passage of *The Revolt of Islam* is cited as part of John Taylor Coleridge's condemnation of the poem for "blasphemy"; see his review, "*Laon and Cythna, or the Revolution of the Golden City*," *Quarterly Review* 42 (April 1819): 464 (rpt. in Albert Mordell, ed., *Notorious Literary Attacks* [New York: Boni and Liveright, 1926] 63–82). Robinson discusses the circumstances of this review; see "Percy Bysshe Shelley, Charles Ollier, and William Blackwood" 196.

Christians, Jews, Buddhists, and Hindus who are equally involved.[42]

The task of defining this poem's treatment of Islam is complicated by the revisions that Shelley's publisher, Charles Ollier, fearing prosecution and loss of business, demanded at the urging of both his printer and his customers.[43] These changes fall into two categories. First, in Shelley's original version, entitled *Laon and Cythna*, the hero and heroine are brother and sister rather than the childhood friends they appear in *The Revolt of Islam*. As in *The Revolt of Islam*, though, they become lovers; Ollier evidently felt that this incest would be too risky to include.[44] Second, the antireligious, and specifically the anti-Christian, views so dominant in the original are muted somewhat.[45]

The moderation of atheistic sentiments can easily be traced in the characterization of the priest who suggests Laon and Cythna's execution. In *Laon and Cythna*, he is introduced as "a Christian Priest" (10.280) and his Christianity is emphasized as the story proceeds. This accentuated Christian identification disappears in the revised *The Revolt of Islam*. The priest is now "an Iberian Priest." His belief in "His cradled Idol, and the sacrifice, / Of God to God's own wrath" is rephrased to convert the attack on Jesus Christ into a mere theological statement: "The expiation and the sacrifice" (10.302–3).[46]

However, the revision's softer approach to Christianity entails a harsher treatment of Islam. For instance, whereas in *Laon and Cythna* the Christian priest's mission is "[t]o quell the rebel Atheists" (10.283), it is in *The Revolt of Islam* "[t]o quell the unbelievers." By replacing "rebel Atheists" with "unbelievers," the stanza shifts the threat away from the Christian domain and

---

[42] Shelley uses another version of the declaration of faith in *Hellas*: "One God is God — Mahomet is His prophet" (274). A more exact translation of the Arabic original would be: "There is no god but God, and Muḥammad is the Messenger of God."

[43] For more information on the circumstances of this revision, see the notes to *Laon and Cythna* in the Ingpen and Peck edition of Shelley's *Complete Works*; and H. Buxton Forman's comments on the poem in his *The Shelley Library: An Essay in Bibliography* (London: Reeves and Turner, 1886) 74–5, 80–1. See also Behrendt, *Shelley and His Audiences* 27–8; Reiman, *Shelley and His Circle* 157–65; and Robinson, "Percy Bysshe Shelley, Charles Ollier, and William Blackwood" 190–3. Shelley's letters at the time are of interest as well; see Shelley, "To Charles Ollier," Dec. 11, 1817, letter 276; "To Charles Ollier," Dec. 13, 1817, letter 278; and "To Thomas Moore," Dec. 16, 1817, letter 279 of *The Letters of Percy Bysshe Shelley* 2: 569–72, 575–7.

[44] Ollier may have been right to worry, if John Coleridge's italicized horror is any indication ("*Laon and Cythna*," *Quarterly Review* 464). For further discussion of this incest and its censorship, see Nathaniel Brown, *Sexuality and Feminism in Shelley* (Cambridge: Harvard UP, 1979) ch. 10; Ruff, *Shelley's* The Revolt of Islam 58–60; and Sperry, "The Sexual Theme in *The Revolt of Islam*" 37.

[45] Reiman reports that "four times as many lines were changed to avoid the charge of blasphemous libel as were altered to remove the subject of incest" (*Shelley and His Circle* 165).

[46] A comparable shift occurs in the passage cited above, where Shelley lists the religious figures to whom the various clergymen appeal. The original list includes Christ; in revision, Christ is replaced by Joshua. However, as Rogers notes, this "substitution [...] was obstinate and artful, the name being a synonym of 'Jesus'" (Shelley, *Complete Poetical Works*, ed. Rogers 2: 393).

into the Muslim one. ("Unbeliever," a word not prevalent in Christian discourse, is the usual English translation of the Arabic "kâfir.") The move to protect Christianity at the expense of Islam is manifested too in the change in the poem's title. Originally *Laon and Cythna; or, The Revolution of the Golden City: A Vision of the Nineteenth Century*, the revised poem was published as *The Revolt of Islam; A Poem in Twelve Cantos*. Although Shelley in a letter glosses "the golden city" as Constantinople,[47] the original title gives no clue to the poem's oriental or Islamic identity. When the title is revised, "Islam" replaces "the golden city" as a location, safely removing Europe and Christianity from the immediate danger of revolution. Moreover, by making "Islam" a region as well as religion, Shelley implicitly posits Islam and the Orient/Middle East as interchangeable terms. In turn, this interchangeability implies and assumes the dominance of religion, specifically Islam, over the Orient. Given that the Orient is affiliated with tyranny, and that religion itself is a manifestation of tyranny, the Orient's identification with Islam is logically consistent, even inevitable. Shelley's revised title simply encapsulates a set of associations already elaborated within the poem but particularly accentuated in the revision.

Like religion, men's oppression of women appears in *The Revolt of Islam* as a form of tyranny with peculiarly intimate connections to the Islamic East. Cythna is his usual mouthpiece on this subject, and she consistently uses terms familiar from the discussion of political tyranny to describe the relationship between men and women.[48] Indeed, what might be considered the best synopsis of Shelley's hopes for political liberty is articulated by Cythna in the context of sexist oppression:

> ye might arise, and will
> That gold should lose its power, and thrones their glory;
> That love, which none may bind, be free to fill
> The world, like light; and evil faith, grown hoary
> With crime, be quenched and die. (8.136–40)

This canto ends with the freeing of women who had been enslaved for the tyrant Othman's pleasure; the effect is to make political tyranny indistinguishable from sexual domination. The relationship between men and

---

[47] Shelley, "To a Publisher," Oct. 13, 1817, letter 266 of *The Letters of Percy Bysshe Shelley* 2: 559.
[48] See esp. 2.42–3 and 8.13–16. For further analysis of Cythna's role and Shelley's "feminism," see Brown, *Sexuality and Feminism in Shelley* 181–7; Gutschera, "The Drama of Reenactment in Shelley's *The Revolt of Islam*" 124–5; E. Douka Kabitoglou, "Shelley's (Feminist) Discourse on the Female: *The Revolt of Islam*," *Arbeiten aus Anglistik und Amerikanistik* 15.2 (1990): 139–50; William Keach, "Cythna's Subtler Language," *Studies in Romanticism* 37.1 (1998): 7–16; Leask, *British Romantic Writers and the East* 130–5; McNiece, *Shelley and the Revolutionary Idea* 198–200; and E.B. Murray, "'Elective Affinity' in *The Revolt of Islam*," *Journal of English and Germanic Philology* 67 (1968): 580–1.

women is functionally equivalent to that between tyrants and slaves, the poem implies. While such a formulation was not commonly applied by Britons to their own culture at this time, it had the status of conventional wisdom when applied to the Islamic East. Much European condemnation of oriental tyranny arose (as it still does) from moral indignation at the presumed oriental subordination of women. As Lisa Lowe explains, the enslavement of Middle Eastern women becomes as a "constructed topos," "a *sign* for oriental barbarism" in orientalist discourse of the period.[49] Indeed, Mary Wollstonecraft, an early feminist and the mother of Shelley's second wife, uses references to "the seraglio" as counterpoints to her remarks on British male-female relations. Her *Vindication of the Rights of Woman* (1792), for example, posed the Islamic Orient as a kind of worst-case scenario where women, "in the true Mohametan strain," are "deprive[d ...] of souls" and, "in blind obedience [to] tyrants and sensualists," "supinely dream life away in the lap of pleasure."[50] By situating his tale in the Islamic Middle East, Shelley lends the ring of truth to his version of relations between the sexes and therefore, by analogy, to the rest of his ideological package, including opposition to political tyranny and to the tyranny of religion.[51]

Orientalism and Shelley's poetics

The Revolt of Islam appears as a long parable: narrative indeed, but with a didactic purpose always in view. Shelley's espousal of didacticism — albeit hidden behind the "narrative" label and form — would be less significant had he not written this poem in an age when didacticism had largely fallen from favor. Aware that poetry's limits as an instructional medium were narrower than they had been for many of his predecessors, Shelley seems intent on testing those limits, just as he tests the limits of conventional political and social morality.

---

[49] Lowe, *Critical Terrains* 51, 43–4, emphasis hers. Daniel argues that in the nineteenth century "[t]here is no subject connected with Islam which Europeans have thought more important than the condition of Muslim women." In the Ottoman context, for instance, he proposes that "the position of Muslim women" was one of the three most important elements "in the European experience of Islam," along with "fear of Turkish power" and "the absence of a gentry." Daniel goes on to explain: "To the mind of aristocratic Europe, tyranny was common to all three, to the external threat, to a polity internally servile and to an enslavement of women" (Daniel, *Islam, Europe and Empire* 36, 11).

[50] Mary Wollstonecraft, *A Vindication of the Rights of Woman*, ed. Carol H. Poston (New York: Norton, 1975) 19, 24, 29. For additional comments on Wollstonecraft in this context, see Keach, "Cythna's Subtler Language" 8.

[51] As usual, Shelley's efforts in this regard were not fully successful. John Coleridge argues in his review that the circumstances Shelley depicts are so extreme as to make his solutions appear irrelevant to ordinary political and social situations. As he says, "We are Englishmen, Christians, free, and independent; we ask Mr. Shelley how his case applies to *us*?" ("*Laon and Cythna*," *Quarterly Review* 466; emphasis his).

Orientalism plays an indispensable role in this endeavor. As I have shown, the Orient's stereotypical characteristics (especially its ahistoricity and its multiple tyrannies) serve Shelley's message well. Equally important, however, is the role orientalism plays in counteracting the poem's didacticism, through two independent mechanisms. First, whereas any return to didacticism is aesthetically retrograde, any treatment of the Orient is, if not cutting-edge, at least up-to-date. Orientalism, then, provides a screen behind which the poem's didactic dimensions can be expanded, since a didactic orientalist poem may appear less offensively didactic than an ordinary didactic poem. Second, oriental(ist) literature's association with entertainment serves to counteract *The Revolt of Islam*'s strong moralizing tendencies. Nineteenth-century readers typically expected plentiful entertainment from any "oriental tale" inspired by the *1001 Nights* and characterized by an ahistorical, nonrealist depiction of the Middle East.[52] Although *The Revolt of Islam* does not directly name the *1001 Nights* as its source or model, certain of its structural aspects, such as the presence of multiple narrative frames, readily recall the *1001 Nights*.[53] The general orientalness of the tale is reinforced throughout by means such as the otherwise gratuitous use of desert images (e.g. "multitudinous as the desert sand / Borne on the storm" [2.403–4]), and the repeated references to dream, which is for various reasons conventionally associated with the Orient. In short, *The Revolt of Islam* takes advantage of the presumption that the Orient is a place where the excitingly implausible — even the impossible — can appear unproblematically verisimilar.

These tactics of orientalization are at least somewhat effective. In his edition of Shelley's works, William Michael Rossetti (brother and editor of Victorian poet Dante Gabriel Rossetti) says of *The Revolt of Islam*: "It affects the mind something like an enchanted palace of the *Arabian Nights*. One is wonderstruck both at the total creation, and at every shifting aspect of it."[54] Would Rossetti have been "wonderstruck" by this poem in the absence of these oriental elements? Perhaps, but not likely, for he goes on to acknowledge that "one does not expect to find in it any detail of the absolute artistic perfection of a Greek gem, nor any inmate of consummate interest to the heart." His admiration, then, depends mainly upon the orientalism of the poem, since despite its "originality" he finds it lacking both artistically and emotionally.[55]

---

[52] See my analysis of Southey below for a fuller discussion of this prevalent view.

[53] Fischer makes a similar observation; see Fischer, *Romantic Verse Narrative* 191.

[54] Shelley, *The Poetical Works of Percy Bysshe Shelley*, ed. W.M. Rossetti, vol. 1 (London: E. Moxon, Son, & Co., 1870) cii.

[55] *The Poetical Works of Percy Bysshe Shelley*, ed. W. M. Rossetti 1: cii. The opposition that Rossetti implies between a Greek standard and the orientalist work at hand may seem innocent, but it depends upon the same political and cultural privileging of the Greek over the Middle Eastern that Shelley affirms in his preface to *The Revolt of Islam* and in *Hellas*. Accordingly, the Greek stands for absolute value; the Middle Eastern for a derivative value bounded by exoticism. The oriental may be admirable, but it can never be Greek.

Given the poem's lack of consistent artistic and emotional appeal (aptly diagnosed by William Rossetti), only the poem's value as amusement is likely to draw the reader through twelve long cantos. The Orient (in its entertaining rather than its timeless and tyrannical guise) is essential to this effort. The strongly narrative form of the *1001 Nights* and, to a lesser degree, of the Europeanized oriental tale lends credibility (at least by association) to Shelley's claim that the poem is "narrative, not didactic." In effect, it is *The Revolt of Islam*'s orientalism that allows Shelley to assert with any legitimacy at all that, for all its moral instruction, the poem is not didactic.

The Revolt of Islam is unconventional chiefly in two respects: first, in its didacticism during a period where didacticism was disfavored; and second, in its morality — liberal, but also atheist and feminist. In both cases, the poem's oriental setting plays an enabling role. As Alan Richardson points out, oriental(ist) literature (especially that related to the *1001 Nights*) was a common basis for morally didactic works in the late eighteenth and early nineteenth centuries.[56] However, the unconventional morality of *The Revolt of Islam* clearly distinguishes it from such texts as Maria Edgeworth's orientalist story "Murad the Unlucky" (1804), which preaches a conservative, almost puritanical message.[57] The poem's engagement with aesthetic experimentation also sets it apart from earlier efforts at orientalist moralizing. As a whole, *The Revolt of Islam* polarizes the terms of the long-standing debate over poetry's purpose. Whereas his predecessors, from Horace to Johnson, assumed that the relationship between amusement and instruction was complementary, Shelley places the two terms in an essentially conflicting relationship in which amusement serves to counteract instruction. At the same time, whereas his contemporaries tended to privilege amusement over instruction, Shelley does the opposite, despite his rhetoric to the contrary. Even while maintaining the tension between instruction and entertainment, he uses entertainment to facilitate the poem's instructional purpose. Through his orientalism, Shelley accentuates the didactic as well as the delightful, developing an approach aesthetically distinct from both his predecessors' moderation and mutuality and his contemporaries' emphasis on pleasure.

---

[56] Alan Richardson, *Literature, Education, and Romanticism: Reading as Social Practice, 1780–1832* (Cambridge: Cambridge UP, 1994) 116–7.

[57] Maria Edgeworth, "Murad the Unlucky," *Oriental Tales*, ed. Robert L. Mack (Oxford: Oxford UP, 1992) 213–77. Originally published in Edgeworth's collection *Popular Tales*, the story advocates an ethic of hard work and self-sufficiency; the title character's misfortune is ascribed to laziness and poor judgement rather than to ill luck.

Morals vs. materials: instruction and pleasure in *Thalaba the Destroyer*

Despite the Islamic Middle East's great importance to the poetics of *The Revolt of Islam*, it remains chiefly a medium. Shelley's choice of the Orient as a setting is subordinate to his aesthetic, moral, social, and political agendas. The opposite is true of Robert Southey's *Thalaba the Destroyer*. This poem is as didactic as *The Revolt of Islam*, but whereas Shelley offers chiefly moral lessons, Southey instructs his reader in the Orient itself. Compared to the elaborate political morality of Shelley's poem, *Thalaba*'s moral values are simplistic; good, in the person of Thalaba, battles evil, represented by denizens of "the Domdaniel [...] a seminary for evil magicians, under the roots of the sea."[58] The scheme remains uncomplicated since there is never any serious doubt about good's ultimate victory. Unlike Shelley, whose aspirations to universality lead him to suppress the Orient, Southey brings the Orient into relief. *Thalaba* shares with *The Revolt of Islam* a relation to the orientalist literature of morality discussed by Richardson, but *Thalaba*'s morality is clearly less important than its orientalism. Motivated by what Richard Hoffpauir has called "[a]n intense desire to explain,"[59] Southey emphasizes all the Orient's particularities with a sort of earnest delight that reminds one of the obsessively detailed orientalist paintings of the nineteenth century.

As a result, the Orient has of course a more prominent status in Southey's poem, but the Orient's tyranny and moral degradation are not emphasized. While Southey would almost certainly have agreed with Shelley's vision of oriental morality, he pointedly avoids pursuing it. He defends what at least one of his critics saw as a "flattering misrepresentation" by explaining that

> Thalaba the Destroyer was professedly an Arabian Tale. The design required that I should bring into view the best features of that system of belief and worship which had been developed under the Covenant with Ishmael, placing in the most favorable light the morality of the Koran, and what the least corrupted of the Mahommedans retain of the patriarchal faith. It would have been altogether incongruous to have touched upon the abominations engrafted upon it.[60]

---

[58] Southey, preface, *Thalaba the Destroyer*, *The Complete Poetical Works of Robert Southey* (New York: D. Appleton; and Philadelphia: George S. Appleton, 1846) 225. This preface is dated October 1800 but is erroneously ascribed to the fourth edition of *Thalaba*; it undoubtedly belongs to the first edition, which appeared in 1801.
This 1846 edition of the *Complete Poetical Works* is my source for Southey's poetry.

[59] Hoffpauir, "The Thematic Structure of Southey's Epic Poetry," *Wordsworth Circle* 6.4 (1975): 240. As Said shows, Southey's brand of informational didacticism is not uncommon; see Said, *Orientalism* 125–9.

[60] Southey, preface (1838), *The Curse of Kehama* (1810) 565.

Tyranny, or in Southey's words, "the spirit of Oriental despotism," is chief among those abominations to be disregarded.[61] In this atmosphere of (implicitly colonialist) relativism, *Thalaba*'s presentation of the Islamic Orient lacks a strong moral component. Instead, it stresses manners, customs, and geography in its portrayal of the region. There is no question that Southey was attracted to his subject mainly by its oriental identity rather than, as in Shelley's case, by its potential as a medium for a culturally generalized message. Southey takes pains in a later preface to *Thalaba* to assure his reader that "this poem was neither crudely conceived nor hastily undertaken. I had fixed upon the ground, four years before, for a Mahommedan tale," the first in a series of narrative poems with "mythological" subjects.[62]

Although Southey identifies *Thalaba* as "a narrative poem" in this preface, there is no corresponding reference, as in Shelley, to didacticism, nor is there any of Shelley's defensiveness. There are at least three possible explanations for Southey's evident self-confidence. First of all, unlike Shelley, Southey is communicating information rather than morals; he can simply offer the information, letting the readers take of it what they will without worrying about their resistance to his preaching. Second, while Shelley, who had done little research on the Orient before portraying it in his poem, made a point of not attempting "minute delineation of Mahometan manners,"[63] Southey was proud of his extensive reading on the subject. In the four years between settling upon the idea of "a Mahommedan tale," and beginning its composition, Southey not only "formed" the "plan" of the poem, but also "collected" the "materials,"[64] many of which appear in the poem's very extensive notes. This process is mentioned several times in his letters, always with enthusiasm despite occasional complaints. On August 22, 1800, for instance, he writes: "I have been polishing and polishing, adding and adding, and my unlearned readers ought to thank me very heartily for the toil, unpleasant and unproductive, of translating so many notes."[65] In short, Southey's research

---

[61] Southey, preface (1838), *The Curse of Kehama* 565. Recent critics have disputed this omission; for further analysis of *Thalaba*'s political dimensions, see Butler, "Plotting the Revolution: The Political Narratives of Romantic Poetry and Criticism," *Romantic Revolutions: Criticism and Theory*, ed. Kenneth R. Johnston et al. (Bloomington: Indiana UP, 1990) 135, 142–52; Butler, "Repossessing the Past: The Case for an Open Literary History," *Rethinking Historicism: Critical Readings in Romantic History*, ed. Marjorie Levinson, Marilyn Bulter, Jerome McGann, Paul Hamilton (Oxford: Basil Blackwell, 1989) 82–3; and Sharafuddin, *Islam and Romantic Orientalism* 54–74, 105–7. See for comparison Balachandra Rajan, "Monstrous Mythologies: Southey and *The Curse of Kehama*," *European Romantic Review* 9.2 (1998): 102–16.

[62] Southey, preface (1837), *Thalaba* 224.

[63] Shelley, "To a Publisher," Oct. 13, 1817, letter 266 of *The Letters of Percy Bysshe Shelley* 2: 559.

[64] Southey, preface (1837), *Thalaba* 224.

[65] Southey, "To John Rickman, Esq.," Aug. 22, 1800, *The Life and Correspondence of Robert Southey,* ed. Charles Cuthbert Southey, vol. 2 (London: Longman, Brown, Green, and

reflects the value he ascribes to the instruction of his poem's "unlearned readers," even while his primary identification of *Thalaba* is as a narrative poem. Unlike Shelley, he seems entirely unconcerned about the possibility of any conflict between his narrative and his didactic intentions. In addition, as Peter Morgan has pointed out, Southey's attitude towards poetry as instruction is relatively favorable;[66] certainly he is less ambivalent on this score than Shelley.

In particular, Southey seems to accept oriental(ist) literature as naturally and desirably informative. This conception of oriental(ist) literature's instructive value underlies *Thalaba*, as we see when Southey explains that he began his planned series of narrative poems with one on

> the Mahommedan religion, as being that with which I was then best acquainted myself, and of which every one who had read the Arabian Nights' Entertainments possessed all the knowledge necessary for readily understanding and entering into the intent and spirit of the poem.[67]

While the *1001 Nights* are "Entertainments," they also leave the reader with "knowledge." This knowledge is "all" that a reader needs to "enter into the intent and spirit of the poem"; in other words, the *1001 Nights* has primed the reader, enabling him or her to take up the much broader stream of information the poem provides. Since "Thalaba the Destroyer [is] professedly an Arabian Tale"[68] and follows from the *1001 Nights*, it complies with the demands of its genre. Southey need make no further explanation or defense of his approach.

Finally, any compunction that Southey might have felt about his didactic ambitions would have been outweighed by his firm belief that the literature of the Orient, whether authentic or orientalist, was a potent source of delight. While Shelley uses the Orient's associations with amusement to take the edge off his poem's moral message, Southey delights in oriental amusement for its own sake. Indeed, he seems to find oriental(ist) literature more pleasurable than any other kind. During an extended stay in Portugal, for example, he laments: "More books are published annually at Bristol than in Portugal. There are no books to induce a love of reading — no Arabian Tales or Seven Champions."[69] Oriental subject matter appeals to him as a poet too. In a letter

---

Longmans, 1850) 104. See also for example Southey, "To Joseph Cottle, Esq.," Sept. 22, 1799, *The Life and Correspondence of Robert Southey* 2: 25.

[66] Peter Morgan, "Southey on Poetry," *Tennessee Studies in Literature* 26 (1971): 80–1.

[67] Southey, preface (1838), *The Curse of Kehama* 565. See Butler, "Repossessing the Past" 76–7 for additional comments on Southey's use of the *1001 Nights*.

[68] Southey, preface (1838), *The Curse of Kehama* 565.

[69] Southey, "To Henry Southey," Aug. 25, 1800, *The Life and Correspondence of Robert Southey* 2: 110. "Seven Champions" refers to *The Seven Champions of Christendom*, a set of tales produced by Richard Johnson (1573–1659) but heavily dependent upon folk legends and traditions of chivalry. Several of the tales include Middle Eastern elements. Mary

written before he began work on *Thalaba*, he tells a friend:

> There are some fine Arabic traditions that would make noble poems. I was about to write one upon the Garden of Irem; the city and garden still exist in the deserts invisibly, and one man only has seen them. This is the tradition, and I had made it the groundwork of what I thought a very fine story; but it seemed too great for a poem of 300 or 400 lines.[70]

Another source of inspiration for Southey is Walter Savage Landor's orientalist poem *Gebir* (1798), which Southey often mentions around the time of composing *Thalaba*.[71] In retrospect, he all but acknowledges *Gebir* as a model for *Thalaba*, remarking, "I am sensible of having derived great improvement from the frequent perusal of Gebir at [the] time" of *Thalaba*'s composition.[72]

Southey's didacticism, then, is a function of two phenomena. First, his attraction to the Orient, both in general and particularly as a poetic subject,

---

Wollstonecraft's husband, William Godwin, recommended both the *1001 Nights* and *The Seven Champions* as books for children.

Southey seems to have more difficulty admiring oriental poetry than prose. Although he occasionally refers to Arabic poetry, especially the famous pre-Islamic Mu'allaqât, the founding poems of the Arabic literary tradition, he is generally critical of oriental poetry. He classes Ferdusi, one of the greatest Persian poets, as "worthless," though admitting that perhaps the translation was bad. "The Arabian Tales," on the other hand, "certainly abound with genius; they have lost their metaphorical rubbish in passing through the filter of a French translation" (notes, *Thalaba* 232).

[70] Southey, "To C.W.W. Wynn, Esq.," Aug. 15, 1798, *The Life and Correspondence of Robert Southey* 1: 346. The legend of the Garden of Irem is incorporated into the first book of *Thalaba*.

[71] In his first reference to *Gebir*, Southey says that the poem contains "some of the most exquisite poetry in the language" (Southey, "To Joseph Cottle, Esq.," Sept. 22, 1799, *The Life and Correspondence of Robert Southey* 2: 24). In this same letter, Southey mentions that he has written a review of the poem; this review acknowledges that the "story of this poem is certainly ill chosen and not sufficiently whole; and the language is frequently deficient in perspicuity." In all other respects, though, Southey's appraisal is extremely high, for the poem "abound[s] with such beauties as it is rarely our good fortune to discover;" "we have read [it] with more than common attention, and with far more than common delight" ("*Gebir; a Poem*," *Critical Review* 27 [Sept. 1799]: 29, 38, 39). From this point on, Southey's pleasure in *Gebir* merely increases. He mentions it again on Dec. 21, 1799, referring to its "miraculous beauties" ("To Grosvenor C. Bedford, Esq., Dec. 21, 1799, *The Life and Correspondence* 2: 33). He recommends it to Samuel Taylor Coleridge on April 1, 1800 ("To S.T. Coleridge, Esq.," April 1, 1800, *The Life and Correspondence* 2: 56.), and again a month later ("To S.T. Coleridge, Esq.," May 1, 1800, *The Life and Correspondence* 2: 64).

Landor (1775–1864) was a poet and prose writer, influential despite his notoriously difficult temperament. For further discussion of his personal and intellectual connections with Southey, see Charles L. Proudfit, "Southey and Landor: A Literary Friendship," *Wordsworth Circle* 5.2 (1974): 105–12. For general analysis of *Gebir*, see Fischer, *Romantic Verse Narrative* 57–61; and Sharafuddin, *Islam and Romantic Orientalism* ch. 1. One of Landor's shorter orientalist poems will be analyzed in chapter 4.

[72] Southey, preface (1837), *Thalaba* 224.

motivates him to undertake an impressive program of research on the culture, geography, and literature of the East. This research and the poem *Thalaba* become mutually supportive structures. The poem justifies the research by providing not only an excuse for its extent but also a medium for its expression, while the research lends the poem a desirable sense of authenticity. Second and more important, Southey's positioning of *Thalaba* as oriental(ist) literature leads him to accept certain genre requirements, including that of extensive instruction accompanied by intense entertainment — in effect, an exaggerated, immoderate version of the classical Horatian model. By announcing in the preface to *Thalaba* that his poem is "an Arabian Tale" following upon "the continuation of the Arabian Tales," Southey requests that his poem be judged according to these oriental(ist) criteria.[73]

Southey's adoption of these alternative criteria is, at bottom, what allows him to avoid such anxiety as Shelley's. As both his *Defence of Poetry* and his preface to *The Revolt of Islam* suggest, Shelley's unease about didactic poetry is grounded in a specific evolution of the old ideal of poetry as a form that "amuses and instructs." According to this evolved position, the ideal permits only a particular mediated type of instruction, one that relies much more upon the sensitive reader's aesthetic and moral receptivity than would Southey's unrestrained flood of information. Southey's disinterest in these refinements depends upon his choice of another, peculiarly oriental(ist), standard, one characterized not only by lack of restraint but also by a marked polarization of terms.

This is much the same polarization evident in *The Revolt of Islam*, but it is underlaid by a different set of concerns. Shelley is interested in the relationship between the terms, whereas Southey prefers to explore the boundaries of each term individually. Southey seems oblivious to the possibility of conflict between terms; Shelley assumes from the outset that entertainment can counteract as well as enable instruction. He also assumes that one term must eventually dominate, claiming victory for amusement ("narrative") even though instruction triumphs in practice. Southey pursues the limits of both terms, favoring neither. If the most pleasurable literature is, as Southey believes, the *1001 Nights*, then his orientalist poem will take that as a model,

---

[73] Southey, preface (1800), *Thalaba* 225. According to Byron Smith, Southey is referring to "*The Arabian Tales, or, a Continuation of the Arabian Nights* (1792) translated by Robert Heron from *La Suite des milles et une nuits, contes arabes* (1788) by Dom Chavis and Jacques Cazotte. The story entitled 'The History of Maugraby the Magician' gave Southey the suggestion for his poem" (Smith, *Islam in English Literature* 180). Martha Conant discusses this tale in some detail; see Conant, *The Oriental Tale in England in the Eighteenth Century* 41–4. Moreover, the term "romance" itself has orientalist connotations in the nineteenth century; see for example John Beer, "Fragmentations and Ironies," *Questioning Romanticism*, ed. John Beer (Baltimore: Johns Hopkins UP, 1995) 262; Fischer, *Romantic Verse Narrative* 191; Metlitzki, *The Matter of Araby in Medieval England* 241–3, 248–50; and Schwab, *The Oriental Renaissance* 108.

aiming for the greatest possible delight. But the *1001 Nights* also instructs successfully; Southey works to replicate its effects by incorporating as much as possible (perhaps more than one would have thought possible) of his accumulated research. Throughout, the model of the *1001 Nights* and its descendants guides his efforts to entertain and inform.[74]

The desert, Islam: foreignness as a hermeneutic category

Thalaba's didacticism emphasizes information rather than morality, but it is nonetheless ideological. Certainly Southey seems unwilling to judge the researched material he presents, except in that selection implies a kind of evaluation. He rarely includes his own comments in the notes, whether independently or as responses to the scholars he cites. On the other hand, foreignness or exoticism — otherness — functions consistently in *Thalaba* as much more than a simple descriptive category; rather, it defines the value of information, whether for instruction or for entertainment. A detailed examination of book 3 will demonstrate the ways in which Southey's articulations of foreignness, specifically the foreignness of the Arabian desert, enable both instruction and entertainment.

By the beginning of book 3, the poem's major conflict — between Thalaba and the Domdaniel's "evil magicians" — has already been established. These sorcerers have killed Thalaba's father. His mother has died after wandering in the desert. Thalaba, just a child and alone, is taken in by a bedouin named Moath, to be cared for until he has grown and is able to avenge his family and destroy the magicians. Book 2 ends with the visit of a sorcerer who has been sent to kill Thalaba, only to be dispatched first by a freak sandstorm.

The opening stanza of book 3 begins with a conversation among Thalaba, Moath, and Thalaba's foster sister and future wife, Oneiza. Thalaba is trying (successfully) to convince the others that he should wear the ring he has found on the body of the dead sorcerer. The basic question is whether an item used by evil can also be used by good; this is universal enough, but Southey is careful to remind his readers of the Middle Eastern setting. When Thalaba notices a cryptic inscription on the ring, for example, he exclaims, "It is not written as the Koran is: / Some other tongue perchance" (3.1). Southey might have indicated the strangeness of the unknown language in another way, but the mention of the Qur'an serves the additional purpose of specifying once

---

[74] However sincerely Southey desires to inform his audience, it is difficult to agree with Sharafuddin that *Thalaba* "became a vehicle for the communication of the nature of the Islamic faith in the West, and in England in particular; it treated Islam with scholarly seriousness" (*Islam and Romantic Orientalism* 87). Part of the entertainment value of texts like the *1001 Nights*, and even *Thalaba*, lies precisely in the exoticism of the information they impart; "scholarly seriousness" must always compete with curiosity, and very often loses to it.

again the Arabian (and Muslim) setting. Towards the same ends, the stanza makes two references to sand, one of them specifically to "desert sands," along with an allusion to the group's "tent." We find this aggressive use of local color again in stanza 3, for instance, where the quietness of the night is described in peculiarly Arabian terms: "the night air had been so calm and still, / It had not from the grove / Shaken a ripe date down" (3.3). In fact, such conventionalized references appear in virtually every stanza, with tents, sand, and palms as the favored (though clichéd) markers of the oriental.[75]

On a pragmatic level, oriental references of this sort allow Southey to integrate information about the Middle East into his text without necessitating recourse to the notes. The group's departure from their campsite, for instance, gives Southey the opportunity to describe the bedouin procedure for breaking camp:

> Thalaba drew up
> The fastening of the cords;
> And Moath furl'd the tent;
> And from the grove of palms Oneiza led
> The Camels, ready to receive their load. (3.5)

The poem's instructional aim can thus be met while requiring minimal effort from the reader — no flipping pages to the notes, no struggling with small print, no deciphering scholarly prose.

More significantly, the markers of the oriental enforce a distance between the reader and the Orient. It may seem that by informing the reader about the East, *Thalaba* is enabling a closeness between them. However, the creation of such a complete picture for readers inevitably casts them as observers and interpreters clearly separate from the scene. By emphasizing the peculiarities of the Orient, the poem stresses this material's exclusion from the reader's experience. The sixth stanza of book 3 is a case in point. A series of nautical references describes the bedouins' passage from one campsite to the next:

> from the Isle of Palms they went their way,
> And when the Sun had reach'd his southern height,

---

[75] This trio of features has been remarkably enduring. A recent travel article on Tunisia includes all three (and little else) in a pull-out quote that precedes the article: "Tunisia offers visitors a glimpse of the great wide sands of the Sahara, with camels and oases formed of springs giving life to date palms, and the brown tents of nomads" (Larry Lindner, "Tunisia: Where the Sands of Time are Still Vibrant," *The Boston Globe* [23 Oct. 1994, Special Section: "Adventures in Travel"] 10.)

It may seem odd that Southey would fasten on such stereotypical Middle Eastern characteristics as tents, sand, and palms when his extensive research would have shown him so much more. Yet while this research enriched his knowledge of the region, it tended, because of its textual derivation, to confirm rather than counter the received ideas and images of the Orient.

> As back they turn'd their eyes,
> The distant Palms arose
> Like to the top-sails of some fleet far-off
> Distinctly seen, where else
> The Ocean bounds had blended with the sky! (3.6)

In a sense, this dressing of the desert caravan in a sailing fleet's costume and of the desert in the sea's makes both caravan and desert more recognizable to the reader. But the (clichéd) disguise cannot cover the differences between the North Atlantic and the Arabian desert, and the very need for disguise accentuates the latter's strangeness. This is a disguise meant to be penetrated. Since the presumed reader is affiliated with the world of the sea, not that of the desert, this "failed" disguise serves more to strengthen that affiliation than to allow a genuine rapprochement between the reader and the scene described.

The most important function of such markers, however, is to specify the scene's orientalness, or rather to orientalize it further. When, for example, Thalaba is visited by the spirit of the ring, he asks Moath if he hears this spirit. Moath responds, "I hear the wind, that flaps / The curtain of the tent" (3.9). The second phrase is superfluous, since Thalaba wants to know only whether Moath can hear the spirit; "I hear the wind" would be sufficient to answer his question. But the allusion to the wind flapping the curtain of the tent reminds the reader once again that the characters are in a bedouin camp. Like so many others, this scene demonstrates a resistance to universality; it comes to have interpretable meaning only in its orientalness. It is in this sense that foreignness (orientalness, otherness) becomes a hermeneutic category.

Seyhan comments that "[m]aking strange, distancing, and exoticizing, are, paradoxically, poetic operations of making an other familiar."[76] She is right, but familiarity is not the same as sameness. Even where Southey's examples are such well known stereotypes that they would be familiar rather than strange to the reader, they are familiar as signs of otherness, not of sameness. Sameness would be antithetical to the purpose of *Thalaba*, for it is difference that gives the poem's subject its appeal, as material for both pleasure and instruction.

Foreignness general and particular: character as archetype

The use of oriental markers is not the only didactic strategy that depends upon foreignness as a category of interpretation. Another crucial one, especially prominent in book 3, is that of the character as archetype. Marilyn Butler argues that *Thalaba* "allegorizes not an individual life, but Everyman travelling

---

[76] Seyhan, *Representation and Its Discontents* 14. MacKenzie makes a similar observation of orientalist painting; see his *Orientalism* 55.

through time and through stages of culture that are the same worldwide."[77] I propose instead that *Thalaba*'s characters are representative in a much more culturally specific way. While each has his or her own life course, that life course, along with the characters' individual features, would be of relatively little instructional value unless the characters were presented as typical of Arabs, and their lives as representative of life in the Arabian desert.[78] *Thalaba*'s notes reinforce Southey's formulation of characters as archetypes, but the poetic text itself engages fully in this project as well.

We may take as an example the depiction of Thalaba's youth in book 3, stanzas 18–25. After a description of his physical appearance (stanza 14) and of his relationship with Moath and Oneiza (stanzas 15–17), stanza 18 begins with the desert rains and the happy domestic scene inside the sodden tent:

> Or comes the Father of the Rains
> From his caves in the uttermost West?
> Comes he in darkness and storms?
> When the blast is loud;
> When the waters fill
> The traveller's tread in the sands;
> When the pouring shower
> Streams adown the roof;
> When the door-curtain hangs in heavier folds:
> When the out-strain'd tent flags loosely:
> Within there is the embers' cheerful glow,
> The sound of the familiar voice,
> The song that lightens toil, —
> Domestic Peace and Comfort are within.
> Under the common shelter, on dry sand,
> The quiet Camels ruminate their food;
> The lengthening cord from Moath falls,
> As patiently the Old Man
> Entwines the strong palm-fibres; by the hearth
> The Damsel shakes the coffee-grains,
> That with warm fragrance fill the tent;
> And while, with dexterous fingers, Thalaba
> Shapes the green basket, haply at his feet.
> Her favorite kidling gnaws the twig,
> Forgiven plunderer, for Oneiza's sake. (3.18)

The juxtaposition of bedouin characters to desert climate in these lines posits the characters as predictable manifestations of their culture and environment

---

[77] Butler, "Repossessing the Past" 77.

[78] Again I must disagree with Sharafuddin, who proposes that Southey's "imaginary Arabs are not merely primitive superstitious people, but cultured beings capable of spiritual experience," characterized by "complexity and aspiration" (*Islam and Romantic Orientalism* 105). Said's analysis of the "life-cycle" of Edward Lane's "modern Egyptian" (*Orientalism* 161) comes closer to the mark.

rather than as human beings acting with free will. The picture Southey paints of each is clearly a composite; his use of present tense is only the most obvious clue. We are to understand that "the Father of the Rains" comes each year in the same way ("From his caves in the uttermost West"), with the same effect ("darkness and storms"). If there is a traveler's footprint in the sand, it will be filled with water in the same way with every storm. Even if Moath does not make rope every evening, his rope making is typical of bedouin rainy-evening activities. That he makes rope, or that Oneiza roasts coffee, or that Thalaba weaves a basket, does not further the narrative in any way. If, however, we assume that Moath, Oneiza, and Thalaba are not simply individual human figures but representative bedouins, we see the importance of their behavior to *Thalaba*'s didactic program. Here, as above, Southey's manipulation of his material becomes legible only through the application of foreignness as a hermeneutic category.

It is clear from the notes accompanying these lines that the characters' specific traits are derived from generalizations about Arabs. The notes' role, though, is to reverse the process, guiding the reader from an understanding of the particular (Moath and his family) to an appreciation of the general (Arabs or bedouins). A brief quotation from Volney explains, for instance, that "The Arabs call the West and South-West winds, which prevail from November to February, *the fathers of the rains*."[79] While Southey's British readers might at first have supposed (based on abundant personal experience) that rainstorms were a universal experience, his citation strips away this universality by stressing the Arabianness of these rains. Moreover, in the next note, Southey quotes Pococke referring to bedouins only as "they," and in the following one Chénier referring only to "these people."[80] In neither case is the group of people at issue explicitly identified. The generality of the references leaves no doubt that readers are to extrapolate from the specific information about these bedouins (provided in the poem) to the habits of bedouins in general (provided in the notes). The effect of such interaction between notes and text is of course to cast Moath and his family principally as individual manifestations of a larger phenomenon of cultural otherness.

The next two stanzas are similar in structure as well as in effect to the one just discussed. They describe the results of the rains: first a "winter torrent," then a "vernal brook." In both cases, these lessons in climate are followed, as above, by a presentation of associated customs. Thalaba, for instance,

---

[79] Southey, notes, *Thalaba* 249; emphasis his. Constantin-François Chasseboeuf Volney (1757–1820) was a French orientalist and author of several books on the Middle East, including the 1787 *Voyage en Egypte et en Syrie* [*Travels in Egypt and Syria*], which chronicles his own travels.

[80] Edward Pococke (1604–1691) was a prolific orientalist at Oxford who had traveled to Syria. Louis de Chénier (1722–1796) spent fifteen years as French consul in Morocco; he published a book on Morocco (1787) and one on the Ottoman Empire (1789).

"wanders" barefoot in the "wet sand" created by the winter torrent, with "The rushing flow, the flowing roar, / Filling his yielded faculties, / A vague, a dizzy, a tumultuous joy" (3.19). Later he "recline[s]" "Beneath the lofty bank," while "With idle eye he views" the vernal brook's "little waves, / Quietly listening to the quiet flow" (3.20). Whereas in stanza 18 the emphasis is on domestic activity, which produced an emotion (contentment), here the emotion itself is accentuated. In neither case, however, can we safely assume that the emotion is individual. The notes to this stanza indicate that the stream described is representative of those "so common in Arabia."[81] Correspondingly, we may suppose that any bedouins who find themselves in a cozy tent during a rainstorm, or next to a flooded channel, or by a quiet stream, might feel as Thalaba and his foster family do. As a result, despite the apparent specificity of the emotion they feel, these characters are not individuals so much as illustrations, the better to contribute to the poem's didactic purpose. Moreover, their status as examples makes them less likely to attract the reader's empathy; as already discussed, such distance between the reader and the poem's subject contributes to the reader's instruction.

With Thalaba's position as a bedouin representative now secure, Moath and Oneiza replace him as the archetypes of choice. The next stanza begins by depicting Moath's circumstances:

> Nor rich, nor poor, was Moath; God hath given
> Enough, and blest him with a mind content.
> No hoarded gold disquieted his dreams;
> But ever round his station he beheld
> Camels that knew his voice,
> And home-birds, grouping at Oneiza's call,
> And goats that, morn and eve,
> Came with full udders to the Damsel's hand. (3.21)

These lines constitute a list of the items that a bedouin male needs in order to feel himself content: camels, poultry, goats, and a capable, hardworking daughter. As above, the image is a composite. Even more than in the preceding stanzas, though, the consistency of the scene is emphasized; his camels are always ("ever") there, and his goats come "morn and eve" for milking. The description is of course specific to Moath and his circumstances, but Southey goes out of his way to identify Moath as average, "Nor rich, nor poor." As usual, the notes complete this movement towards generality, making Moath's situation and attitude emblematic of bedouins as a group:

> All the wealth of a family consists of movables, of which the following is a pretty exact inventory: — A few male and female camels, some goats and poultry, a mare and her bridle and saddle,

---

[81] Southey, notes, *Thalaba* 250.

a tent, a lance sixteen feet long, a crooked sabre, a rusty musket, with a flint or matchlock; a pipe, a portable mill, a pot for cooking, a leathern bucket, a small coffee-roaster; a mat, some clothes, a mantle of black woollen, and a few glass or silver rings, which the women wear upon their legs and arms; if none of these are wanting, their furniture is complete.[82]

The note prepares the way for Southey's next topic: bedouin women. Oneiza is his example:

> Dear child! the tent beneath whose shade they dwelt,
> It was her work; and she had twined
> His girdle's many hues;
> And he had seen his robe
> Grow in Oneiza's loom.
> How often, with a memory-mingled joy
> Which made her Mother live before his sight,
> He watch'd her nimble fingers thread the woof!
> Or at the hand-mill, when she knelt and toil'd,
> Toss'd the thin cake on spreading palm,
> Or fix'd it on the glowing oven's side,
> With bare, wet arm, and safe dexterity. (3.21)

The fact that Oneiza is representative of bedouin women generally is supported by the mention of her mother. These lines characterize both women by their involvement in work, especially weaving. Such a characterization is confirmed in the notes, all three of which refer primarily and explicitly to women's labor — weaving, grinding, and baking.

Having identified the daytime activities of these supposedly typical bedouins, the poem shifts to evening, when "The Tamarind from the dew / Sheathes its young fruit, yet green" (3.22). This reference to the tamarind (elaborated upon in the notes) serves the same purpose as the introductory references to climate in earlier stanzas; it sets the scene, but in such a way as to emphasize its difference from an assumed European standard. This accomplished, the entire remainder of the stanza is devoted to the characters' habits of prayer. Again, they are offered as representative, even though their worship might seem primitive compared with other Muslims', whose more elaborate arrangements might be more familiar to readers. But, the speaker asks rhetorically,

> What if beneath no lamp-illumined dome,
> Its marble walls bedeck'd with flourish'd truth,
> Azure and gold adornment? Sinks the word
> With deeper influence from the Imam's voice,
> Where, in the day of congregation, crowds
> Perform the duty-task? (3.22)

---

[82] Southey, notes, *Thalaba* 250; the quotation is from Volney.

Now that these pious Muslims have prayed as required, they are at leisure.[83] Oneiza is of course still working, "knitting light palm-leaves for her brother's brow," but Moath is "tranquilly" smoking his pipe (3.23). Thalaba has let "The slacken'd bow, the quiver, the long lance / Rest on the pillar of the Tent," while he plays a reed flute or recites love poetry to his companions (3.23–4).[84]

Beneath all this peace there is passion, however. We soon suspect that Oneiza is in love with Thalaba, which creates an opportunity for the delineation of oriental feminine adornments:

> was it sister-love
> For which the silver rings
> Round her smooth ankles and her tawny arms
> Shone daily brighten'd? for a brother's eye
> Were her long fingers tinged,
> As when she trimm'd the lamp,
> And through the veins and delicate skin
> The light shone rosy? that the darken'd lids
> Gave yet a softer lustre to her eye?
> That with such pride she trick'd
> Her glossy tresses, and on holyday
> Wreathed the red flower-crown round
> Their waves of glossy jet? (3.25)

It is difficult to imagine how Oneiza would find time for all of these cosmetic refinements, given that she must also weave the family's shelter and clothing, prepare their food, care for their livestock, and so forth. This is clearly of no concern to Southey; the important thing is that the reader know about these ornaments, not that Oneiza (or any other single individual) make use of them. The notes emphasize the Arabness of the adornments, observing for instance that the "tinge" on Oneiza's fingers is from henna and that her eyelids are darkened by kohl. (The henna is especially problematic because it requires some time to set; Oneiza would probably have had to miss a milking.) However, it is important also to observe that, as elsewhere, these notes draw upon non-Arab as well as Arab materials. India, Persia, West Africa, Poland, Hungary, Italy, Portugal, and Greece all are mentioned, after which Southey remarks that "The females of the rest of Europe have never added [kohl and

---

[83] Southey takes this opportunity to include more than half a page of notes on oriental singing, mosque architecture, and the direction in which Muslims are required to face while praying.

[84] This reference to the "pillar of the Tent" is explained in a long footnote that discusses not only tent materials and construction but also the particulars of tent use. Bedouins, it is pointed out, have no "bed, mattrass [sic], or pillow," but sleep "lying, as they find room, upon a mat or carpet, in the middle or corner of the tent." We will be relieved to learn, however, that "[t]hose who are married, have each of them a corner of the tent, cantoned off with a curtain" (Southey, notes, *Thalaba* 251; he is citing Thomas Shaw [1694–1751], who published several books based on his travels in North Africa and the Levant).

henna] to their list of ornaments."[85] Clearly, then, the crucial interpretive category in play here is not that of Arabness, orientalness, or even exoticism, but rather once again of foreignness in general, even while the Arab and the oriental remain the essential points of reference for Southey's implied definition of the other.

This stanza concludes Southey's summary of Thalaba's youth. The remainder of book 3 describes how Thalaba finds upon the forehead of a locust instructions to depart "when the sun shall be darkened at noon" (3.34). The eclipse arrives that very day, and Thalaba leaves immediately, despite the distress of Moath and Oneiza. This turn of events gives Southey an excuse for lengthy notes on locust plagues, predators on locusts, the physical characteristics of locusts (including their forehead markings), and the appearance of a solar eclipse. The remaining nine books of *Thalaba* describe the protagonist's wanderings through the Middle East and his repeated encounters with villainous magicians. After many travails, and with his piety reaffirmed, Thalaba finally uses his father's sword to kill all the magicians but one, who repents and is spared. Urged on by his mother's spirit, he then kills "the Idol," who represents the Devil, Eblis. At last, in an ending recalled in *The Revolt of Islam*, Thalaba himself is killed as the "Ocean-vault" of the Domdaniel collapses.

> In the same moment, at the gate
> Of Paradise, Oneiza's Houri form
> Welcomed her Husband to eternal bliss. (12.36)[86]

Extremes: too many notes?

Although book 3 has especially extensive notes (and especially little action), the other books of *Thalaba* are also heavily annotated. One cannot argue that the Islamic Orient per se called Southey to this approach; his other long poems on exotic subjects are also annotated, though not quite so heavily.[87] However, conventional perceptions of the Orient clearly encourage annotation. If orientalist literature is already assumed to be edifying, its instructive capacity

---

[85] Southey, notes, *Thalaba* 253.

[86] More extended summaries and general analyses of *Thalaba* may be found in Beyer, *The Enchanted Forest* (Oxford: Basil Blackwell, 1963) 237–44; Butler, "Plotting the Revolution" 143–52 and "Repossessing the Past" 73–80; Hoffpauir, "The Thematic Structure of Southey's Epic Poetry" 246–8; Sharafuddin, *Islam and Romantic Orientalism* 50–133; and Smith, *Islam in English Literature* 181–6.

[87] Diego Saglia's analysis of the notes to Southey's long poem on Moorish Spain, *Roderick, the Last of the Goths* (1814), confirms the significance of such marginalia; see Saglia, "Nationalist Texts and Counter-Texts: Southey's *Roderick* and the Dissensions of the Annotated Romance," *Nineteenth-Century Literature* 53:4 (1999): 421–51.

can be practically increased by the use of notes. Indeed, notes, along with explanatory prefaces and other paratextual framing devices, are so common in orientalist works as to be characteristic of the genre. Southey's use of them is simply more extensive than usual.[88]

Further, while keeping in mind how the oriental (specifically the Arab) is subsumed within the hermeneutic category of foreignness, it is essential to remember that the oriental is the standard for other types of foreignness, exoticism, and indeed weirdness of every kind. In *Thalaba* we see this not only in the indistinct relationship between the Arabian setting and the information about Persia, Poland, Portugal, etc., brought to bear upon it, but also especially in the unconcern with which the poem mingles the natural and supernatural, the explicable and the magical; in the Orient, it seems, there is no need to differentiate one from the other. In short, *Thalaba* implies that the strange is necessarily relevant. For instance, during one of Thalaba's encounters with the evil sorcerers, the mummified hand of a hanged man is burned so that its fumes will subdue the vicious guardian of a cave (5.27–9). This scene reveals the union of natural and supernatural; Southey's note associates the burning with the supernatural by labeling it "superstition," yet the same note also includes detailed instructions on how to prepare such a hand, almost as if Southey expects his (presumably nonsupernatural) readers to try the recipe themselves. Similarly, the text specifies that "No eye of mortal man, / If unenabled by enchanted spell, / Had pierced those fearful depths" (5.23), but those evidently supernatural "fearful depths," are found at the edge of a "bitumen-lake" (5.22), which is described in both text and notes as a natural phenomenon.[89] The blurring of these various boundaries recalls once again the importance of the Orient as a locus for both amusement and instruction. Indeed, it is here that we see most clearly the extent to which instruction and entertainment overlap. When we are acquiring information about what is weird we enjoy ourselves; the origin of the weirdness matters very little. But precisely because Southey's Orient is so inclusive of weirdness, virtually any odd bit of information becomes pertinent; one result is the massing of information we see in *Thalaba*'s notes and poetic text.[90]

Finally, the Orient (with the partial exception of the desert) is

---

[88] Sharafuddin's comments on this phenomenon are useful; see *Islam and Romantic Orientalism* xxix–xxx, 117.

[89] Southey's tactics here may be modeled in part upon what Haddawy describes as the *1001 Nights*' "interweaving the unusual, the extraordinary, the marvelous, and the supernatural into the fabric of everyday life. [...] Thus the phantasmagoric is based on the concrete, the supernatural grounded in the natural" (*The Arabian Nights* x–xi).

[90] Said makes a related argument about Gustave Flaubert's orientalism: "The Orient is *watched* [...]; the European, whose sensibility tours the Orient, is a watcher, never involved, always detached, always ready for new examples of what [Le Mascrier's 1735] *Description de l'Égypte* called 'bizarre jouissance.' The Orient becomes a living tableau of queerness" (*Orientalism* 103; emphasis his).

conventionally perceived as jumbled, detail-ridden, and otherwise excessive.[91] The desert, for instance, is a dry, vacant wasteland, as Southey establishes early on by having Thalaba nearly die in it. The great force of the winter rains then contrasts sharply with the dryness of the desert in other seasons; similarly, the familial comfort of Moath's tent contrasts with the empty solitude of its surroundings (book 3). The heat of the desert finds its opposite extreme in the snows of Lebanon, where Thalaba almost dies of hypothermia (book 10). Less physical extremes also predominate. Thalaba, for instance, goes repeatedly from a state of abandonment and mortal danger to one of being cherished and honored. Moath and Oneiza are absolutely good and loyal, while the sorcerers of the Domdaniel are (with one exception) utterly deceitful villains. In short, the Islamic Orient in this poem is stereotypically constituted as a place of extremes.

Indeed, one could argue that *Thalaba*'s overflowing notes exemplify a sort of corresponding structural excess. These notes are occasionally inconsistent with the text, as when Southey praises the domestic scene in Moath's tent but then in the notes cites Chénier's negative comment: "being black, [these tents] produce a disagreeable effect at a distant view."[92] More often, though, the notes are simply disproportionate or irrelevant. In book 8, for instance, a false version of Oneiza's spirit appears, lasting less than two stanzas of verse before her real spirit emerges (8.9–10). The false spirit is called a "vampire corpse," which gives rise to two full pages of notes on vampires in the Middle East and elsewhere.[93] Clearly such extensive annotation cannot be justified on the basis of the incident's importance, especially since, unlike the lengthy descriptions of tent construction, for example, it does little to help the reader visualize the scene at hand.

In this case, as in numerous others, we may justifiably suspect that the incident occurs for the sake of the notes. Indeed, Southey's letters suggest that he considered the notes ahead of the text.[94] While still in the midst of writing

---

[91] This perception applies to any number of spheres of life, from government to architecture and urban planning to interior decoration to interpersonal relations. See for instance Asad, "Two European Images of Non-European Rule" 110–1. Timothy Mitchell explores this view's obvious implications for colonialism: "The Orient was backward, irrational, and disordered, and therefore in need of European order and authority" (*Colonising Egypt* 166). The problem of disorder will be addressed more fully in chapter 2.

[92] Southey, notes, *Thalaba* 251.

[93] Southey, notes, *Thalaba* 292–4.

[94] Butler concludes that "Southey's notes must have existed before he went off to Portugal in the summer of 1800 to write the text of his poem, since he sent *Thalaba* directly to the publisher from Portugal the following year" ("Plotting the Revolution" 148). Francis Jeffrey, whose notorious review of *Thalaba* appeared in 1802, would have shared her suspicions; he says with dismay that "It is impossible to peruse this poem, with the notes, without feeling that it is the fruit of much reading undertaken for the express purpose of fabricating some such performance" ("*Thalaba the Destroyer*," *Edinburgh Review* 1 [Oct.

the sixth book of *Thalaba*, for instance, he comments, "my notes are ready for the whole, at least there is only the trouble of arranging and seasoning them."[95] Later, as he describes the process of revision, he again gives priority to the notes: "The work before me is almost of terrifying labour; folio after folio to be gutted, for the immense mass of collateral knowledge which is indispensable."[96]

Diego Saglia argues that the notes to Southey's 1814 *Roderick, the Last of the Goths* constitute "an additional discourse" that operates as a Derridean supplement, "work[ing] against textual unity." He sees the relationship between the poetic text and the notes as "both collaborative and antagonistic, completing and supplanting."[97] Such a reading would be largely valid for *Thalaba* as well, with one important qualification. Saglia's argument assumes that, in the absence of the notes, the signification of the poetic text would be relatively unproblematic; it is "the notes [that] expose the impossibility of origins and seminal histories within a textuality that is always a reproduction and a transcription of other texts."[98] In *Thalaba*, however, it is clear that even without what Saglia calls the "series of discourses" "staged" by the notes,[99] the poetic text itself resists unitary meaning. This resistance is particularly evident in the impulse towards excessive information that affects the text as well as the notes. The crowding in the description of Moath's tent (3.18, cited above) is unexceptional; *Thalaba* seems driven by an urge for completeness that often results in a list rather than a full picture. When, for example, Southey describes Oneiza's efforts to make herself attractive to Thalaba, the minute detail tends to atomize the image. It takes great effort on the reader's part to gather Southey's description of her ankles, arms, fingers, veins, skin, eyelids, eyes, and hair into a composite picture of a beautiful young woman (3.25).[100]

The polarization of amusement and instruction in *Thalaba*, then, is supported not only by Southey's choice of discursive models (the *1001 Nights* and scholarly orientalism), as I suggest above, but also by those excesses characteristic of the conventionalized Orient. The structural excesses (notes

---

1802] 77). For discussion of this review, see Alison Hickey, "Coleridge, Southey, 'and Co.': Collaboration and Authority," *Studies in Romanticism* 37.3 (1998): 305, 307.

[95] Southey, "To S.T. Coleridge, Esq.," Dec. 27, 1799, *The Life and Correspondence of Robert Southey* 2: 36.

[96] Southey, "To S.T. Coleridge, Esq.," May 1, 1800, *The Life and Correspondence of Robert Southey* 2: 64.

[97] Saglia, "Nationalist Texts" 427–9.

[98] Saglia, "Nationalist Texts" 428.

[99] Saglia, "Nationalist Texts" 429.

[100] As Lowe observes, the descriptive dismemberment of the love object has strong roots in Western literary traditions, independent of orientalism; she cites Petrarch's praise of Laura as an example (*Critical Terrains* 48). However, the tendency towards atomization pervades orientalists' descriptions of Orientals in circumstances that have nothing to do with love; Southey's portrayal of Oneiza here is clearly part of that tradition as well as of Petrarch's.

disproportionate to the text, extraordinarily complete but atomized descriptions) extend the instructional aspects of *Thalaba*, while the excesses integral to the depiction of the Orient itself (extremes of heat, opulence, and danger) enhance the poem's amusement value.

Southey and his readers: delighted, informed, or distressed

It is difficult to know how effectively Southey's contemporary readers were either instructed or entertained. *Thalaba* did not sell particularly well.[101] The *Monthly Review*, the *Critical Review* and the *Edinburgh Review* each offered mixed evaluations in their articles on *Thalaba*. The *Monthly* reviewer criticizes Southey on several counts. "The more minute description," he complains, "is rather tedious, and is very particular without being distinct."[102] Although he praises certain descriptive passages, he concludes that

> Throughout the poem [...] the author has interspersed too much description; and the notes, though sometimes curious and amusing, are too bulky, and contain rather an ostentasious [sic] display of the author's assiduity in collecting materials for his undertaking.[103]

Portions of the poem are "not very intelligible," "fatiguing," "tedious," and "dull."[104] Southey's "mongrel metre" shows "a degree of presumption which we are not much inclined to pardon."[105] Despite

> poetical beauties of the first order, [...] the poem is deficient not only in probability, but in connection and consistency of fiction. The death of every new sorcerer is the end of an entire fable and course of action; and there is no more connection nor dependency of parts in the different enterprizes [sic] of the Destroyer, than in the seven voyages of Sinbad the sailor. We find no discrimination of character, nor any extended delineation of human actions.[106]

The *Critical* reviewer, Southey's friend William Taylor, too notes that "there is a want of concatenation, of mutual dependence, of natural arrangement [...]: the fable somewhat wants cohesion: nor is it wholly consistent."[107] Although he is intrigued by the characters in *Thalaba*, he finds that they

---

[101] Rajan speculates on the reasons for the poem's poor performance; see "Monstrous Mythologies" 202.
[102] *"Thalaba the Destroyer," Monthly Review* 39 (Sept. 1802): 241.
[103] *"Thalaba the Destroyer," Monthly Review* 251.
[104] *"Thalaba the Destroyer," Monthly Review* 243, 244, 245, 247.
[105] *"Thalaba the Destroyer," Monthly Review* 251.
[106] *"Thalaba the Destroyer," Monthly Review* 250.
[107] [Taylor], *"Thalaba the Destroyer," Critical Review* 39 (Sept. 1803): 370.

> have something supernatural in their turn of mind, which surely intercepts very much our fellow-feeling. [... L]ike the figures of landscape-painters, [they] are often almost lost in the scene: they appear as the episodical or accessory objects. [...] It is theatric representation reversed: the places seem the realities; the actors the fictitious existences.[108]

Writing for the *Edinburgh Review*, Francis Jeffrey praises certain passages but devotes himself mainly to complaints. The style is "feeble, low, and disjointed." The "exaggerat[ed ...] characters must be in agonies and ecstasies, from their entrance to their exit," to the point that "[t]here is little of human character in the poem." The versification is "a jumble," and "the conduct of the fable is as disorderly as the versification." Finally, "the story [...] consists altogether of the most wild and extravagant fictions, and openly sets nature and probability at defiance."[109]

These reviewers' criticisms, then, focus on two problems: the inaccessibility of the characters, and the disjointedness and artificiality of the plot. Southey's manipulations of entertainment and instruction appear quite beside the point; the reviewers seem to be saying that they would prefer a psychologically satisfying experience, which is made impossible by the nature of the characters and the plot. The reviewers' critique is largely explicable if we consider *Thalaba*'s relationship with the oriental tale as genre. The classic "Arabian tale," such as that recounting "the seven voyages of Sinbad the sailor" mentioned by the *Monthly* reviewer, is episodic and/or composed of stories enframed by other stories. As a rule, the characters are not developed sufficiently to arouse empathy even when their misfortunes inspire sympathy. In fact, the entertainment derived from such a tale depends upon its not making demands upon the psyche of the reader. In Rae Beth Gordon's terms, these are "Arabian tales where complicated imaginary events are intertwined, and where the readers' pleasure lies in losing themselves along with the narrator, then in untying the plot."[110] This is a principally intellectual pleasure that does not entail the reader's emotional involvement with psychologically complex characters. So too, it is the intellect, not the psyche, that engages with the instructional component of such tales. Thus the reviewers' dissatisfaction with *Thalaba* is in an odd sense a mark of the poem's success; it has alienated them for all the right reasons. This leaves the poem in an ambiguous position, since the fulfillment of its aesthetic aims causes its rejection.

The problem is essentially one of conflicting expectations. The reviewer

---

[108] [Taylor], "*Thalaba the Destroyer*," 371, 369. I will return in chapter 3 to this question of the relative position of people and places.

[109] [Jeffrey], "*Thalaba the Destroyer*," 69, 69, 80, 72, 74, 75. The context of this review is discussed in Butler, "Plotting the Revolution" 141; and Fischer, *Romantic Verse Narrative* 80–1.

[110] Gordon, *Ornament, Fantasy, and Desire in Nineteenth-Century French Literature* (Princeton: Princeton UP, 1992) 13. See also Smith, *Islam in English Literature* 84.

looks for a poem with coherent narrative flow and emotionally developed figures, whereas the poet is working within a genre (the "Arabian tale") with opposite expectations. That two of the reviewers recognize this problem of genre on some level is clear from their uneasy attempts to categorize *Thalaba*. Taylor begins his review with the question of whether to call *Thalaba* a "metrical romance" or a "lyrical one;" he also calls it a "story," and compares it to the ode and the "epopoeia."[111] The *Monthly*'s review starts with the sentence "It is not easy either to class or to appreciate this singular performance," and then, as if to explain, announces that "[t]he story and action of the poem are altogether oriental."[112] In neither case does the reviewer's recognition of genre as an issue in the interpretation of *Thalaba* lead to substantially greater enthusiasm for the poem.[113] Nor does the *Monthly* reviewer's attribution of orientalness to story and action inspire him to articulate expectations consistent with the genre of the oriental tale. Like the other reviewers, his standards rely on the moderated opposition between pleasure (the favored term) and instruction typical of mainstream early-nineteenth-century aesthetics.

Representation and the "Arabesque ornament"

Presumably, Southey's reviewers' would have preferred a poem with emotionally developed, verisimilar characters; a credible plot; and description that was "distinct" as well as "particular." Such characters, plot, and description would all be based upon a classical assumption of realistic representation; mimesis would be such a poem's dominant mode. In contrast, as Jeffrey says rather truculently, *Thalaba*,

> [i]n its action, [...] is not an imitation of any thing. [...] The pleasure afforded by performances of this sort is very much akin

---

[111] [Taylor], "*Thalaba the Destroyer*," 369. "Epopoeia" is an alternative to "epopee," an epic poem or a "composition comparable to an epic poem" (*OED*).

[112] "*Thalaba the Destroyer*," *Monthly Review* 240.

[113] The genre of Southey's long poems (and other nineteenth-century poets' work of the same scope) is a complex problem that has been debated at some length; see for instance Fischer, *Romantic Verse Narrative* 72–85. Fischer points out that Jeffrey simply adopts Southey's term, "metrical romance," but then judges the poem according to epic criteria (81). Fischer also observes correctly that Southey himself obscures *Thalaba*'s genre by using at least three different terms ("romance," "poem," and "Arabian Tale") to identify the poem. However, it is important to note, as Fischer does not, that two of these three terms refer to the work's orientalism, strongly suggesting that Southey privileged that aspect of *Thalaba* above any other. The remaining term, "poem," is so general as to appear virtually meaningless until we notice that the reviewers' reactions to *Thalaba*'s plot and characters seem better suited to a discussion of prose fiction than of poetry; perhaps Southey really did need to remind his readers that this was a poem.

> to that which may be derived from the exhibition of a harlequin farce; where, instead of just imitations of nature and human character, we are entertained with the transformation of cauliflowers and beer-barrels, the apparition of ghosts and devils, and all the other magic of the wooden sword.[114]

From a (neo)classical perspective, moreover, it would be reasonable to expect representation in a poem whose goals are to amuse and instruct. The link between these goals and representation is forged in Greek aesthetic theory and persists throughout the development of English criticism. Sidney associates them when he declares that "Poesy therefore is an art of imitation, for so Aristotle termeth it in his word *Mimesis*, that is to say, a representing, counterfeiting, or figuring forth [...]; with this end, to teach and delight."[115] Joseph Addison resumes the more explicitly causal connection suggested by Aristotle, explaining that representation is itself a source of delight:

> this [...] Pleasure of the Imagination proceeds from that Action of the Mind, which compares the Ideas arising from the Original Objects, with the Ideas we receive from the Statue, Picture, Description, or Sound that represents them. It is impossible for us to give the necessary Reason, why this Operation of the Mind is attended with so much Pleasure, as I have before observed on the same Occasion; but we find a great variety of Entertainments derived from this single Principle.[116]

Johnson specifies this connection between pleasure and representation. Representations of "particular manners" will be unsuccessful, he predicts, whereas "[n]othing can please many, and please long, but just representations of general nature." He also tries to articulate the "necessary Reason" for this pleasure that Addison found it "impossible for us to give": "Imitations produce pain or pleasure, not because they are mistaken for realities, but because they bring realities to mind."[117] Unfortunately, since Johnson is unable then to explain why "bringing realities to mind" should produce pleasure, his attempt is hardly more satisfying than Addison's evasion. Hazlitt tries again, emphasizing new impressions rather than familiar realities:

> One chief reason, it should seem then, why imitation pleases, is, because, by exciting curiosity, and inviting a comparison between

---

[114] [Jeffrey], "*Thalaba the Destroyer*," 75–6.

[115] Sidney, *An Apology for Poetry* 86.

[116] Addison, "The Pleasures of the Imagination" (1712), *Criticism: The Major Texts*, ed. W.J. Bate 186. Aristotle's version, briefly, is as follows: "there are some things that distress us when we see them in reality, but the most accurate representations of these same things we view with pleasure [... M]en find pleasure in viewing representations because it turns out that they learn and infer what each thing is" (Aristotle, *Poetics* 7).

[117] Johnson, "Preface to Shakespeare" 208, 215.

the object and the representation, it opens a new field of inquiry, and leads the attention to a variety of details and distinctions not perceived before.[118]

Shelley's version stresses formal conventions instead: "there is a certain order or rhythm belonging to each of these classes of mimetic representation, from which the hearer and the spectator receive an intenser and purer pleasure than from other."[119]

This progression of views suggests that while English critics remain convinced that instruction and pleasure have something to do with representation, they have trouble fixing upon the connection. Though the question of pleasure concerns them more urgently than that of instruction, their underlying assumption is evidently that representation enables both instruction and pleasure.[120] These critics seem not to have considered seriously the possibility of a poetry which may seek earnestly to amuse and instruct but in which representation is neither based in a verifiable, experiential reality nor accorded the ultimate aesthetic value.[121] Yet at least in certain respects, *Thalaba the Destroyer* explores just such a possibility. The poem's consistent unwillingness to separate natural from supernatural, or fact from fantasy, distorts the supposed reality in which this representation is grounded. Because the "reality" that it imitates is unreliable, the resulting imitation appears unreliable as well, however solidly referential it might still be. In addition, because this representation is, like so much of nineteenth-century orientalism, heavily dependent on texts instead of on empirical reality, and because it incorporates so much non-Middle Eastern (textual) material, it evokes the Islamic Middle East as an unstable referent only insecurely grounded in reality:

---

[118] Hazlitt, "On Imitation" 298.

[119] Shelley, *A Defence of Poetry* 430.

[120] For more recent reflection upon this problem, see Jacques Derrida's discussion of Kant in *The Truth in Painting*, 1978, trans. Geoff Bennington and Ian McLeod (Chicago: U of Chicago P, 1987) esp. 45.

[121] Boyd argues persuasively that mimesis had begun to fade by the end of the eighteenth century. However, it remains for poets of the early nineteenth century a "given" (Boyd's term) against which they must judge their own critical and poetic positions (see Boyd, *The Function of Mimesis and Its Decline* 304–5). Comprehensive book-length studies of this hugely important issue include Boyd, *The Function of Mimesis and Its Decline*; Gunter Gebauer and Christoph Wulf, *Mimesis: Culture, Art, Society*, trans. Don Reneau (Berkeley: U of California P, 1995); Arne Melberg, *Theories of Mimesis* (Cambridge: Cambridge UP, 1995); Seyhan, *Representation and Its Discontents*; and Michael Taussig, *Mimesis and Alterity: A Particular History of the Senses* (New York: Routledge, 1993). See also Frederick Burwick, "The Romantic Concept of Mimesis: *Idem et Alter*," *Questioning Romanticism*, ed. John Beer (Baltimore: Johns Hopkins UP, 1995) 179–208; Derrida, *The Truth in Painting* ch. 1; and Thomas McFarland, *Romanticism and the Forms of Ruin: Wordsworth, Coleridge, and Modalities of Fragmentation* (Princeton: Princeton UP, 1981) 382–418.

in Said's terms, a simulacrum.¹²² *Thalaba*'s use of foreignness as a hermeneutic category becomes especially significant in this context since it implies an aesthetic standard other than the (neo)classical fidelity to nature.

Equally important, though, is Southey's attempt to use the arabesque as a challenge to representation itself. This ambivalent and understated effort is based an a surprisingly simplistic vision of the arabesque, compared for instance to the complex consideration of this subject presented by Friedrich Schlegel in the same year that Southey wrote *Thalaba*.¹²³ Be that as it may, Southey uses the notion of the arabesque primarily as a justification for his chosen meter. In his original preface to *Thalaba*, he announces:

> Let me not be supposed to prefer the rhythm in which [*Thalaba*] is written, abstractedly considered, to the regular blank verse — the noblest measure, in my judgment, of which our admirable language is capable. For the following Poem I have preferred it, because it suits the varied subject: it is the *Arabesque* ornament of an Arabian tale.¹²⁴

In his much later preface to *The Curse of Kehama*, he states again that the "reason why the irregular, rhymeless lyrics [...] were preferred for Thalaba was, that the freedom and variety of such verse were suited to the story." While *Kehama* demanded "moral sublimity" and "the utmost richness of versification," *Thalaba*, as an "Arabian Tale," called for "the simplest and easiest form of verse."¹²⁵

Southey's comments in both prefaces present this aspect of the poem's form as dictated by its content (its "story") and specifically by the "Arabian" identity of that story. Whereas ornament is usually, by definition, understood to be supplemental and nonessential, he indicates that this "Arabesque ornament" is actually necessary to the effect he seeks. The relationship between the "Arabian tale" and its "Arabesque ornament" thus becomes oddly reciprocal. On the one hand, the tale's Arabian affiliation calls for the arabesque ornament, while on the other hand, the ornament completes that

---

¹²² Said, *Orientalism* 166. Others have extended Said's analysis; see Lowe, *Critical Terrains* x; Mitchell, *Colonising Egypt* esp. chs. 1, 5; and Sharafuddin, *Islam and Romantic Orientalism* 228.

¹²³ See F. Schlegel, *Dialogue on Poetry* (1799–1800), *Dialogue on Poetry and Literary Aphorisms*, trans. Ernst Behler and Roman Struc, (University Park: Pennsylvania State UP, 1968) 86, 96, 103–4. For discussion of Schlegel's arabesque, see Gordon, *Ornament, Fantasy, and Desire* 31–6. General analysis of the arabesque, with reference to its origin in the visual arts, may be found in Ernst Kühnel, *The Arabesque: Meaning and Transformation of an Ornament*, 1949, trans. Richard Ettinghausen (Graz, Austria: Verlag für Sammler, 1976). For discussion of the arabesque as it relates to narrative and to Islamic aesthetics, see Sandra Naddaff, *Arabesque: Narrative Structure and the Aesthetics of Repetition in* 1001 *Nights* (Evanston, IL: Northwestern UP, 1991) 111–9.

¹²⁴ Southey, preface (1800), *Thalaba* 225; emphasis his.

¹²⁵ Southey, preface (1838), *The Curse of Kehama* 566.

affiliation, confirming the tale's fundamental Arabianness. The arabesque is thereby put in the position of representing the oriental nature of the poem, even though the essence of the arabesque is of course that it is purely ornament, that it does not represent — or, in Sandra Naddaff's words, that it is "[n]onfigural and thus necessarily antimimetic, [...] at once the means of signification and the thing signified."[126]

Southey's prefaces do not comment, of course, either upon the representational role of the "Arabesque ornament" or upon *Thalaba*'s other formal allusions to the arabesque, including repeated lines and episodic narrative structures. Such features are strongly associated with oriental literary models. Moreover, like the arabesque of meter, these arabesque characteristics are not in themselves representational or referential. Southey's unwillingness to acknowledge the arabesque in any less "ornamental" aspect of the poem than its meter indicates an ambivalence about the arabesque. His equivocal, even suspicious attitude can also be discerned in one of the very few directly judgmental comments he makes in the notes to *Thalaba*.

> A waste of ornament and labor characterizes all the works of the Orientalists [that is, the Orientals]. I have seen illuminated Persian manuscripts that must each have been the toil of many years, every page painted, not with representations of life and manners, but usually like the curves and lines of a Turkey carpet, conveying no idea whatever, as absurd to the eye as nonsense-verses to the ear. The little of their literature that has reached us is equally worthless.[127]

This note takes a fundamentally neoclassical position in favor of the "representations of life and manners" and against arabesque ornamentation "like the curves and lines of a Turkey carpet."

However, in yet another instance of the sort of discursive diffusion Saglia observes, *Thalaba*'s orientalism itself forces this prejudice to be compromised. Certainly, too much arabesque would interfere with the representation upon which both the entertainment and the instruction of the poem depend, as Jeffrey implies when he charges Southey with "disproportioned and

---

[126] Naddaff, *Arabesque* 115. Derrida identifies a similar phenomenon: "[t]he *parergon* can [...] contribute to the proper and intrinsically aesthetic representation if it intervenes *by its form* and only by its form" (*The Truth in Painting* 64, emphasis his). One can glimpse too in Southey's arabesque the prototype of what Lowe calls Roland Barthes's "'poetics of escape,' a desire to transcend semiology and the ideology of signifier and signified, to invent a place that exceeds binary structure itself" (*Critical Terrains* 154).

[127] Southey, notes, *Thalaba* 232. Smith comments briefly on this passage; see *Islam in English Literature* 184–5. In accordance with current critical conventions, I use "oriental" to refer to things of the Orient, and "orientalist" to refer to things produced through European signification upon the Orient. Nineteenth-century distinctions between the terms are typically imprecise — hence Southey's reference to Persian artists as "Orientalists."

injudicious ornaments."[128] On the other hand, as an "Arabian tale," the poem must have something arabesque about it. Southey's solution to this dilemma is to include arabesque, restrictively labeled as such, in an area — meter, rhyme — which is already chiefly ornamental and nonrepresentational. Indeed, the ornamental aspect of the arabesque remains the only important one for him, to the point that his interpretation of the arabesque as "irregular" and "free" disregards the customary view (based mainly on Islamic art) of the arabesque as orderly, repetitive, geometric, and symmetrical.[129]

Thalaba remains relentlessly and obsessively referential even though, as I have shown, mimetic representation is undermined throughout, especially by the Islamic Middle East's instability as a referent and by the (partial) substitution of foreignness for fidelity to nature as an aesthetic criterion. It is only through the arabesque that *Thalaba* begins to bring referentiality itself into question.[130] Gordon argues that "one of the primary functions of ornament is to carry meaning and intent that have been suppressed or excluded from the central field." Among ornaments, the arabesque in particular "is pure form, nonreferential ornament."[131] Given that, as Seyhan explains, "such figures as the arabesque [...] challenge the notion of total representation,"[132] *Thalaba*'s "Arabesque ornament" enables a query about the privileged status of referentiality, a query that is firmly suppressed within *Thalaba*'s emphatically referential "central field."

Thalaba's staged meeting of form and content through the "Arabesque ornament" is important as an experiment with nonrepresentation, despite the experiment's superficiality and tentativeness and despite Southey's reliance on a dubious interpretation of the arabesque. Shelley's approach is closer to Southey's than might first appear, and not only because of Southey's well-known and formidable influence on his younger contemporary.[133] *The Revolt of Islam*'s allegorical displacement of European events onto an Eastern setting indicates a parallel endeavor to reach beyond the conventional bounds of representation. To borrow the terms of Seyhan's argument, allegory

---

[128] [Jeffrey], *"Thalaba the Destroyer,"* 78.

[129] See Gordon, *Ornament, Fantasy, and Desire* 201; and Naddaff, *Arabesque* 112, 115.

[130] Saglia remarks that "irony in [Southey's] *Roderick* cannot be explained in terms of authorial intention" ("Nationalist Texts" 443). The same is true of *Thalaba*'s counter-referential experimentation. It is instead, as Saglia says, "a feature that escapes authorial control; it is rather an aspect of the work's internal organization" (p. 443).

[131] Gordon, *Ornament, Fantasy, and Desire* 4, 34. For a summary of Southey's views on ornament in literary style, see Morgan, "Southey on Poetry" 81–3. Butler argues that Southey's "experimental metres [...] suspend [...] the automatic superior prestige of forms and metres from the corpus of polished written literature," but she does not address the extent to which the mimetic assumptions of that corpus are also opened to question ("Repossessing the Past" 75–6).

[132] Seyhan, *Representation and Its Discontents* 28.

[133] Butler's comments on Shelley's mixed reactions to Southey are useful; see "Byron and the Empire in the East" 70; and "Repossessing the Past" 79–81. For additional discussion, see Keach, "Cythna's Subtler Language" 9–11.

"confirm[s] the impossibility of the mimetic project [and] signif[ies] the absence of an ultimate referent."[134] In *The Revolt of Islam*, the Orient as a discrete and empirically verifiable referent disappears, subsumed into the allegory that is its raison d'être. *Thalaba*'s Orient derives from descriptions in texts and remains merely a (very exhaustive) description in Southey's text; "reality" is deferred through referential instability and discursive diffusion. Both *The Revolt of Islam* and *Thalaba the Destroyer* produce representations of the Islamic Middle East that are in an essential respect not representational. The "Arabesque ornament" becomes the Arabian tale.

Given the English literary critical tradition's linkage of mimesis with the mandate that poetry amuse and instruct its readers, it is no surprise that the challenge to mimetic representation in these poems is accompanied by a disrupted implementation of the twin purposes claimed for poetry. Through the mediation of the Orient as a setting, pleasure and edification are both accentuated and polarized. Although Shelley suppresses the exoticism of the Orient, seeing instruction as a matter of universal humanistic morality, whereas Southey affirms it vigorously, with conveying information as his instructional goal, instruction supercedes pleasure in each case. The emphasis on instruction runs counter to the inclinations of the time, which privilege amusement at the expense of edification. So too, both poems undermine the notion that the two purposes of poetry exist in a moderate, balanced, and mutually reinforcing relationship. These important divergences from contemporary norms in poetics depend upon the poets' conventionalizing manipulation of the Islamic Middle East.

---

[134] Seyhan, *Representation and Its Discontents* 67.

Chapter 2

Representing, misrepresenting, not representing: Victor Hugo's *Les Orientales* and Alfred de Musset's "Namouna"

Like their British contemporaries, the French poets of the early nineteenth century were interested in the problem of representation in poetry, especially as it related to the portrayal of the Islamic Middle East. This and other common preoccupations seem to me of greater significance than the differences between French and English approaches to orientalism during this period. For example, Lisa Lowe's analysis of these differences concludes that

> Even though both French and British orientalisms are products of European colonial encounters with non-Europeans, the French tradition does not often directly represent French colonial situations. Rather, the allegories about otherness in French orientalism tend to be literary figurations that detour or displace the problems of colonial encounter; in effect, colonialism is often not named or addressed. Furthermore, the French tradition frequently alludes to the literary figures and iconography of an Orient drawn from the previous literary tradition of orientalism.[1]

Such an argument is valuable as an antidote to Edward Said's presentation of a totalizing, monolithic orientalism, but the exceptions to it are numerous, especially in poetry. In important respects, both *Thalaba the Destroyer* and *The Revolt of Islam* could, for instance, fit within Lowe's model of French orientalism — *Thalaba* for its reliance on "the previous literary tradition of orientalism," and *The Revolt of Islam* for the way its "allegories of otherness [...] displace the problems of colonial encounter." Certainly neither of these texts directly represents colonial relationships between England and the East, despite the obvious importance of colonialism to both texts.

Thus even if we assume that the English literary tradition's appropriation of the Orient differs substantially from the French tradition's, the precise

---
[1] Lowe, *Critical Terrains* 107.

articulation of such differences appears problematic, in part because of the persistent, bidirectional exchange of ideas and texts across the Channel. The aim of this chapter, which focuses on works by Victor Hugo (1802–1885) and Alfred de Musset (1810–1857), is not then to delineate their connection with or divergence from their English counterparts on the basis of national origin. Instead, the chapter will emphasize the way in which both Hugo and Musset negotiate the relationship of poetic language with representation and referentiality. For both of these poets, as well as for George Gordon Byron (1788–1824), who plays a lesser role in this chapter, orientalism is essential to that negotiation.

In Hugo's case, neoclassicism constitutes the principal counterpoint to romantic orientalism. His collection *Les Orientales* [*The Orientals*] (1829) achieves a complex aesthetic compromise with neoclassicism, accepting neoclassical standards for representation but rejecting, via orientalism, neoclassical restrictions upon the subject matter to be represented. Musset engages less with neoclassicism than with the romanticisms of Hugo and Byron. Musset's "Namouna: conte oriental" ["Namouna: An Oriental Tale"] (1832) investigates problems of representation and referentiality without Shelley's defensiveness or Southey's ambivalence.[2] Its orientalism is a pastiche, a parody of orientalism — especially of Hugo's *Les Orientales*, with which I will begin this chapter. "Namouna" reveals the great potential of the Orient as a romantic subject and of orientalism as an approach, only then to show how readily the limits of that potential might be exhausted. By the time of the romantics, generations of critical reinterpretations had tended to preserve as a standard Aristotle's view that "the capacity to produce an imitation [mimesis] is the essential characteristic of the poet"[3] even when they questioned the universality of that view. Yet "Namouna" reaches well beyond both *Les Orientales* and its other major antecedent text, Byron's *Don Juan* (1819–24), to question representation and even referentiality as bases for poetic production.

Hugo's preface: poetic ideals and the Orient as subject

Despite his claim that a poem's subject has no bearing on its merit, Hugo devotes most of the preface to *Les Orientales* to justifying his choice of the

---

[2] "Namouna" was first printed as part of Musset's *Un spectacle dans un fauteuil* [*A Spectacle in an Armchair*]. Musset wrote a few other poems with orientalist components; see especially "L'Andalouse" ["The Andalusian Woman"] (1829). Of particular interest among his prose fiction and dramatic works are his version of Thomas de Quincey's *Confessions of an English Opium-Eater* and his *Contes d'Espagne et d'Italie* [*Tales of Spain and Italy*].

[3] Aristotle, *Poetics* 4.

Orient as a subject.[4] With a good deal of excitement, as well as some defensiveness, he explains that whereas "[a]u siècle Louis XIV on était helléniste, maintenant on est orientaliste" [in the century of Louis XIV people were Hellenists; now they are orientalists].[5] In particular, he observes, scholarly study of the Orient has made great advances:

> Jamais tant d'intelligences n'ont fouillé à la fois ce grand abîme de l'Asie. Nous avons aujourd'hui un savant cantonné dans chacun des idiomes de l'Orient, depuis Chine jusqu'à l'Egypte.[6]
>
> [Never have so many intellects probed this great abyss of Asia at once. Today we have an expert devoted to each of the dialects of the Orient, from China to Egypt.]

The result of this heightened interest and activity is, as he explains,

> que l'Orient, soit comme image, soit comme pensée, est devenu pour les intelligences autant que pour les imaginations une sorte de préoccupation générale à laquelle l'auteur de ce livre a obéi peut-être à son insu.[7]
>
> [that the Orient, be it as an image or as a concept, has become, for the intellect as much as for the imagination, a sort of general preoccupation to which the author of this book has yielded perhaps unbeknownst to himself.]

In selecting the Orient as his subject, then, the poet claims to be simply following the passion of his times.

However, Hugo's choice of the Orient is not merely the choice of a subject; it is the adoption of an entire approach to poetry. Hugo signals this in a variety of ways. His mention of scholarly orientalism, and especially of oriental philology, is also a reference to a methodology. By citing that field as a precursor to his own endeavor in *Les Orientales*, he implicitly claims an affiliation with an orientalist approach already defined and established. His claim that orientalism has replaced Hellenism has much the same effect; the orientalism that he has adopted himself is thereby identified less as a topic than as a mode of intellectual and creative engagement.

Most important in delineating orientalism as an aesthetic approach, though, is Hugo's explanation of his poetic ideal in terms of a medieval Spanish city. Why, he asks,

---

[4] Schwab comments extensively on this preface; see *The Oriental Renaissance* 11–12, 263, 289, 363–5.

[5] Hugo, preface, *Les Orientales*, ed. Jean Gaudon, *Odes et Ballades, Les Orientales* (Paris: Flammarion, 1968) 322. This edition will be my source for Hugo's poems as well.

[6] Hugo, preface, *Les Orientales* 322.

[7] Hugo, preface, *Les Orientales* 322.

> n'en serait-il pas d'une littérature dans son ensemble, et en particulier de l'oeuvre d'un poète, comme de ces belles vieilles villes d'Espagne, par exemple, où vous trouvez tout?[8]
>
> [might not a literature as a whole, and in particular the oeuvre of a poet, be like those beautiful old cities of Spain, for example, where you find everything?]

A very detailed, descriptive list of the components of such a city follows:

> fraîche promenade d'orangers le long d'une rivière; larges places ouvertes au grand soleil pour les fêtes; rues étroites, tortueuses, quelquefois obscures, où se lient les unes aux autres mille maisons de toute forme.[9]
>
> [a cool promenade of orange trees along a river; wide, open, sunny squares for festivals; narrow, twisted, sometimes dark streets where a thousand houses of every shape connect to one another.]

He includes palaces, asylums, convents, barracks, cemeteries, a theater, a gallows, and with an especially long description, a Gothic cathedral. But the final item on his list is a mosque:

> et enfin, à l'autre bout de la ville, cachée dans les sycomores et les palmiers, la mosquée orientale, aux dômes de cuivre et d'étain, aux portes peintes, aux parois vernissées, avec son jour d'en haut, ses grêles arcades, ses cassolettes qui fument jour et nuit, ses versets du Koran sur chaque porte, ses sanctuaires éblouissants, et la mosaïque de son pavé et la mosaïque de ses murailles; épanouie au soleil comme une large fleur pleine de parfums.[10]
>
> [and finally, at the other end of the city, hidden in the sycamores and palms, the oriental mosque, with domes of copper and tin, painted doors, varnished partitions, with its aperture above, its slender arches, its censers burning day and night, its Koranic verses above each door, its dazzling sanctuaries, and the mosaic of its floor tiles and its walls, blooming in the sun like a large flower full of fragrance.]

Despite the geographically central location of the cathedral and the hidden, obscure site of the mosque, it is the mosque that commands the writer's attention:

> Certes, ce n'est pas l'auteur de ce livre qui réalisera jamais un ensemble d'oeuvres auquel puisse s'appliquer la comparaison

---

[8] Hugo, preface, *Les Orientales* 320.
[9] Hugo, preface, *Les Orientales* 320.
[10] Hugo, preface, *Les Orientales* 321.

qu'il a cru pouvoir hasarder. Toutefois, sans espérer que l'on trouve dans ce qu'il a déjà bâti même quelque ébauche informe des monuments qu'il vient d'indiquer, soit la cathédrale gothique, soit le théâtre, soit encore le hideux gibet; si on lui demandait ce qu'il a voulu faire ici, il dirait que c'est la mosquée.[11]

[Indeed, it is not the author of this book who will ever produce a group of works to which could be applied the comparison he has thought might be ventured. Yet — without hoping that one will find in what he has already constructed even some crude outline of the monuments he has just mentioned, be it the Gothic cathedral, the theater, even the hideous gallows — if one asked him what he wanted to do here, he would say it was the mosque.]

The oriental mosque constitutes both the essence of this archetypal old Spanish city and the substance of Hugo's poetic aim. Its prominence situates orientalism as the defining feature of the poet's project.

The characteristics of Hugo's orientalism are poorly sketched in this preface. The scholarly orientalism that he cites is grounded in philology and in supposedly factual details about the history and culture of the East, but his own literary orientalism clearly is not. As described in the preface, Hugo's orientalism relies upon a fantasized local color that apparently occurs to the poet without any effort on his part:

Les couleurs orientales sont venues comme d'elles-mêmes empreindre toutes ses pensées, toutes ses rêveries; et ses rêveries et ses pénsées se sont trouvées tour à tour, et presque sans l'avoir voulu, hebraïques, turques, grecques, persanes, arabes, espagnoles même.[12]

[Oriental colors seem to have come of their own accord to imprint all his thoughts, all his reveries; and his reveries and thoughts have found themselves in turn, and nearly without having wished it, Hebrew, Turkish, Greek, Persian, Arabic, even Spanish.]

Moreover, because of the emphasis on reverie rather than research in the development of orientalist elements, the mimetic representation of empirical reality is not given privileged status. Although Hugo acknowledges the actual existence of the Orient in political terms, he does so to stress its importance as

---

[11] Hugo, preface, *Les Orientales* 321. Citing Hugo as her example, Grossir speaks of a "preoccupation with the buildings of Islam's religious vocation. [...] Domes, minarets, mosques, palms, gardens, and terraces constitute above all the romantic repertoire for evoking oriental cities and houses" (Grossir, *L'Islam des Romantiques* 97).

[12] Hugo, preface, *Les Orientales* 322. Hugo's claim of automatic orientalism is reminiscent of Coleridge's in his introductory note to "Kubla Khan."

a subject, not to indicate his poems' portrayal of a verifiable Middle East.[13] If he were to pause over the relationship between that genuine political entity and the fantastic one he creates in his poems, he would have to accept that reality has a determining effect on the subjects of poems, and consequently that the autonomy of the poet's imagination is limited by the contents of the real world. This he refuses to do. Not only does he remove the question of the poetic subject from the purview of critics, but he also explicitly denies the existence of *"les limites de l'art"* [*the limits of art*].[14] These limits are the dictates of convention, as represented by the critics who would denigrate Hugo's Spanish city as "le désordre, la profusion, la bizarrerie, le mauvais goût" [disorder, profusion, oddity, bad taste].[15]

Instead, Hugo advocates for a vision of poetry as a "grand jardin [...], où il n'y a pas de fruit défendu" [large garden, where there is no forbidden fruit] and where "[l]e poëte est libre" [the poet is free].[16] In depicting the poet as liberated from aesthetic convention, Hugo is also suggesting that he need not, and in fact should not, accept the traditional (neoclassical) mode of representation — "une belle et correcte nudité" [a beautiful, correct nudity], for example — but should instead welcome the guidance of "sa fantaisie" [his fantasy].[17] The relationship between the empirical world and the world portrayed in poetry becomes quite tenuous here. Thus while Hugo does not raise the possibility of nonreferentiality, he does license poets to abandon representation of reality in favor of referents drawn from fantasy. Both the trope for this new poetics (the mosque) and the subject matter of the collection that attempts to implement it are drawn from the Orient, which then becomes the locus for the poems' experimentation with the limits of mimesis.

"La Douleur du pacha": the Orient as origin or as end

While Hugo speaks of creating a total world through a group of poems, each individual poem of *Les Orientales* seems also to be attempting the same thing, even though the forty-one poems of the collection vary in length, form, setting, and the prominence of local color. Before turning to "Novembre" ["November"], the final poem of the volume, I will discuss "La Douleur du

---

[13] Hugo, preface, *Les Orientales* 322–3. As Mary J. Harper observes, Hugo takes note of "recent political events — most notably the Greek war of independence, and the growing French interest in Algeria — as well as [of] the writings of scholars and travelers. [...] Yet the Orient of Hugo's poetry reveals little of these immediate concerns" (Harper, "Recovering the Other: Women and the Orient in Writings of Early Nineteenth-Century France," *Critical Matrix: Princeton Working Papers in Women's Studies* 1.3 [1985]: 1).
[14] Hugo, preface, *Les Orientales* 320; emphasis his.
[15] Hugo, preface, *Les Orientales* 321.
[16] Hugo, preface, *Les Orientales* 319.
[17] Hugo, preface, *Les Orientales* 321, 319.

pacha" ["The Sorrow of the Pasha"] and "Adieux de l'hôtesse arabe" ["Farewells of the Arab Hostess"], two poems that particularly emphasize problems of representation.[18] In each of these three poems, Hugo implements various elements of the program he sets out in his preface. Mainly through manipulations of form, "La Douleur" and "Adieux" not only depict a fantasized Orient but also supercede their own depictions to offer orientalism as a aesthetic strategy tentatively emptied of oriental content. "Novembre" replaces the oriental with the personal but nonetheless maintains a prominent place for orientalist poetics; Hugo's reinstatement of mimetic representation to replace the purer referentiality with which he had experimented in the two preceding poems does not constitute a total capitulation to the dictates of neoclassicism.

"La Douleur du pacha" has the repetitive structure of a fairy tale or a nursery rhyme.[19] In each of the first five stanzas a member of the pasha's household asks a version of the question, "Qu'a donc le pacha?" [So what is (wrong) with the pasha?]. Each guesses a cause for the pasha's melancholy: perhaps he has broken his father's saber, or perhaps he has not kept the Ramadan fast and has been punished by seeing the angel of death in a dream, or perhaps he has surprised his son under a plane-tree with his own favorite concubine. But all of these speculations are wrong, and the poem retraces its steps, listing once again all the reasons already suggested, and adding others equally incorrect. The poem ends with the right answer:

> Qu'a-t-il donc ce pacha que la guerre réclame,
> Et qui, triste et rêveur, pleure comme une femme...?
> Son tigre de Nubie est mort. (52–4)

> [So what is with this pasha for whose presence the war clamors, /
> And who, thoughtful and sad, weeps like a woman...? / His
> Nubian tiger is dead.]

"La Douleur" marks its orientalism in its structure. The repetitive, here-we-go-again form of this poem constitutes an oriental allusion, a kind of arabesque. As the various speculations are reembedded in the second part of "La Douleur," the poem also becomes a more specific allusion to the *1001 Nights*, whose narrative structure is characterized not only by repetition but also by the successive framing or embedding of stories. Moreover, even more obvious than the poem's formal orientalism is the explicitly orientalist content of the household's speculations. The members of the household are clearly

---

[18] The poems of *Les Orientales* were composed 1827–28; for further information, see Hugo, *Les Orientales*, ed. Élisabeth Barineau, vol. 1 (Paris: Marcel Didier, 1952) xviii–xx.

[19] Grossir discusses this poem briefly; see *L'Islam des Romantiques* 105. Barineau comments that "La Douleur" is the first poem of the collection composed with no other purpose than to depict an oriental world (Hugo, *Les Orientales*, ed. Barineau 1: 112).

Middle Eastern; they include a "humble derviche" [humble dervish], "icoglans stupides" [stupid palace attachés], "sultanes" [sultanas], and "esclaves" [slaves].[20] Their suggestions are not only fanciful (e.g., perhaps the pasha has lost the bottle of perfume that would give him back his youth) but also implausibly numerous. Each group, with the exception of the slaves, offers several guesses, to which the speaker adds many others. The speaker's suggestions are especially superfluous, since his presentation of them makes clear that they are incorrect even before he proposes them. Their function is rather to provide yet more of the oriental "facts" surrounding this pasha and his doldrums.

Like Southey's *Thalaba*, then, "La Douleur" is characterized by a seeming excess of information, information that is justifiable and relevant only because it is Middle Eastern. Yet Southey's many details — even the unlikely and supernatural ones — are marked as the result of years of research, while Hugo's appear mainly the products of his imagination, inspired (as Lowe's analysis of French orientalism would predict) more by the conventionalized literary motifs of orientalism than by any scholarly investigation of the subject. Indeed, this lack of research is essential to Hugo's endeavor; "ce livre inutile de pure poésie" [this useless book of pure poetry] is, he promises, the result of a whim, an idea that occurred to him while he was watching a summer sunset.[21] Certainly such an assertion has little in common with Southey's methodical, albeit idiosyncratic, scholarship. Even though Hugo's tactics (excess information, for instance) may resemble Southey's, he does not share Southey's fundamental assumption that the Orient is interesting and valuable in its own right. Instead, the Orient becomes important for Hugo not as an end but as an origin, a channel to that "pure poésie," "une source à laquelle il désirait depuis longtemps se désaltérer. Là, en effet, tout est grand, riche, fécond, comme dans le Moyen Age, cette autre mer de poésie" [a spring at which he had long desired to quench his thirst. There, indeed, everything is great, rich, fertile, as in the Middle Ages, that other sea of poetry].[22] This shift of emphasis away from the Orient's particular features and towards its generative aesthetic value is an essential step in Hugo's assimilation of orientalism as the basis for a poetics.

Thus, despite Hugo's insistence that the poet be free to select a subject, his chosen subject in *Les Orientales* turns out to be relatively unimportant in itself, though critically important to the author's poetic aims. "La Douleur du pacha" is an enactment — an imitation, a mimesis, a re-presentation — of these conditions. The origin of the pasha's melancholy is the death of his Nubian tiger, just as the origin of *Les Orientales* is the East. Yet the revelation that the

---

[20] Note that the word "icoglans" refers explicitly to aides in a Turkish palace.
[21] Hugo, preface, *Les Orientales* 320.
[22] Hugo, preface, *Les Orientales* 322.

pasha is grieving for a tiger is as much an afterthought as a climax. The poem's more important revelation is of the fantastic exoticism of the pasha's household and lifestyle, but this is already made in the string of faulty guesses that precedes the correct answer. Both in the poem's relationship with the tiger and in the collection's relationship with the Orient, what might be essential (the tiger, the Orient) ends up instead as a mere origin, superceded by that to which it has given rise.

"Adieux de l'hôtesse arabe": stasis

Although the Middle East's difference from Europe is at the heart of "La Douleur du pacha," Europe is present in the poem only implicitly, as a concealed point of reference for the odd, oriental traits depicted. In "Adieux de l'hôtesse arabe," on the other hand, Europe is very much present, figured in the person of a "voyageur blanc" [white traveler], a European man to whom the Arab speaker is bidding farewell. In the face of this explicit East-West encounter, the general characteristics of the Middle East are crystallized more distinctly than in "La Douleur." These characteristics are among the most stereotypical and conventionalized of the time; clearly Hugo's stated resistance to the limits of convention has its own limits. The use of a female speaker/protagonist, for instance, suggests the femininity of the Orient, especially as this "hôtesse arabe" situates herself as representative both of those around her and of the place itself.[23] Affirming the Middle East's reputation for both luxury and danger, the speaker emphasizes "le repos" [tranquillity] and "l'abondance" [abundance] of "cet heureux pays" [this fortunate country] (1, 3), while worrying frantically about the misfortunes — from blind demons to sunburn — that might befall her visitor as he travels through "l'Arabie infranchissable" [insurmountable Arabia] (45). Similarly, the Middle East is subservient to the West; had he been willing to stay, she promises that she would have "aimé te servir à genoux" [liked to serve you on bended knee] (20).

The most prominent of Hugo's hand-me-down Middle Eastern images is that of the Orient as a static, backward place — the stereotype so essential to

---

[23] Several critics have analyzed the trope of the Orient as woman. Grossir, *L'Islam des Romantiques* 99–102; Harper, "Recovering the Orient" 1–3, 8; Jennifer Yee, "La Tahoser de Gautier et la Salammbo de Flaubert: l'orientale et le voyage au-delà de l'histoire," *Australian Journal of French Studies* 36.2 (1999): 189, 197–9; and esp. Lowe, *Critical Terrains* ch. 3. *Les Orientales* includes numerous examples of this trope; see for instance "La Sultane favorite," "Sara la baigneuse," and "Nourmahal-la-rousse" ["The Favorite Sultana," "Sara the bather," "Nourmahal-the-redhead"]. Moreover, the collection's title, *Les Orientales*, is grammatically feminine, a feature not reflected in English translation.

Shelley's manipulation of the Orient in *The Revolt of Islam*.[24] The speaker makes clear that if her foreign beloved ever returns to look for her (it being evidently inconceivable that she could go looking for him), he will find her still thinking of him fondly in her "hutte fidèle" [faithful hut] (33), still in the same hamlet on the same hill. While he walks on "sans cesse" [ceaselessly] (13), she is among those

> Qui donnent pour limite à leurs pieds paresseux
>   Leur toit de branches ou de toiles!
> Qui, rêveurs, sans en faire, écoutent les récits,
> Et souhaitent, le soir, devant leur porte assis,
>   De s'en aller dans les étoiles! (14–18)

[Who set as a boundary for their lazy feet / Their walls of boughs or canvas! / Who listen dreamily to tales, effortlessly, / And in the evening, sitting before their door, / Wish to disappear into the stars!]

To the catalogue of stereotypical Middle Eastern traits, these lines add laziness, storytelling, and dreaming, but the key feature emphasized here remains the unchangeability of the Middle East.

This trite and clichéd assumption of a static Orient, staying forever in its place (geographically and politically), is enacted in the structure of the poem as well. Like "La Douleur du pacha," "Adieux de l'hôtesse arabe" rejects progress, but it achieves its stasis without "La Douleur"'s blatant repetitions. Although "Adieux" looks to the past and to the future, both are subsumed into the present moment, in which the speaker is coming to terms with her visitor's decision to leave. Moreover, the speaker's reflections during this moment are relatively disordered. The second stanza, for instance, confirms the central fact of the traveler's departure, but four of the stanza's seven lines are spent describing the beauty of his horse. Then at the beginning of the fifth stanza, the speaker suddenly announces, as if it were news, "Mais tu pars!" [But you are leaving!] (25). She returns in the next lines to the image of the horse and then mentions the traveler's lance, envisioning how it shines ("reluit") in the shadows. The use of this word, in conjunction with the return to the horse,

---

[24] Schwab's rendition of this stereotype is succinct: "[t]he Orient rigid and faithful, the Occident fickle" (*The Oriental Renaissance* 242); see also Nichola Haxell, "Hugo, Gautier and the Obelisk of Luxor (Place de la Concorde) During the Second Republic," *Nineteenth-Century French Studies* 18.1–2 (1989–90): 68–9, 74–5; MacKenzie, *Orientalism* 58–9; Said, *Orientalism* 96, 161, 167, 240; Makdisi, *Romantic Imperialism* 113; and Seyhan, *Representation and Its Discontents* 80.

This aspect of "Adieux" could also be interpreted according to Lowe's contention that "French colonialism is often buried beneath literary representations of the Orient as temporally remote, or fictions of a distanced and imaginary oriental world" (*Critical Terrains* 107). After all, the context of the encounter depicted here is clearly colonial, yet the setting is both "temporally remote" and largely "imaginary."

which is described previously in very similar terms ("luisant"), reveals a more subtle strategy of repetition than that of "La Douleur."

The final stanza of "Adieux" offers another example. Beginning like the second with "Adieu," this stanza picks up three motifs already introduced: the pale skin of the traveler, the danger of the Middle East, and the inherent difference between the Oriental and the European — all in the course of warning the traveler against sunburn, to which his light complexion makes him more vulnerable than an Arab would be:

> Adieu donc! — Va tout droit. Garde-toi du soleil,
> Qui dore nos fronts bruns, mais brûle un teint vermeil. (43–4)
>
> [Farewell then! — Go straight on. Protect yourself from the sun, / Which turns our dark faces golden, but burns a ruddy complexion.]

The repetitions and the disinterest in priority, along with the tendency (as in the final stanza just cited) to gather multiple previously mentioned elements into a single image, create a poem that remains static.

Such stasis on the level of form has two effects. First, it reminds us that Hugo's Orient offers not only a subject but also a way of thinking, and therefore a way of writing. This is much the same point that *Thalaba*'s preface makes (albeit in a much more limited way) by claiming to include an "Arabesque ornament." Hugo's use of repetition, whether subtle ("Adieux") or blatant ("La Douleur"), serves the same purpose, as does his rejection of logical or chronological prioritization in the structure of his poems. The second effect of formal stasis is to confirm the static nature of the Orient. A presumption of immutability frees the poet from the need to take chronology or historical progression into account in his depictions. In effect, this liberty amounts to a license for endless improvisation; the results will have the air of reality (since the Orient always is how it is), but will be grounded more firmly in imagination than in reality. The resulting poetry's referents will be more fantastic than real; mimetic representation will have given way to a referentiality of the imagination.

This ideal situation is precisely what Hugo seeks when he proclaims a correspondence between the Middle East and the Middle Ages.[25] The depiction of the European traveler in this poem as a kind of medieval knight-errant bidding farewell to a lady emblematizes this connection. Like the Middle Ages, the Middle East exists unto itself, a chronologically and geographically indivisible unit standing in a "synchronic, rather than diachronic, relation to Europe," as Saree Makdisi argues in another context.[26] It remains always

---

[25] Hugo, preface, *Les Orientales* 322.
[26] Makdisi, *Romantic Orientalism* 111.

distinctive and distant; to borrow Said's formulation, it is "a closed system, in which objects are what they are *because* they are what they are, for once, for all time, for ontological reasons that no empirical material can either dislodge or alter."[27] Just as there are no survivors of the Middle Ages to correct our modern misconceptions of it, there are no authentic Middle Easterners in a position to speak against Hugo. The Arab woman in "Adieux" appears to stand for the Middle East, yet her emphasis on such ordinary details as the rump of the traveler's horse or the construction of her home marks her own constructedness. Even more importantly, as the manifestation of oriental changelessness, she is herself presented as heavily complicit in the region's evident inferiority.

The Arab hostess's lack of authenticity, is — like the unlikely range of explanations for the pasha's distress in "La Douleur" — nonetheless evidence of Hugo's pragmatic attitude towards the Orient. Hugo is relatively uninterested in the Islamic Middle East as an actual geographic, social, or political entity; in his work the Middle East serves instead an aesthetic purpose dependent more upon the accumulated European assumptions about an essentialized Orient than on its reality. Both "La Douleur du pacha" and "Adieux de l'hôtesse arabe" manifest Homi Bhabha's formulation of the stereotype as "requir[ing], for its successful signification, a continual and repetitive chain of other stereotypes."[28] At the same time, however, the poems' interdependent, repetitive, stereotypical representations of the Middle East offer an opportunity for the elaboration of an orientalist aesthetic that implements itself as an arabesque of formal repetition. Thus, though the Orient is, as I explained above, an approach as well as a subject, it becomes in this context more an approach than a subject. The essential feature of this approach is its experimental substitution of a fantasy- and text-based referentiality for the mimetic representation advocated by neoclassical aesthetics.

"Novembre": returning to Paris, the self, and mimesis

Hugo's subordination of the Orient as a subject is completed in "Novembre," the final poem of *Les Orientales*. "Novembre" describes how the speaker's muse, and consequently the speaker himself, are deserted by the "beau rêve d'Asie" [beautiful dream of Asia] (9) when faced with the oncoming Parisian winter. The speaker replaces his muse with memories of his own explicitly European youth, which will from now on serve as his inspiration. In effect, the poem's transition from Asia to Europe distributes the Orient into the Occident, opening the way for the application of orientalism as an aesthetic approach to

---

[27] Said, *Orientalism* 70; emphasis his.
[28] Homi Bhabha, *The Location of Culture* (London: Routledge, 1994) 77.

definitively occidental subject matter.

The final stanza of "Novembre" makes clear that even though the muse of the Orient is now powerless and the Orient has been dismissed as a subject, a kind of orientalist sensibility will guide the speaker's future poetic endeavors. After the muse suggests that the speaker look within his "coeur jeune encor" [still youthful heart] for "Quelque chose à chanter" [Something to sing] (33–4), he explains how he will take her tastes into account as he selects his new material:

> Mais surtout tu te plais aux premières amours,
> Frais papillons dont l'aile, en fuyant rajeunie,
> Sous le doigt qui la fixe est si vite ternie,
> Essaim doré qui n'a qu'un jour dans tous nos jours! (57–60)

> [But above all you take pleasure in (those) first loves, / Lively butterflies whose wings, revived in flight, / Are so quickly dulled under the finger that holds them down: / A golden swarm, which has only one day among all of ours!]

Not only will the muse influence his choice of subject matter (first loves), but she will also affect his depiction of it. These love affairs, like the "beau rêve d'Asie" [beautiful dream of Asia], are very short-lived, lasting only a day and quickly becoming dulled and deadened by reality, in the guise either of adulthood or of Parisian weather. But while they last, both the Orient and young love are golden, the one "un soleil d'or" [a sun of gold] (36) and the other an "essaim doré" [golden swarm] (60).[29] In this fashion, the speaker/poet finds his portrayal of his own highly domestic experience being orientalized (gilded, if you will) under the gentle direction of his (former) muse.[30] Assigning the Orient the role of muse, a figure emblematic of the art of classical antiquity, "Novembre" presents orientalism as an aesthetic source and standard entirely independent of the Orient as a subject. In this respect, the poem's assimilationist strategy completes the implementation of orientalism as a poetics.

On the other hand, the abandonment of the Middle East as a subject, together with the concomitant resumption of the self as the origin of poetry, signals a return to mimetic representation. "Novembre" offers a fully developed contrast between Paris and the Orient, such that the one appears as firm reality and the other as a fantasy destined to fade. The poem begins by

---

[29] The imagery of the Orient in "Novembre" has much in common with that of Baudelaire's "L'Invitation au voyage" (1855), another poem in which stereotypical oriental splendor appears infinitely attractive but not sustainable.

[30] Barineau sees this poem as a "transition" between *Les Orientales* and the more "personal" and "intimate" poetry of Hugo's next collection, *Les Feuilles d'Automne*, published in 1831 (*Les Orientales*, ed. Barineau, 1: xx, 2: 192).

lamenting autumn's cold, its mist, its shortened days, and its falling leaves. The speaker then addresses his muse:

> Devant le sombre hiver de Paris qui bourdonne,
> Ton soleil d'orient s'éclipse et t'abandonne,
> Ton beau rêve d'Asie avorte, et tu ne vois,
> Sous tes yeux, que la rue au bruit accoutumée,
> Brouillard à ta fenêtre, et longs flots de fumée
> Qui baignent en fuyant l'angle noirci des toits. (7–12)

> [Faced with the somber winter of busy Paris, / Your Eastern sun disappears and abandons you, / Your beautiful dream of Asia fails, and you see nothing / Before your eyes but the street with its usual noise, / Fog at your window, and long billows of smoke / That envelop, as they recede, the blackened corners of the roofs.]

Paris and the Orient oppose one another directly here for the first time in the poem; Paris is somber, busy, foggy, and dark, whereas "Asie" is bright and beautiful. But it is Paris that survives when the shining sun of the Orient has disappeared. Along with it,

> Alors s'en vont en foule et sultans et sultanes,
> Pyramides, palmiers, galères capitanes,
> Et le tigre vorace et le chameau frugal,
> Djinns au vol furieux, danses des bayadères,
> L'Arabe qui se penche au cou des dromadaires,
> Et la fauve girafe au galop inégal!
>
> Alors, éléphants blancs chargés de femmes brunes,
> Cités aux dômes d'or où les mois sont des lunes,
> Imams de Mahomet, mages, prêtres de Bel,
> Tout fuit, tout disparaît: — plus de minaret maure,
> Plus de sérail fleuri, plus d'ardente Gomorrhe
> Qui jette un reflet rouge au front noir de Babel! (13–24)

> [Then all together both sultans and sultanas vanish, / Pyramids, palm trees, admiral's galleys, / Both the voracious tiger and the frugal camel, / Genies flying madly, the dances of bayaderes, / The Arab who leans over dromedaries' necks, / And the tawny giraffe with the uneven gallop!
>
> Then, white elephants loaded with dark women, / Towns with domes of gold where months are moons, / Imams of Mohammed, magi, priests of Baal, / Everything flies, everything disappears — no more Moorish minaret, / No more ornate seraglio, no more fiery Gomorrah / Which casts a red reflection on the black face of Babel!]

All of these stereotypical oriental accoutrements, as well as a few others (odalisques, emirs, pashas, peris, the Nile, and the roses of Bengal) mentioned in the next stanza, are unable to endure the rigors of the European climate. "C'est Paris, c'est hiver. / [...] / A ce soleil brumeux les Péris auraient froid" [It is Paris, it is winter / ... / In this hazy sunshine the peris would be cold] (25, 30). This should not surprise us, however, since it is clear from the start of the poem that the Orient is a fantasy or a dream, not something that could survive the chill of reality. And Paris (both in particular and as a stand-in for Europe) is from the beginning that reality. Paris preexists the speaker and his muse, and it will outlive them as well, whereas the Middle East is merely "ton Orient" [your Orient] (31), a lovely artifact of the muse's ingenuity.

In the course of acknowledging the Orient as a fantasy, the speaker also discounts it as a stable referent; he speaks of approaching his oriental muse like a cold child drawing near the fire, only to find it gone when he reaches it. This analogy, which indirectly figures the fire (a feature of the European nursery) as a mirage (a feature of the Eastern desert), itself implies that the Orient is inherently unreliable, even illusory. The Orient may appear amenable to representation, but its inaccessibility to empirical verification makes it an ultimately unsuitable referent despite its great appeal. By reverting to the self as his subject matter, the speaker avails himself of a more reliable and verifiable referent.

The greater security thus afforded is manifested in the later stanzas of the poem, in which the speaker recounts the events of his youth that will now serve as material for his poetry. His descriptions here are full but staid, quite unlike the frenzied lists of key words that described the Middle East in earlier stanzas. I will cite one example:

> Je te raconte aussi comment aux Feuillantines,
> [...]
>   jeune et sauvage, errait ma liberté,
> Et qu'à dix ans, parfois, resté seul à la brune,
> Rêveur, mes yeux cherchaient les deux yeux de la lune,
> Comme la fleur qui s'ouvre aux tièdes nuits d'été. (43–8)[31]
>
> [I recount to you as well how, at the Feuillantines, / ... / young and wild, I wandered freely, / And at ten years of age, sometimes, left alone at nightfall, / Dreaming, my eyes sought the two eyes of the moon, / Like the flower that opens in the mild nights of summer.]

Detail is scant; the emphasis in these lines falls on the speaker's recollected experience, not on local color. In the speaker's comfortable intimacy with nature, there is no sense that poetic language is struggling to grasp or contain a problematic referent.

---

[31] The Feuillantines is a Paris convent where Hugo spent part of his childhood.

In "Novembre" Hugo abandons the Orient as a subject for the same reasons he was initially drawn to it. For him, the Orient is a fantasy, one that enables the production of "pure poésie." Even after concluding that pure poetry is fragile and unsustainable because of its insecure connection with the empirical world, a reality figured in this poem as Paris in autumn, he retains an affiliation with the oriental fantasy that allowed him to explore this "pure poésie." The muse that brought the speaker the Middle East is still at his side, guiding him as he outlines his new approach, with its domestic subject matter and its attachment to mimetic representation of an experienced reality. In the lines just cited, for example, this link with orientalism is manifested twice. First, the speaker presents himself as wandering; because wandering is a stereotypical Arab (bedouin) activity, the reference subtly orientalizes the speaker even while he situates himself firmly in Europe. Second, the poem continues to resist narrative. Despite its adoption of European subject matter, "Novembre" is, like both "La Douleur du pacha" and "Adieux de l'hôtesse arabe," grounded in the moment.

Hugo's orientalism is that of an art founded on imagination but disconnected from reality, a kind of prototypical version of art for art's sake. Unable to develop or accept this philosophy fully but at the same time resistant to the notion that poetry must be limited by the poet's relationship with reality, Hugo sketches a compromise in "Novembre" by detaching orientalist poetics from the stereotypical oriental components that generate it. As the preface promises, the poet is free to go "où il veut en faisant ce qui lui plaît" [where he wants, doing what pleases him], no matter whether

> il prenne pied dans tel siècle ou dans tel climat; qu'il soit du midi, du nord, de l'occident, de l'orient; qu'il soit antique ou moderne; que sa muse soit une Muse ou une fée.[32]
>
> [he settles in such and such a century or such and such a region; whether it be of the south, the north, the Occident, or the Orient; whether it be ancient or modern; whether his muse be a Muse or a fairy.]

The muse of "Novembre" functions as both Muse and fairy. Hearing the Muse, Hugo accepts the neoclassical demand for mimetic representation. Under the fairy's direction, however, he continues to ignore neoclassical restrictions on subject matter, choosing instead as his topic a version of personal experience with a slight oriental flavor.

---

[32] Hugo, Preface, *Les Orientales* 319.

Hugo's critics: E.J. Chételat

Hugo's distance from neoclassicism exposed him often to criticism and parody. Barbara Cooper cites seven separate contemporary parodies of Hugo's play *Hernani*, which was first performed about a year after the publication of *Les Orientales* and three years before Musset's "Namouna."[33] Cooper argues that the aim of these parodies is to reveal and ridicule *Hernani*'s romanticism and its divergence from "the tenets of French neoclassicism."[34] Writing on *Les Orientales*, E.J. Chételat shares this goal, seeking in particular to affirm the privileged status of mimesis again the orientalist threat. Chételat (probably Emmanuel Joseph Chételat [b. 1800], a secondary-school instructor in grammar) published *Les Occidentales, ou lettres critiques sur les Orientales* [*The Occidentals, or Critical Letters on* The Orientals] a few months after the appearance of Hugo's collection in 1829.[35] The volume consists of a series of letters from an unidentified (and possibly fictional) correspondent.

Chételat's conservative and paranoid foreword to *Les Occidentales* makes his (and the letter writer's) essentially neoclassical outlook clear:

> C'est aussi, ce me semble, un intérêt sérieux pour la France que le maintien de sa gloire littéraire, et elle doit être assez fière de ses propres grandeurs pour repousser avec dédain toutes les influences étrangères sur son génie comme sur sa puissance. Or, voici venir de l'Orient, c'est-à-dire de la Barbarie, des inspirations nouvelles faites pour altérer la pureté de notre belle littérature: un cri général de réprobation doit donc s'élever contre cette invasion offensante.[36]
>
> [The maintenance of her literary glory is, it seems to me, a serious concern for France, and she should be proud enough of her own grandeur to reject with disdain all foreign influences upon her genius as upon her sovereignty. But here come from the Orient, that is to say from Barbar(it)y, these new inspirations meant to corrupt the purity of our beautiful literature.[37] A general cry of reprobation should be raised against this offensive invasion.]

In response to this frightening onslaught of alien influences, Chételat presents these letters, with the intent to "venger de tant d'outrages le bon sens et le bon goût, la nature et Racine" [avenge good sense and good taste, nature and

---

[33] Cooper, "Parodying Hugo," *European Romantic Review* 2.1 (1991): 23, n. 4.
[34] Cooper, "Parodying Hugo" 25.
[35] E.J. Chételat, ed., *Les Occidentales, ou lettres critiques sur Les Orientales de M. Victor Hugo*, Paris: Hautecoeur-Martinet, 1829; rpt. 1970.
[36] Chételat, ed., *Les Occidentales* 6.
[37] The French "Barbarie" means "Barbary," but if printed in lowercase ("barbarie") means "barbarity."

Racine, for so many outrages (against them)].[38] Chételat's highest priority is preserving the traditions that constitute the literary glory of France. However, by appealing to nature as well as to good sense, good taste, and Racine, Chételat is introducing an element of universality; the value of the other three items might be defined by French culture, but nature is a transnational concept. The inclusion of this key term refocuses the debate; the problem at hand is now how to maintain the correct relationship between literature and nature. By introducing the Orient — Barbar(it)y — Hugo has disrupted this relationship.

Neither Chételat nor his anonymous correspondent explains which particular oriental traits are particularly at fault. Yet the supposed barbarity (difference) of the Orient certainly troubles both of these Frenchmen. For example, when discussing Hugo's "Adieux de l'hôtesse arabe" the letter writer complains:

> Le caractère essentiel de l'Arabe est la vie errante et voyageuse, et placer l'idée d'hospitalité, idée qui implique le repos, sur un caractère arabe, c'est, à mon avis, vouloir bâtir sur le sable.[39]
>
> [The essential disposition of the Arab is the wandering, traveling life, and to place the idea of hospitality, an idea that implies settlement, upon an Arab character, is, in my opinion, to build upon sand.]

The writer evidently associates hospitality with a permanent home, determines that Arabs have none, and logically concludes that they must be inhospitable. Not only is he apparently unaware that many Arabs are not nomadic (certainly the Arab depicted in this poem is not), but he also betrays here the assumption underlying his entire argument: Arabs are barbaric, and barbarians are inhospitable, so Arabs must be inhospitable. While other accusations of inauthenticity might be justifiable, as suggested in my discussion of this poem above, the letter writer misses them. Ironically, he becomes guilty of the same crime with which he is charging Hugo here, that of falsely representing the Orient. His metaphorical reference to sand suggests that he has even been somehow infected by Hugo's orientalism; certainly his idea could have been expressed without resorting to a premiere trope of orientalist literature.[40]

As we see from this example, Chételat cannot disengage the otherness/barbarism of the Arabs from the aesthetic issue at hand, that of the degree to which the poems of *Les Orientales* truly or accurately represent the

---

[38] Chételat, ed., *Les Occidentales* 6. Jean Racine (1639–1699) was a celebrated neoclassical dramatist.

[39] Chételat, ed., *Les Occidentales* 79.

[40] Indeed, the last two lines of "Adieux de l'hôtesse arabe" are based on precisely this trope: "Et de ceux qui le soir, avec un bâton blanc, / Tracent des cercles sur le sable!" [And of those who, in the evening, with a white stick, / Trace circles in the sand!] (47–8).

empirical reality of the Middle East. The first of his correspondent's letters, labeled an "avant-propos" [preamble], addresses that issue specifically, in terms not only of truth but also of the relationship between nature and mimesis. The writer begins by praising the ancients and explaining:

> Quand j'interroge les immortels écrits de toutes les antiquités de la Grèce, de l'Italie, et même de la France [...], j'entends toujours à la fois un écho dans la nature qui me rend toutes leurs images, et une voix dans mon intelligence qui les approuve et les admire.[41]

> [When I examine the immortal writings of all the antiquities of Greece, of Italy, and even of France ... , I always hear at the same time (both) an echo in nature that conveys to me all their images, and a voice in my mind that approves of and admires them.]

He goes on to affirm that "ce n'est pas la nature qui manque jamais au génie de l'homme, c'est l'homme qui manque à son propre génie en manquant à l'imitation fidèle de la nature" [it is never nature that fails the genius of man; it is man who fails his own genius by neglecting the faithful imitation of nature].[42] Literature's "vocation première" [primary vocation] is "l'expression véritable de la nature ou de la société" [the genuine expression of nature or of society].[43]

In light of this high calling, "poésie nouvelle" [new poetry] such as Hugo's is both horrifying and laughable, given

> ces affectations de l'esprit aux dépens de la vérité, ces imaginations tantôt monstrueuses, tantôt grotesques, qui ont la prétention d'être merveilleuses tandis qu'elles ne sont qu'insensées, d'être naturelles tandis qu'elles ne sont que triviales.[44]

> [these pretences of fancy at the expense of the truth, these inventions [that are] sometimes monstrous, sometimes grotesque, that claim to be marvelous whereas they are nothing but foolish, to be natural whereas they are nothing but vulgar.]

From the letter writer's neoclassical perspective, poetry is valuable to the extent that it is true, and true to the extent that it represents (imitates) nature. The implied definition of nature here is a limited one; we may be quite safe in assuming, for example, that Southey's supernatural would be excluded as foolish, if not monstrous or grotesque.

---

[41] Chételat, ed., *Les Occidentales* 10.
[42] Chételat, ed., *Les Occidentales* 10.
[43] Chétalat, ed., *Les Occidentales* 10.
[44] Chételat, ed., *Les Occidentales* 10.

Although in this case the writer is referring specifically to Hugo's romanticism rather than his orientalism, the references to the marvelous, and especially to the grotesque, may fairly be read as allusions to orientalism. Moreover, the writer's next letter shows how difficult it is for him to separate romanticism from orientalism in Hugo's poetry. This letter, which describes itself as a postscript to the first one, is a critique of *Les Orientales*'s preface. It begins by blaming Hugo for his lack of modesty and particularly for his arrogance in allowing a critic to judge only a poem's quality, not its poet's choice of subject. Since one of the letter writer's chief complaints is the choice of subject (trivial when it should be natural, and so forth), it is not surprising that he objects to Hugo's prohibiting comments on this topic. For him, the essential question, "à quoi servira l'art?" [what (purpose) will art serve?] cannot be answered without reference to art's subject matter.[45] He looks in vain for traces of classical or neoclassical topics in *Les Orientales*, but "Andromaque, Zaïre et Mérope" are all missing.[46] Asking again the question Hugo explicitly refuses to answer in his preface, the letter writer queries: "Pourquoi [...] s'embarquer pour cet Orient [...] *A quoi bon ce voyage oriental?*" [Why ... set off for this Orient ... What is the use of this oriental voyage?].[47] Hugo's choice of an oriental subject, then, constitutes his most blatant violation of the letter writer's neoclassical precepts. In short, it is Hugo's orientalism that typifies, defines, and ultimately convicts his romanticism.

This orientalist romanticism is characterized not only by new and unpalatable subjects for poetry but also by a vexing disregard for the obligations of the poet. Hugo is negligent in his duty to represent reality in his poetry, as we saw in the case of the Arab hostess's supposedly implausible hospitality. In addition, Chételat's correspondent observes with dismay Hugo's abdication of responsibility for his own poetic production, quoting Hugo's explanation, cited above, of oriental colors coming of their own accord and tinting the poet's thoughts Hebrew, Turkish, Greek, etc., almost without his having wished it. When the letter writer reproduces this citation, however, he omits Hugo's reference to Spain; in his rendition, the absolute foreignness of the Orient remains uncontaminated by any allusion to a European country, even one with Moorish associations. He also glosses Hugo's list of Eastern nationalities: "c'est-à-dire, en termes plus clairs, prosaïques, brusques, grotesques, barbares" [that is to say, in clearer terms, prosaic, uncouth, grotesque, barbaric].[48] Once again we find that the inclusion of the Eastern is

---

[45] Chételat, ed., *Les Occidentales* 15.
[46] Chételat, ed., *Les Occidentales* 16. *Andromaque* (1667) is a tragedy by Racine. *Zaïre* and *Mérope* are early-eighteenth-century tragedies.
[47] Chételat, ed., *Les Occidentales* 16; emphasis his. Compare Hugo, preface, *Les Orientales* 320.
[48] Chételat, ed., *Les Occidentales* 17.

the single most important factor militating against the writer's acceptance of *Les Orientales*. The oriental — prosaic, uncouth, grotesque, barbaric — is not merely offensive; it is also a corrupting influence, inciting the poet to ignore his obligation to uphold the traditional ideals of poetry.

In essence, the writer is charging that *Les Orientales* is not poetry because it is oriental(ist). Whereas the neoclassical aesthetics to which Chételat and his correspondent adhere place a high value on traditional, tried-and-true subject matter, and on poetry as an imitator of nature, orientalism seems to have allowed Hugo to abandon both. What remains is of course imitation without nature, representation without truth — perhaps prosaic or barbaric, but in Hugo's terms, "pure poésie."

George Gordon Byron's *Don Juan*: "But what's reality?"

Byron addresses in *Don Juan* the same two irresolvable problems that Hugo explores in *Les Orientales*: first, the nature of reality, and second, the ability of (poetic) language to represent that reality.[49] Hugo first experiments with the notion of "pure poetry" as a response to these problems and then returns to the more classical view of an empirically verifiable reality adequately represented by poetic language. Byron claims to eschew the possibility of representation without "facts" as referents while often producing just that, thereby calling into question both the existence of an empirically verifiable reality and the capacities of language at precisely the same time that he is supposedly reaffirming each. Thus while the poetics of both *Les Orientales* and *Don Juan* depend largely upon the construction of a relationship between reality and representation, *Don Juan* differs from *Les Orientales* first in questioning more rigorously the nature of the real and second in suggesting that mimesis is not fully capable of representing the real, whatever its nature.

Byron introduces the awkwardness of reality's link with representation in his draft preface to the first two cantos of *Don Juan*, where he explains the speaker's indeterminate identity (a "Spanish gentleman" who is "either an Englishman settled in Spain — or a Spaniard who had travelled in England") and asks the reader to "suppose" numerous elements of setting and character.[50] He continues, "Having supposed as much of this as the utter impossibility of such a supposition will admit, the reader is requested to extend his supposed

---

[49] A caveat here: what follows is meant as a preliminary investigation opening the way for my reading of Musset's "Namouna," a text strongly influenced by *Don Juan*; it does not pretend to serve as an exhaustive analysis of *Don Juan*.

[50] Byron, preface, *Don Juan*, ed. Jerome J. McGann, *The Complete Poetical Works*, vol. 5 (Oxford: Clarendon, 1986) 83; reprinted by permission of Oxford University Press. As McGann points out, Byron neither completed the preface nor ever published it with his poem; see *The Complete Poetical Works* 665. I have used McGann's edition as my source for *Don Juan*.

power of supposing so far as to conceive that the Dedication to Mr. Southey, and several stanzas of the poem itself, are interpolated by the English editor."[51] The opening stanza of the first canto acknowledges that the poem's "hero" is drawn from the world of art (pantomime), since the reality of "the present age" (1.5) offers no one so suitable.[52] Thus we cannot assume — as the speaker later invites us on so many occasions to do — that there is a verifiable reality represented in this poem.

On the other hand, the speaker's much later query "But what's reality?" (15.89) reveals that the issue here is not whether the reality represented is subject to verification through experience (evidently it never entirely is), but rather whether the representation has captured it adequately. The difficulty of determining whether this standard has been met is obvious; neoclassical critics like Chételat judge a text according to the fidelity of its representation of "nature" and "society," but in *Don Juan*, it is never quite clear how "nature" and "society" are constituted. The speaker offers alternative standards for mimetic accuracy; at one point, for instance, he distinguishes his work from past epics on the grounds that "this story's actually true" (1.202), and

> If any person doubt it, I appeal
>   To history, tradition and to facts,
> To newspapers, whose truth all know and feel. (1.203)

However, his distinction between the "true" *Don Juan* and the "untrue" epics is instantly undone when he sets up a notoriously untruthful medium (newspapers) as his standard for truthfulness.

The speaker's insistence throughout *Don Juan* that the value of his work rests upon its truth and accuracy privileges representation, but only through representation's relationship with the notion of reality; we see here, as in *Les Orientales*, an operative difference between referentiality (language expressing the products of the imagination) and mimetic representation (language expressing an empirically verifiable reality). While the reader easily perceives the text as essentially fictional rather than documentary, the speaker continues to assert its sincerity and truthfulness. Analyzing *Don Juan*'s form, Suzanne Ferriss argues convincingly that

> [i]n the process of creating the narrative, Byron self-consciously undermines and destructs it, simultaneously demonstrating the limits of all literary systems which refuse to acknowledge the chaos of experience and the value of works, such as his own,

---

[51] Byron, preface, *Don Juan* 83–4.
[52] A summary of Byron's sources for *Don Juan* may be found in Byron, *Don Juan*, eds. T.G. Steffan, E. Steffan, and W.W. Pratt, rev. ed. (Harmondsworth, UK: Penguin, 1977) 8. For a comprehensive analysis, see Moyra Haslett, *Byron's* Don Juan *and the Don Juan Legend* (Oxford: Clarendon, 1997).

which not only acknowledge but embrace the world of infinite becoming.[53]

If the poem's function is to reflect "real" experience, mimetic representation will remain the foundation of its aesthetic. It may violate literary conventions in order to "embrace the world of infinite becoming," but it does so with the very conventional goal of imitating reality (a disordered narrative structure to match "the chaos of experience," for instance). Thus while *Don Juan* suggests that mimetic representation is rarely, if ever, adequate to its task, it does not discard mimesis as a standard.

Unlike *Les Orientales*, *Don Juan* is not, of course, an orientalist work in the usual sense. To begin with, it does not label its affiliation with the Orient in the way that Hugo's collection does, or Musset's "Namouna: conte oriental," or even Byron's own "Turkish Tales." As Alan Richardson observes, "Byron makes a point in *Don Juan* of deliberately avoiding the more purely decorative exoticism of his Oriental tales."[54] The central character and the original setting are Spanish, with only vague Moorish associations.[55] On the other hand, orientalist elements recur throughout the poem. Several key characters, including three of Don Juan's lovers (Donna Julia, Haidée, and Gulbeyaz) as well as his protégée (Leila), are orientalized to various degrees. The events of cantos 5, 6, and 7 take place in Turkey; settings include a slave market and a sultan's harem. One of the models for the figure of Don Juan himself is no doubt that of the sexually capricious sultan. Orientalist tropes ("These words went through his soul like Arab-spears" [5.117], "ready money *is* Aladdin's lamp" [12.12; emphasis his], and the like) and other such allusions are frequent even when the setting is not oriental.

The link between orientalism and the struggle with representation is less obvious in *Don Juan* than in either *Les Orientales* or "Namouna," but it is nonetheless significant. The principal factor here is the poem's narrative disorder. As Timothy Mitchell and others have observed, nineteenth-century orientalism's Orient is typically characterized as disordered.[56] Byron's own presentation of Turkey participates heavily in this stereotype. Juan's childhood environment in Spain, for instance, is presented as highly regimented, its orderliness disrupted only by Donna Julia and the seductive "darkness of her oriental eye" (1.56). In contrast, the Constantinople slave market appears random and disorganized:

---

[53] Suzanne Ferriss, "Romantic Carnivalesque: Byron's *Tale of Calil, Beppo,* and *Don Juan*," *Rereading Byron: Essays Selected from Hofstra University's Byron Bicentennial Conference*, ed. Alice Levine and Robert N. Keane (New York: Garland, 1993) 144.

[54] Alan Richardson, "Escape from the Seraglio: Cultural Transvestism in *Don Juan*," *Rereading Byron: Essays Selected from Hofstra University's Byron Bicentennial Conference*, ed. Alice Levine and Robert N. Keane (New York: Garland, 1993) 176.

[55] Diego Saglia argues for a closer association between Spain and the Orient in *Don Juan*; see Saglia, "Spain and Byron's Construction of Place," *Byron Journal* 22 (1994): 31–42.

[56] See for example Mitchell, *Colonising Egypt* 21–2.

> Like a backgammon board the place was dotted
> With whites and blacks, in groups on show for sale,
> Though rather more irregularly spotted. (5.10)

The description of the sultan's palace follows the same model. Once inside, Juan is led

> Into a room still nobler than the last;
> A rich confusion form'd a disarray
> In such sort, that the eye along it cast
> Could hardly carry anything away,
>   Object on object flash'd so bright and fast;
> A dazzling mass of gems, and gold, and glitter,
> Magnificently mingled in a litter. (5.93)

Formally, *Don Juan* constitutes a similarly magnificent muddle. The speaker asserts time and again the importance of consistency, but even more often indulges in digressions. Early in the first canto, for example, he explains that

> My way is to begin with the beginning;
> The regularity of my design
> Forbids all wandering as the worst of sinning (1.7)

Although he does "begin with the beginning" (Juan's parents and childhood), "wandering" becomes his primary modus operandi, as Suzanne Ferriss has remarked.[57] Over and over, he must drag himself back to the main thread of the narrative: "Return we to our story" (1.134), "Return we to Don Juan" (2.167), "T' our tale" (3.101), and so on throughout the poem's seventeen cantos (five more than promised at the outset [1.200]). He repeats himself ("But I have spoken of all this already — / And repetition's tiresome and unwise" [2.171]) and often loses his place ("The coast — I think it was the coast that I / Was just describing — Yes, it *was* the coast" [2.181; emphasis his]). By canto 9 he feels the need to confess, "I never know the word which will come next. / So on I ramble" (9.41–2). In canto 12 (the final one, according to the plan he announced in the first canto), he proclaims:

> But now I will begin my poem — 'Tis
> Perhaps a little strange, if not quite new,
> That from the first of Cantos up to this
> I've not begun what we have to go through. (12.54)

Under the pressure of such digressions, the narrative's progression becomes fitful at best.

---

[57] See Ferriss, "Romantic Carnivalesque" 140–5.

The poem's digressive quality functions in turn as a symptom of its difficulties with representation, or as another manifestation of the poem's resistance to a straightforward relationship between representation and reality. As I mentioned above, reality is often presented in *Don Juan* as exceeding the grasp of representation. In particular, the speaker frequently either confesses ignorance of or explicitly declines to include elements of the tale he is telling, with the result that the boundaries of the tale emerge well outside those of the narration. The speaker usually functions as an omniscient narrator but repeatedly claims to lack knowledge that an omniscient narrator would normally possess: "I cannot know what Juan thought of this" (1.112), "I know not if he had domestic cares" (5.148), and so forth. On other occasions he implies an inability to communicate what he knows: "I can't describe it" (2.5), "it would strike you blind / Could I do justice to the full detail; / So, luckily [...], my phrases fail" (5.97), etc. In adopting such a stance, the speaker indicates that his representation (the poem) is insufficient as a mimesis of the reality it attempts to depict. His digressions, I would argue, are a product of the same phenomenon. Reality (and it does not matter here whether this "reality" is "real") is, as Ferriss says, "too large and too complex to be captured and arranged in any aesthetic order"[58] — or to be reproduced mimetically. Consequently, the speaker moves distracted through it, settling briefly here and there but then always wandering on.

Analysis of Hugo's "Adieux de l'hôtesse arabe" showed how the speaker's ethnically overdetermined psychological stasis plays out in the poem's lack of formal progression. The connection between the East and *Don Juan*'s stymied progress is channeled not through the central character, as in "Adieux," but through the association of disorder with the Orient. *Don Juan*'s distracted speaker becomes, figuratively, the eye scanning the Turkish palace room: the eye "[c]ould hardly carry anything away, / Object on object flash'd so bright and fast" (5.93). Thus the speaker's penchant for digression, his lapses into ignorance, and his refusal to describe, all become metaphoric instances of orientalization, thereby throwing the entire problematic relationship between representation and reality into relief against the background of *Don Juan*'s orientalism.[59] When the speaker labels "wandering" as "the worst of sinning," but then in effect confesses to the same sin, he is casting himself as an oriental, a kind of narrative nomad. He himself comes near to acknowledging such an oriental identification in canto 4, when he observes:

---

[58] Ferriss, "Romantic Carnivalesque" 141.

[59] McGann comments extensively on these issues in *Don Juan*, concluding that in Byron's view, the poet is to "'arrange' the elements of his poem not on the aesthetic principles of 'the poem itself,' but on the rhetorical principles of the poem in its relations with men and affairs outside itself' (McGann, "*Don Juan*: Form," *Lord Byron's* Don Juan, ed. Harold Bloom [New York: Chelsea, 1987] 37). McGann does not take any account of the role played here by Byron's orientalism, however.

> Some have accused me of a strange design
>   Against the creed and morals of the land,
> [...]
> To the kind reader of our sober clime
> This way of writing will appear exotic. (4.5, 6)

"Namouna": fragmentary representation

In assimilating *Don Juan* as one of "Namouna"'s two most important literary ancestors, Musset seems to have looked to Byron's poem less for its orientalism than for its protagonist and its self-conscious, ironic style of narration, the influence of which is very clear in "Namouna."[60] "Namouna" also takes *Don Juan* as a point of departure for its handling of representation, but it mounts a stronger challenge to the privileged relationship between reality and representation. In this respect, *Don Juan* occupies an intermediate position between "Namouna" and Hugo's *Les Orientales*, which remains "Namouna"'s most immediate orientalist precedent (and object of scorn). "Namouna" uses some of the same tactics observed by Cooper in the parodies of Hugo's *Hernani*, including directly addressing the audience (often self-referentially), shifting the locale away from that of the original piece, and "diminish[ing] the ability of illusion and identification to overwhelm one's faculty for judgment."[61] However, Musset's strategy is clearly different. The *Hernani* parodists exaggerate the "illogic" and "unintelligibility" of Hugo's play so as to advocate a return to a more reasoned, neoclassical approach.[62] And in "Novembre," Hugo himself proposes much the same move, reasserting the value of a traditional mimetic model despite his insistence on unconventional subject matter. Musset, on the other hand, is inclined to point out the impossibility of such an orderly, rational endeavor; if the parodists of *Hernani* felt that Hugo was going too far, Musset seems to feel that he is not going far enough.

"Namouna" is one of several works in which Musset challenges the conventions and assumptions of his time. Pierre-André Reiben bases his analysis of Musset's *Lorenzaccio* (1834), for example, on the premise that this play, "not only by its subject matter, but also by its structure, its dramaturgical characteristics, implies a will to disrupt, to challenge a certain order in

---

[60] "Namouna" is not the only poem by Musset to contend with Byron; see for example his "Lettre à Lamartine" (1836). Musset also engages with Byron in his dramatic fragment entitled *La Matinée de Don Juan* [*Don Juan's Morning*] (1833). For an overview of Musset's relations with Byron's work, see Loïc Chotard, "A propos du byronisme de Musset: la réception de Lord Byron à l'Académie Française," *Revue de littérature comparée* 2 (1990) 347–54.

[61] Cooper, "Parodying Hugo" 27, 31, 32.

[62] Cooper, "Parodying Hugo" 25.

theatrical discourse."[63] Margaret Rees notes that Musset's verse comedy *A quoi rêvent les jeunes filles* [*What Girls Dream Of*], whose sole setting instruction is "La scène est où l'on voudra." [The setting is wherever one wishes.], pointedly disregards "Victor Hugo's insistence on the importance of characteristic setting" — at a time when Hugo was the dominant literary presence in France.[64]

A quoi rêvent les jeunes filles was originally published in the same volume as "Namouna," which is even more persistent in disrespecting the conventional demands of setting. Moreover, the first poem in the volume is preceded by a verse dedication of several pages, in which the speaker claims to reject politics, patriotism, Catholicism, wisdom, nature, and wealth. He announces:

> il n'entre pas dans mes prétentions
> D'être l'homme du siècle et de ses passions.
> C'est un triste métier que de suivre la foule,
> Et de vouloir crier plus fort que les meneurs,
> Pendant qu'on se raccroche au manteau des traîneurs.[65]

> [I make no pretense / Of being the man of the times and of its passions. / It is such a sorry calling to follow the mob, / And to want to shout louder than the ringleaders / While one clings to the coattails of the stragglers.]

Such a dismissive attitude towards the literary scene and presumed mentors of the young poet would be unlikely to inspire sympathy for "Namouna" and the other two works that follow the dedication. It is no surprise that the first public reading of this volume was poorly received, given that those present were very much part of the literary establishment.[66] According to Pierre Gastinel, "Namouna" was especially provocative.[67] Despite its apparent levity, "Namouna" follows the dedication in rejecting, or at least challenging, much of the accepted wisdom of Musset's older peers. But where the dedication is a relatively abstract manifesto, "Namouna" endeavors to implement the manifesto's principles.

---

[63] Pierre-André Rieben, *Délires Romantiques: Musset, Nodier, Gautier, Hugo* (Paris: José Corti, 1989) 19–20.

[64] Margaret Rees, *Alfred de Musset* (New York: Twayne, 1971) 74.

[65] Musset, "Dédicace à M. Alfred T[attet]," *Poésies complètes*, ed. Maurice Allem (Paris: Gallimard, 1957) 155. Byron's *Don Juan* is preceded by a shorter "Dedication," to Robert Southey. Like Musset's opening, it addresses various issues in poetics. However, whereas Musset addresses his dedication to a close and admired friend, Byron takes his as an opportunity to attack Southey for arrogance and poetic bungling.

[66] See Henry Dwight Sedgwick, *Alfred de Musset: 1810–1857* (Indianapolis: Bobbs-Merrill, 1931) 47–48. Pierre Gastinel notes that Musset also had difficulty getting his volume accepted by the publisher (see Gastinel, *Le Romantisme d'Alfred de Musset* [Paris: Hachette, (1933)] 221).

[67] Gastinel, *Le Romantisme d'Alfred de Musset* 588.

"Namouna" is a loosely structured poem, consisting of three cantos ("Chants") of unequal length, all written in sestets. The first canto (seventy-eight stanzas) describes the situation of Hassan, who is originally French but lives like a stereotypical sultan, luxuriating in women. This first canto is interrupted by frequent digressions, many of them commenting explicitly upon the progress of the poem, with the result that the narrative makes no progress at all. The second canto (fifty-five stanzas) continues the self-referential commentary on the poem but makes no mention of Hassan until the last two lines of the last stanza. Instead, the speaker delineates two types of "roué" [rake].[68] The first corresponds more or less to the Hassan of the first canto, but the second, a "don Juan ordinaire" [ordinary Don Juan] (2.23) who is an idealist rather than a cynic, is clearly the speaker's favorite. The final canto (fourteen stanzas) begins with more discussion of the poem itself, at last commencing the tale of Namouna in the fifth stanza. Namouna, it appears, is a Spanish slave girl who has been abducted by a Greek pirate and later purchased by Hassan. When he tires of her, he sets her free with sufficient funds to buy her passage home. But she is smitten with him and refuses to leave. When she sees a group of African women displayed for sale as slaves, she convinces their dealer to offer her as well, disguised with makeup and a wig, in the hope that Hassan will repurchase her.[69] This entire story is told in only eight stanzas, with the canto's final two stanzas refusing to supply a happy or satisfying ending, which the speaker could do only "si la vérité ne m'était pas sacrée" [if the truth were not sacred to me] (3.13).

Like *Don Juan*, which is an extended exercise in romantic irony, "Namouna" depends heavily upon irony to establish its aesthetic stance; the speaker's final dubious profession of sincerity, for instance, clearly echoes Byron's.[70] Irony is essential to "Namouna"'s effort at parody, but it is also engaged in the poem's exploration of representation per se. Azade Seyhan suggests this connection in general terms when she observes that "Romantic irony was a self-conscious reflection on the contingent nature of

---

[68] My source for "Namouna" is Musset, *Premières poésies, Poésies nouvelles*, ed. Patrick Berthier (Paris: Gallimard, 1976).

[69] Both Namouna's (racial) cross-dressing and her sexual assertiveness have clear antecedents in *Don Juan*. For further discussion of these issues in Byron's poem, see for example Caroline Franklin, "Haidée and Neuha: Byron's Heroines of the South," *Byron Journal* 18 (1990) 39, 41; Malcolm Kelsall, "Byron and the Women of the Harem," *Rereading Byron: Essays Selected from Hofstra University's Byron Bicentennial Conference*, ed. Alice Levine and Robert N. Keane (New York: Garland, 1993) 171; and Susan Wolfson, "'Their She Condition': Cross-Dressing and the Politics of Gender in *Don Juan*," *ELH* 54.3 (1987): 585–617.

[70] Critics consistently cite *Don Juan* as a major example of romantic irony. See for instance Frederick Garber, *Self, Text, and Romantic Irony: The Example of Byron* (Princeton: Princeton UP, 1988) esp. ch. 9; John Francis Fetzer, "Romantic Irony," *European Romanticism: Literary Cross-Currents, Modes, and Models*, ed. Gerhart Hoffmeister (Detroit: Wayne State UP, 1990) 19–36; and Anne Mellor, *English Romantic Irony* (Cambridge: Harvard UP, 1980) esp. ch. 2.

'representational reality.'"[71] Seyhan argues persuasively that "such figures and tropes as the arabesque and irony, which challenge the notion of total representation, become the formal staples of Romantic narratives;" and further, that "the popular twin tropes of Romantic writing, allegory and irony, confirm the impossibility of the mimetic project."[72]

Seyhan, who focuses on German romanticism, does not discuss Musset, but there are substantial links between "Namouna" and Seyhan's German model. Not only is "Namouna" ironic, but it is also, as I will argue later, legible as an allegory of the process of representation. Seyhan shows how the presence of allegory can be antimimetic in itself; this antimimetic tendency is compounded in "Namouna" by the participation of mimesis as a component of the allegory. Moreover, while Musset nowhere mentions the term "arabesque" in connection with "Namouna," certainly some features of the poem recall the arabesque. One of these is "Namouna"'s emphatic repetition of detail, which is less researched than *Thalaba*'s but in its own way as overwhelming. One could also look to Seyhan's definition of the arabesque as "mimic[ing] an unending spiral."[73] "Namouna"'s tendency to return to its starting point and its inability to make narrative progress both suggest an arabesque type of spiral structure, comparable to that employed in Hugo's "Adieux de l'hotêsse arabe" but much more blatant.

Further, Seyhan proposes that the fragment "enacts both interruption and subversion of closure. In narrative form, the fragment resists all claims to truth and desires of system building."[74] "Namouna" has much in common with the fragment in this sense. The story of Namouna herself is abbreviated; more importantly, the speaker interrupts his own story through most of the poem and tells it finally without an ending. As a result, closure is denied, in accordance with Seyhan's model. Because the poem's conclusion is pointedly incomplete rather than, as in the case of *Don Juan*, absent in that the poet never definitively finished the poem, it becomes a distinctive element of "Namouna"'s poetic strategy.[75] Finally, at the same time that the speaker's last, coy allusion to truth claims to elevate truth as a literary ideal, it reflects the poem's resistance to truth, for in the end the truth (if there is one) will not be told. Again, Seyhan's model holds.

While Seyhan does not refer to it, there is a link between certain aspects of

---

[71] Seyhan, *Representation and Its Discontents* 166.
[72] Seyhan, *Representation and Its Discontents* 28, 67.
[73] Seyhan, *Representation and Its Discontents* 72.
[74] Seyhan, *Representation and Its Discontents* 72.
[75] The status of *Don Juan*'s ending aside, Ferriss is right to point out that the work appears by design "fragmented and incomplete" throughout (Ferriss, "Romantic Carnivalesque" 144).

orientalism and the concept of the fragment.[76] Archaeological material from the Middle East had been attracting significant interest at this time; much of what had been discovered was of course fragmentary. Oriental texts too (with the complicated exception of the *1001 Nights*) were known primarily in the form of fragments. Even those texts available in their entirety, including some of William Jones's translations, lent themselves to being read more as collections of fragments than as whole poems, since, for example, the conventional structure of the Arabic qaṣîda [ode] form probably would not have given nineteenth-century European readers an impression of unity or cohesion. The English translations of the Muʻallaqât (pre-Islamic odes) in Jones's 1807 *Works* are even printed as if they were collections of fragments, with each Arabic line appearing as a numbered, three- or four-line "fragment" separated from the next by a space.[77] His French translations of Hâfiz's poems are more traditionally presented, in stanzas, but these relatively short poems may well have seemed fragmentary in themselves. Moreover, the poems translated are also selected from Hâfiz's much larger opus, and as such represent a fragment of the Persian poet's work.[78]

Such texts may well have been more appealing in a fragmentary state than whole, perhaps because they could thereby profit from the preexisting aesthetic of the ruin, perhaps because their incompleteness offered a greater opportunity for free play to the romantic imagination.[79] Following Marjorie Levinson's analysis, John Beer argues that the "Romantic Fragment Poem" developed as a distinct genre in the late eighteenth century; poets, he says, tended "to find a possible virtue in incompleteness."[80] Seyhan connects the romantic appreciation for the fragment with early-nineteenth-century approaches to mimesis: "[f]ragment," she says, "negates the philosophical postulate of continuous representation and induces cracks in the fundament of the idea."[81]

---

[76] Speaking of Silvestre de Sacy, the most influential French orientalist of the late eighteenth and early nineteenth centuries, Said says: "the Orientalist is required to *present* the Orient by a series of representative fragments, fragments republished, explicated, annotated, and surrounded with still more fragments" (*Orientalism* 128; emphasis his).

[77] Jones, *Works*, vol. 10 (London: Stockdale and Walker, 1807).

[78] Jones, *Works*, vol. 12. In his preface to *Poems, Consisting Chiefly of Translations from the Asiatick Languages* (1772), Jones also explains that in more than one instance he combined fragments of several poems to create a single "poem"; see Jones, *Works* 10:200–201.

[79] See Seyhan, *Representation and Its Discontents* 29; and Sharafuddin, *Islam and Romantic Orientalism* 9. "Incompleteness, fragmentation, and ruin" are the concepts underlying Thomas McFarland's useful analysis of romantic aesthetics; see *Romanticism and the Forms of Ruin* 5.

[80] Beer, "Fragmentations and Ironies" 238, 239–40; see Marjorie Levinson, *The Romantic Fragment Poem: A Critique of a Form* (Chapel Hill: U of North Carolina P, 1986).

[81] Seyhan, *Representation and Its Discontents* 29; see also 9. Although Gordon delineates a different relationship between fragment and arabesque, she reaches much the same conclusion as Seyhan: "The radical implications of the arabesque are those of ornament in general: it works to break down limits (between figure and background, frame and subject, fragment and continuity) as it elevates the notion of pure nonrepresentational art, thereby

Addressing the same issue in different terms, Thomas McFarland posits a contrast between the mimetic mode and what he calls the "meontic mode," which is "the imitation of [...] what is not there," or, in other words, of a referent (like Hugo's Orient) that originates in the imagination but not in any empirical reality.[82] (I have generally used the term "referentiality" to include McFarland's "meontic mode"; to clarify, a text can be referential whether or not its referents are part of a reality that has been or could be experienced, whereas in order to be mimetic or representational a text must "imitate" an empirically available entity.) According to McFarland, at the same time that the mimetic, like the meontic, "desire[s] and pursu[es ...] the whole," it must contend with the fact that "the only wholes encountered in experience are themselves fragments [...] The only true whole is a transcendently constituted whole."[83] Such a "true whole" may be available through the meontic mode, but not — as my discussion of the digressions and ellipses of *Don Juan* suggests — through the mimetic.

Beer observes that an orientalist poem, Coleridge's "Kubla Khan," is for the English tradition "in many respects *the* Romantic fragment."[84] Using Coleridge as his example, he then notes that poets who are concerned with the relationship between fragments and the whole often resort to the Orient. "Why," Beer asks, "should Arabia have been for [Coleridge] the place where the riddle of the One and the Many might be solved?"[85] He answers the question in terms of William Wordsworth's *Prelude*:

> the East provided for some imaginative writers [...] the suggestion not only of a delight in sensuousness, which might be refracting memories of a paradisal state that had been more decisively lost in Western culture, but in its most primitive forms of a desert simplicity that could cradle a unified culture, reconciling mathematics and artistic harmony, one which still might have a solution to offer for Western intellects, increasingly bewildered by the contradictions and fissures opening up in their own more "advanced" societies.[86]

Hugo might have shared Wordsworth's nostalgic idealism, but Musset does not. He welcomes the fragment, and he delights to show how multiple fragments do not in fact create a whole. For him, the whole is not elusive, but frankly illusory. Any representation of such a (nonexistent) whole is fraudulent and deserves to be exposed, as he exposes Hugo's.

---

according a limitless freedom to the hand of the artisan/poet" (*Ornament, Fantasy, and Desire* 53).

[82] McFarland, *Romanticism and the Forms of Ruin* 384.
[83] McFarland, *Romanticism and the Forms of Ruin* 409.
[84] Beer, "Fragmentations and Ironies" 241; emphasis his. Byron's *The Giaour* is of course another romantic-period poem often cited for its fragmentation.
[85] Beer, "Fragmentations and Ironies" 261.
[86] Beer, "Fragmentations and Ironies" 263.

No narrative, no representation

Musset does not articulate a principle of representation per se, either in his dedicatory poem or in "Namouna." Yet in "Namouna," more than in the dedication, representation appears the fundamental issue, even where it arises in the guise of more superficial problems.[87] Using exaggerated versions of tactics familiar from *Don Juan* and *Les Orientales*, "Namouna" disappoints certain conventions of literary representation. The narrative fails to progress as expected, the speaker appears unreliable, and the poem casts doubt upon the truth-value of the referents it represents. "Namouna" is experimenting, in effect, with the transmutation of what is proper to the meontic into a semblance of the mimetic, thereby devaluing the mimetic to a significantly greater degree than either *Les Orientales* or *Don Juan*.

Musset's disrespect for conventions begins with the poem's title: "Namouna: conte oriental." Each of the title's three words raises expectations that the poem disappoints. One might reasonably (neoclassically) expect that, as the title character, Namouna would be the poem's protagonist. Yet although Namouna is a central figure in the only story the poem really tells, she does not appear until the 138th of the poem's 147 stanzas. Her place as protagonist in the remainder of the poem is filled in the first canto by Hassan, and in the second left empty, or perhaps filled in the abstract by the second of the rakes. "Conte" is equally misleading; there is a story here, but its hurried, pro forma presentation at the very end of the poem is undoubtedly not what a reader trained on the *1001 Nights* and its imitations would anticipate with pleasure.[88] If one attempts to read the entire poem, rather than simply sestets 3.5–12, as a "conte," the resulting narrative is even further from the reader's expectation. Jacques Bony is right to label the poem "an anti-tale," but "Namouna" becomes, more precisely, also the story of the failed writing of a "conte oriental" — or, in other words, the representation of an ineffectual representation of the Orient.[89] Indeed, despite the "oriental' in the title, "Namouna" refuses to be orientalist in many of the conventional ways. There is not a single Middle Eastern character in the poem. Hassan, despite his Arabic name and sultanlike habits, is of French origin; Namouna is Spanish; the minor characters introduced at the end are Greek, Jewish, and African. Nor

---

[87] Musset's long-standing reputation as a poet who is, as Baudelaire charges, "totally unable to understand the process by which a reverie becomes a work of art," is unfounded, as Jacques Bony points out; see Bony, "Musset et les formes poétiques," *Revue d'histoire littéraire de la France* 96.3 (1996): 483.

[88] Like virtually all his contemporaries, Musset had read the *1001 Nights*; see Gastinel, *Le Romantisme d'Alfred de Musset* 9, 212; and Sedgwick, *Alfred de Musset* 304. As I will show later, certain essentials of Hassan's character are derived from the *1001 Nights* as well.

[89] Bony, "Musset et les formes poétiques" 487. For an overview of the romantic "conte oriental" as well as of its relations with the *1001 Nights*, see Bruneau, *Le "Conte oriental"* ch. 1.

does Musset go out of his way to create an orientalized setting, as Hugo tends to do; local color is scant. In short, the poem seems to be more interested in representing orientalism than in depicting the Orient.

Of these numerous unconventionalities, the most substantial is the resistance to narrative progression, which a reader expects in a story. In this case, the inclusion of the adjective "oriental" in the title may, on the model of the *1001 Nights*, prepare the reader for an unusual or contorted plot, but not for no plot at all; indeed, as I noted in my discussion of Southey, oriental tales tend to have prominent plots (at the expense of psychological characterization, for instance). But "Namouna" provides virtually no plot, at least until its very end. The poem outdoes *Don Juan* in this respect; after all, Byron's narrative does advance despite all the irregularities and obstacles. The basis for "Namouna"'s failure to progress is, however, approximately the same as *Don Juan*'s. In the first canto, the speaker makes a point of his frequent digressions from the supposed subject at hand (Hassan). For instance, after a dozen stanzas having no direct bearing on the story of Hassan, the speaker recollects himself:

> En vérité, lecteur, je crois que je radote.
> Si tout ce que je dis vient à propos de botte,
> Comment goûteras-tu ce que je dis de bon?
> J'ai fait un hiatus indigne de pardon;
> Je compte là-dessus rédiger une note.
> J'en suis donc à te dire... Où diable en suis-je donc?
>
> M'y voilà. — Je disais qu'Hassan, près d'une femme,
> Était très expansif, — il voulait tout ou rien. (1.61–2)

> [Truly, reader, I believe that I am talking drivel. / If everything I say comes out about nothing, / How will you appreciate what I say that is worthwhile? / I've created an unpardonable hiatus; / I figure on drafting a remark on that. / I am going, then, to tell you ... Where the devil am I then?
>
> Here I am. I was saying that Hassan, (when) near a woman, / Was very unreserved — he wanted all or nothing.]

Not only has no progress been made in the telling of the story during the "hiatus," but the speaker also acknowledges that he has been talking about nothing, "à propos de botte."[90]

These lines also constitute one of Musset's most concrete appropriations of *Don Juan*; Byron uses a variant of the same expression, and in a similar context: "Oh ye great authors! *Apropos de bottes*, / I have forgotten what I meant to say" (9.36; italics in original). Musset's production here of a

---

[90] Berthier reads "hiatus" as a reference to a line in the preceding stanza, but this seems a limited interpretation; see Musset, *Premières poésies*, ed. Berthier, 455.

supposedly orientalist poem based on, and even in part borrowed directly from, another writer's semiorientalist work is standard procedure in nineteenth-century European orientalism, as Said observes on several occasions.[91] As a result, Musset's use of Byron's phrase in this explicitly orientalist context (marked here by the inclusion of Hassan's obviously Arabic name) sets "Namouna" up to reflect upon orientalism and upon orientalist narrative in particular (the "conte oriental"). Finally, the appropriation of Byron's phrase becomes a reappropriation if we consider that the expression is French (Musset's language, not Byron's). The possibility of a legitimate literary original thus recedes along with that of an empirically verifiable referent; in its assimilation of precedent text, "Namouna" mirrors the ontological status of orientalism in a way that sets it apart from *Don Juan*.

Both the reuse of a Byronic phrase and the poem's evident inability here to represent much besides its own narrative constipation also suggest a more general reflection on the nature of the poetic narrative itself. These lines trope on the idea of an empty mimesis, representation somehow disassociated from any referent — even a fantasized, Hugoesque, meontic one. The speaker implies a link between his inability to stick to the (as-yet-undeveloped) story line, and the poem's lapse from mimesis; as Seyhan's analysis would predict, the existence of an uninterrupted narrative structure appears as the (here absent) prerequisite for representation. Of the two problems, the failure of representation is evidently the more urgent for the speaker; his mimetic "hiatus" is unpardonable, whereas the fragmented narrative can be resumed with a simple "M'y voilà." [Here I am.].

Such situations arise repeatedly in "Namouna." At the end of canto 1, for example, the speaker again finds himself distracted. This time, he has written the word "mahométanisme," but then realized that it should be "mahométisme,"

> et j'en suis bien fâché.
> Il fallait me lever pour prendre un dictionnaire,
> Et j'avais fait mon vers avant d'avoir cherché.
> Je me suis retourné, — ma plume était par terre.
> J'avais marché dessus, — j'ai soufflé, de colère,
> Ma bougie et ma verve, et je me suis couché.
>
> Tu vois, ami lecteur, jusqu'où va ma franchise.
> Mon héros est tout nu, — moi, je suis en chemise. (1.74–5)

[and I was very annoyed. / I ought to have gotten up to fetch a dictionary, / And I had made my verse without having looked. / I turned around — my pen was on the floor. / I had stepped on it — out of anger I extinguished / My candle and my zeal, and I went to bed.

---

[91] See for example Said, *Orientalism* 23.

> You see, dear reader, the extent of my frankness. / My hero is entirely naked — me, I am in shirtsleeves.]

The speaker/poet's initial error (the misspelling of "mahométisme") confirms his rejection of the researched orientalism whose aims include the authenticated representation of the Orient in literature.[92] He has already indicated his distaste for such orientalism:

> Considérez aussi que je n'ai rien volé
> À la Bibliothèque; — et bien que cette histoire
> Se passe en Orient, je n'en ai point parlé.
> Il est vrai que, pour moi, je n'y suis point allé.
> Mais c'est si grand, si loin! (1.23)
>
> [Consider that I have taken nothing / From the *Bibliothèque* — and although this story / Takes place in the Orient, I have said nothing at all about it. / As for me, it is true that I have not gone there at all. / Why, it is so big, so far away!]

This scholarly orientalism, for which Barthélemy d'Herbelot's *Bibliothèque orientale* (1697) is a major historical source,[93] is emblematic of the romantic drive for truth and knowledge, which Seyhan aptly describes:

> The search for artistic tools of representation and exotic icons of expression sends the Romantics on textual voyages to every corner of history. The expeditions to libraries, archives, museums, mausoleums, and ruins underline the Romantic desire to face the crisis of representation by creating a new mythology. This desire is also at the heart of the Romantics' encyclopedia project, an undertaking of colossal proportions which aimed to unearth, weld together, or reconstruct fragments of what was considered to have been a unified body of human knowledge.[94]

In the specific context of the Orient, Seyhan concludes, "[t]he investigation and appropriation or appropriative representation of otherness constitutes the essential gesture of Romantic hermeneutics."[95]

Once we recognize this diffuse cultural project as the background to Musset's endeavor, we see clearly how subversive and reactionary it is for him to ascribe to his speaker such unwillingness even to check a dictionary for a basic item of information about the Orient. Musset (or at least his speaker)

---

[92] This episode too has Byronic antecedents, but they are not orientalist; see *Don Juan* 5.61, 7.14. As Berthier notes, "mahométanisme" was in use (Musset, *Premières poésies*, ed. Berthier, 455), but clearly it was not the preferred spelling. It is also possible in this context to read "mahométanisme" ironically, as an anglicism on the model of "Mohammedanism."
[93] Said emphasizes the significance of this text; see *Orientalism* 63–7.
[94] Seyhan, *Representation and Its Discontents* 15.
[95] Seyhan, *Representation and Its Discontents* 23.

seems to resent and resist the totalizing operation of orientalism. He has no use for the notion of an empirical, textually representable Orient, or for the textualized discourse about such an Orient. Further, by perforating the boundaries between Orient and Occident (through Hassan's Frenchness, for example, or through his own orientalist appropriation of a French phrase used by an orientalist English writer) and by destabilizing the very definition of the Orient with his exclusion of identifiably oriental characters and of local color, Musset declines to participate in what Seyhan calls the "appropriative representation" of the East. Since the Orient is no longer absolutely "other" in "Namouna," it has lost its capacity to represent the Occident to Occidentals. In other words, it has lost its status as what Seyhan, following Roland Barthes, terms a "second-order semiological system," or the ability to function as a language, with signifiers, signifieds, and the capability of signifying — and thereby of representing.[96] Thus the speaker/poet's apparently simple objection to looking in a dictionary actually becomes a statement on the entire romantic orientalist project (including the work of both Hugo and Byron) and particularly on the use of the Orient as a (secondary) representational system.

The dictionary incident also foregrounds the process of literary representation per se, independent of the status of the Orient. The speaker/poet's insertion of the mundane circumstances of composition into the flow of the poem calls attention more to the role of the representer than to that of the representation.[97] The small acts that become the great act of literary representation (sitting down to write, using an ink pen, checking in a dictionary), but are conventionally excluded from the consciousness of the reader, now demand notice. Their material presence bars the representation from attaining its classical transparency; instead of representing the poem's supposed subject, the representation now calls attention to its own petty mechanical origins. The intrusive presence of the poet (or rather of a speaker who lays claim to the position of poet) interferes with mimesis. Secondarily, it thereby also interferes with the text's ability to offer readers the (vicarious) experience of an empirical Middle East through mimesis.

Finally, the episode of the dictionary serves to remind us of how far we have come, which is — in narrative terms — no distance at all. The poem's very first lines reveal that Hassan is naked, and here, seventy-five stanzas later, we find that he is (still) naked.[98] Thus far, nothing has happened, the poem is still "à propos de botte" [about nothing] (1.61) — and the very concreteness of "botte" in its usual usage (meaning "boot") makes the poem's persistently

---

[96] Seyhan, *Representation and Its Discontents* 40.

[97] Byron makes occasional references in *Don Juan* to the materiality of the process of composition, but the topic's place in "Namouna" is much more prominent; see for comparison *Don Juan* 2.216, 3.88, 111.

[98] This is perhaps the best example of the arabesque spiral structure of "Namouna" mentioned above.

antimimetic course appear all the more ironic. As the speaker/poet admits in the second canto,

> Mon premier chant est fait. – Je viens de le relire.
> J'ai bien mal expliqué ce que je voulais dire;
> Je n'ai pas dit un mot de ce que j'aurais dit
> Si j'avais fait un plan une heure avant d'écrire;
> Je crève de dégoût, de rage et de dépit. (2.13)

> [My first canto is done. I just reread it. / I have explained very badly what I wanted to say; / I have said not a word of what I would have said / If I had made a plan an hour before writing. / I am bursting with disgust, rage, and vexation.]

Authority, referents, and representation

Unlike canto 1, canto 2 focuses for the most part on a single subject, though it is one not well suited to narrative. The presentation is quite orderly, with few digressions. Stanzas 2.14–22 depict the first of "Deux sortes de roués [...] sur la terre" [Two types of rake in the world] (2.14). This first rake is an arrogant, narcissistic cynic, "sans coeur" [heartless] (2.20) and only "l'écorce d'un homme" [the shell of a man] (2.14). "Son idéal, c'est lui / [...] / Il est l'axe du monde, et lui permet d'aller" [He is his own ideal. He is the axis of the world; he enables it to turn.] (2.16). In the remainder of the canto, however, this fellow is overshadowed by the second type of rake, one that resembles Byron's Don Juan more closely:

> [le] roué Français, [le] don Juan ordinaire,
> Ivre, riche, joyeux, raillant l'homme de pierre,
> Ne demandant partout qu'à trouver le vin bon. (2.23)[99]

> [the French rake, the ordinary Don Juan, / Drunken, rich, joyous, mocking the man of stone, / Everywhere asking only to find good wine.]

The next fourteen stanzas continue to elaborate and to admire, before the speaker comes to question his own capacity. "C'est don Juan" [This is Don Juan], he says,

---

[99] The "homme de pierre" [man of stone] in these lines relates "Namouna" to Molière's version of the Don Juan legend (*Dom Juan ou le festin de pierre*; 1665), in which the protagonist is visited by, and ultimately taken off to Hell by, the stone statue marking the tomb of a man he had killed; Mozart's rendition in *Don Giovanni* is similar (libretto by Lorenzo Da Ponte; 1787). For Molière's sources on this aspect of the legend, see David Whitton, *Molière: Dom Juan* (Cambridge: Cambridge UP, 1995) 1–2. A summary of Musset's Don Juan sources is included in Magda Campanini Catani, "Le *Don Juan* d'Alfred de Musset," *Don Giovanni a più voci*, ed. Anna Maria Finoli (Bologna: Cisalpino, 1996) 196–7.

> Oui, don Juan. Le voilà, ce nom que tout répète,
> Ce nom mystérieux que tout l'univers prend,
> Dont chacun vient parler, et que nul ne comprend;
> Si vaste et si puissant qu'il n'est pas de poète
> Qui ne l'ait soulevé dans son coeur et sa tête,
> Et pour l'avoir tenté ne soit resté plus grand.
>
> Insensé que je suis! que fais-je ici moi-même?
> Était-ce donc mon tour de leur parler de toi,
> Grande ombre, et d'où viens-tu pour tomber jusqu'à moi?
> (2.38–9)

[Yes, Don Juan. There it is, that name which everything echoes, / That mysterious name which all the universe seizes upon, / Of which everyone comes to speak and which no one understands; / So vast and so powerful that there is no poet / Who has not taken it up into his heart and his mind, / And who is not diminished for having attempted it.

How foolish I am! What am I doing here myself? / Was this then my turn to speak to them of you, / And whence do you come to fall as far as me, great shade?]

Not only does this passage interrupt the flow of the speaker's presentation, with all the consequences described above, but it also casts doubt upon the validity of that presentation, much as Byron's speaker's confessions of ignorance do. In effect, it violates both the convention of authorial control and that of narrative progression; as we have seen, both are also at issue in Byron's and Hugo's work.

The speaker's claim of authorial incapacity, of the referent exceeding the representational capabilities of the speaker/poet, bears upon the poem's mimetic status. This becomes especially clear in one of the speaker's asides during a long speech of Hassan's:

> — Je rappelle au lecteur qu'ici comme là-bas
> C'est mon héros qui parle, et je mourrais de honte
> S'il croyait un instant que ce que je raconte,
> Ici plus que jamais, ne me révolte pas. (1.39)

[— I remind the reader that here as above / It is my hero who is speaking, and I would die of shame / If he (the reader) believed for an instant that what I am recounting, / Here more than ever, does not revolt me.]

Whereas in the preceding case the speaker seemed overwhelmed by the hugeness of his project, here he simply reconfigures his task so that he is no longer responsible for the characters he claims to have created. In one sense this approach might appear to enhance the representational value of Hassan's speech, since the speaker would then simply be recording what is said, "representing" it in the most basic sense. But since the text has already indicated its abstraction from the real (oriental or not), this documentary pose is patently fraudulent; the poem's subject is a fabrication for which the poet, here proxied by the speaker, is already wholly responsible. At the same time, however, the speaker/poet's stance implicitly casts doubt on the integrity of other orientalist poets (Southey, for example), who encourage readers to assume that their supposedly mimetic work describes an oriental reality, even though it may be as fictional as Musset's (approximately meontic) text.

Musset uses another version of this same tactic later in canto 1 when the speaker, again echoing Byron's, claims to be ignorant of Hassan's character and behavior:

> Je ne sais pas non plus s'il était bon chrétien;
>
> Je ne sais même pas quelle était sa croyance,
> Ni quel secret si tendre il avait confié,
> Ni de quelle façon. (1.62–3)
>
> [I do not know either if he was a good Christian;
>
> I do not even know what his creed was, / Nor what so tender secret he had confided, / Nor in what fashion.]

As when he dissociates himself from Hassan's speech in the example above, the speaker/poet appears here to be ascribing an independent status to the products of literary creation, claiming a place in empirical reality for referents (Hassan, his beliefs, his secrets) originating in the imagination. While in the preceding case the speaker/poet's stance seemed critical of the assumption of veracity underlying much of oriental(ist) literature's appeal, here we see more clearly how he offers the pure product of the imagination as a competitor. This invented figure, Hassan, is just as complete, just as mysterious, as any genuine oriental character could ever be. Why then, Musset seems to ask, should we be so intrigued by the Middle East as a real (mimetically accessible) place, when a fabricated (meontically based) version is just as good? In effect, Musset eliminates the space allowed in Hugo's preface for the Orient as a geopolitical entity; what remains, in revised form, is Hugo's construction of orientalism as fantastic.

It might be possible to understand this position as one that valorizes literary representation as a creative act. However, the speaker's stated ignorance about his subject subverts mimesis by exposing it as inadequate to capture what it purports to represent. This is true whether we assume an empirically verifiable reality (the domain of the mimetic) or a referent originating mainly in the imagination (the domain of the meontic). If Hassan is supposed to have a life outside the text (as the speaker/poet claims), the text is evidently incapable of representing it fully. If instead we accept that Hassan is completely without authenticity as either a "real Oriental" or a "real person," the conventions of literary representation require that his creator (the speaker/poet) know him as if he were real — or rather, better than if he were, since authors are conventionally assumed to have complete knowledge of the characters they create. Yet in this case, the author (or his stand-in) refuses that obligation. Consequently, the text falls into a sort of representational limbo, where an obviously unreal, even fraudulent character has pretended to the status of the real. To recast this supposition in McFarland's terms: Musset is suggesting that the meontic mode supplant or replace the mimetic entirely, rather than continuing to coexist with it on what McFarland describes as a "continuum."[100] As a result, it becomes possible, theoretically, for referentiality to exist as an activity entirely of the imagination, divorced from the representation of an empirical or experiential external reality.

Elsewhere in "Namouna," Musset's challenge to mimesis is grounded upon an implied critique of the validity of the Middle East as a referent. This critique is channeled first through his handling of characterization and second through his treatment of dream as a motif. The problem of characterization centers on the relationship between canto 2, which depicts the two rakes, and cantos 1 and 3, which deal with the individual character of Hassan. There is a sharp break between the depiction of Hassan in canto 1 and the development of the two types of rake in canto 2. Only in the final stanza of the second canto is Hassan mentioned, and even there the connection drawn between his character and the types is oblique. Canto 3 takes up the story of Hassan as if canto 2 did not exist. Thus whereas in Southey's *Thalaba* we perceive a distinct relationship between archetype and individual character, in "Namouna" the sudden and complete shifts from one to the other prevent this sort of mutual complementarity.

The inclusion of the archetype in *Thalaba* enhances the supposed authenticity of the individuals depicted, both as characters and more particularly as Arabs, but in "Namouna" it has the opposite effect. First of all, the assumption that permits Southey's bedouin characters to be absorbed into an archetypal norm of bedouin behavior is that Arabs are essentially types anyway and have no particular individuality; the depiction of any one such Arab can therefore easily shed light on the others. By disconnecting the Hassan of cantos 1 and 3 from the rakes of canto 2, Musset obstructs this process. Thus while Hassan is explicitly modeled on an archetype, that of the womanizing sultan, he is able, unlike Southey's characters, to attain an individual identity. Secondly, except in that they reflect the vaguely and intermittently orientalized

---

[100] McFarland, *Romanticism and the Forms of Ruin* 385.

figure of Byron's Don Juan, the rake archetypes Musset presents are not definitively oriental. As such, they tend to diminish rather than support Hassan's legitimacy as a Middle Easterner, and thus also "Namouna"'s trustworthiness as a depiction of things Middle Eastern. Therefore the entire scenario undermines both Hassan's validity as an oriental referent and concomitantly the poem's value as a text representing the Orient.

Oriental referents are not the only ones whose validity is called into question by "Namouna," however. By repeatedly presenting the referent as a product of fantasy, the poem challenges its value in a mimetic system. Altered states of consciousness, including fantasy-generating dreams, constitute a significant motif in the latter half of canto 1. The speaker's concern with this issue begins with his description of Hassan's orgasm (1.44–5), after which he concludes that

> Ce n'est vraiment pas vrai que tout soit pour le mieux.
>
> Et la preuve, lecteur, la preuve irrécusable
> Que le monde est mauvais, c'est que pour y rester
> Il a fallu s'en faire un autre, et l'inventer. (1.49–50)
>
> [It is truly not true that everything is for the best.
>
> And the proof, reader, the irrefutable proof / That the world is wicked, is that to stay there / It was necessary to make it something other, to invent it.]

Such fantasy is inseparable from dream:

> dormir — et rêver! — Ah! que la vie est belle,
> Quand un rêve divin fait sur sa nudité
> Pleuvoir les rayons d'or de son prisme enchanté!
> Frais comme la rosée, et fils du ciel comme elle!
> Jeune oiseau de la nuit, qui, sans mouiller son aile,
> Voltige sur les mers de la réalité!
>
> Ah! si la rêverie était toujours possible!
> Et si le somnambule, en étandant la main,
> Ne trouvait pas toujours la nature inflexible
> Qui lui heurte le front contre un pilier d'airain! (1.55–6)
>
> [to sleep — and to dream! Oh, how beautiful life is, / When a divine dream on his nudity makes / Shower rays of gold from its enchanted prism! / Fresh like the dew, and like it offspring of the heavens! / A young bird of the night, who, without wetting its wings, / Hovers over the seas of reality!

Oh, if only reverie were always possible! / And if only the somnambulist, stretching out a hand, / Did not always find inflexible nature, / Which knocks his forehead against a pillar of bronze!]

By indicating a preference for an alternative "reality" — dream, fantasy, "jouissance" — the speaker implicitly rejects the notion that the purpose of representation is to imitate (in the sense of mimesis) empirical reality. Deprived (or freed?) of its privileged relationship with reality, representation degenerates (or evolves?) into a referentiality that hovers over the seas of reality instead of imitating it.

Hassan is at the center of this problem of alternative realities, in part because of his own exploration of dream, sexual pleasure, and other such states with persistent oriental associations for Europeans.[101] More important, though, is the fact that Hassan, in a seemingly infinite retreat from reality, is not only "invented" in the sense that all fictional characters are, but is also portrayed as having invented himself, and on the basis of a literary text, which is of course also an invention:

> certain soir qu'il ne savait que faire,
> Se trouvant mal en train vis-à-vis de son verre,
> Pour tuer un quart d'heure il prit monsieur Galland.
> Dieu voulut qu'il y vît comme quoi le sultan
> Envoyait tous les jours une sultane en terre,
> Et ce fut là-dessus qu'il se fit musulman. (1.64)

[a certain evening when he did not know what to do, / Finding himself not in the mood for drinking, / He took up Mr. Galland to kill a quarter of an hour. / God wanted him to see there how the sultan / Dispatched a sultana every day, / And it was on that basis that he became a Muslim.]

Through this process the normal action of mimesis, from object to representation, has been inverted; the starting point is now not an object in reality but instead a literary representation. While "Namouna" represents Hassan, he is also himself a representation, an "imitation" of a figure represented in Antoine Galland's translation of the *1001 Nights*, a text that stood as the quintessential alternative reality for nineteenth-century readers. Hassan kills only a quarter of an hour, whereas the sultan (Shahrazad's

---

[101] Musset is one of many nineteenth-century writers to connect the Orient with dream, fantasy, and even hallucination. Coleridge's "Kubla Khan" (1797) is perhaps the most famous example, though it does not deal with the Islamic Middle East per se. I would also cite Baudelaire's essays "Du vin et du hachish [sic]" ["On Wine and Hashish"] (1851) and "Les Paradis artificiels" ["Artificial Paradises"] (1858–60), as well as de Quincey's "Confessions of an English Opium-Eater" (1822).

husband-to-be Shahrayar) kills every morning the wife he had married the previous day. "Hassan" the Frenchman may have become a Muslim on the basis of a sexual fantasy redirected (reoriented?) by a fictional text, but his imitation appears severely attenuated.

In a move that is especially subversive because oriental(ist) texts, especially the *1001 Nights*, are so commonly read for the Middle Eastern reality they are supposed to depict, "Namouna" warns us specifically against assuming a close relationship between a literary text and reality. The speaker/poet asks rhetorically:

> Eh! depuis quand un livre est-il donc autre chose
> Que le rêve d'un jour qu'on raconte un instant;
> Un oiseau qui gazouille et s'envole; — une rose
> Qu'on respire et qu'on jette, et qui meurt en tombant; —
> [...]
> Aujourd'hui, par exemple, il plaît à ma cervelle
> De rimer en sixains le conte que voici.
> Va-t-on le maltraiter et lui chercher querelle?
> Est-ce sa faute, à lui, si je l'écris ainsi?
> "Byron, me direz-vous, m'a servi de modèle."
> Vous ne savez donc pas qu'il imitait Pulci?[102] (2.7–8)

> [Eh! Since when is a book, then, anything other / Than a (single) day's dream which one recounts for an instant, / A bird that chirps and flies off — a rose / That one inhales and throws away, and that dies falling —
> ...
> Today, for example, it pleases my mind / To write this tale here in sestets. / Will one insult it or pick a quarrel with it? / Is it its own fault if I write it thus? / Byron, you tell me, served me as a model. / You do not know, then, that he imitated Pulci?]

Here, in contrast to the examples cited earlier, the speaker/poet appears in control of the text; he chooses the poem's format, and in the final line cited, he makes clear that the poem has no independent authority. Moreover, as the final reference to Byron and Pulci reveals, what a literary work represents ("imitates") is as likely to be textual as actual. On the other hand, not only is the experience depicted by literature ephemeral, but the literature itself is as well. In a sense, then, whether or not a literary work succeeds as representation (of reality, of fantasy, or of precedent text) becomes relatively unimportant, since both it and what it appears to represent are fleeting and insignificant. What Seyhan describes elegantly as "the free and seamless association of the mimetic-representational and the fantastic"[103] allows, or even requires, that mimesis-representation cede to a more inclusive referentiality, one in which a

---

[102] Luigi Pulci was a fifteenth-century Italian poet.
[103] Seyhan, *Representation and Its Discontents* 127.

referent can be substantially disconnected from "reality," or at least distanced from it by several layers of text.

The insecure position of representation is reaffirmed by the speaker/poet's emphasis on his choice of rhymed sestets as a form. With no mention being made of the sestets' content, the speaker/poet's function becomes vested entirely in the poem's form. We might be reminded here of Southey's locating the arabesque in *Thalaba*'s meter so that that aspect of the poem's form stands for the poem's oriental content. Musset's focus here on the choice of form makes form into content in a much more direct way than Southey's; the poem's form becomes explicitly, if only briefly, the poem's subject as well. In other words, the technical, superficial aspects of representation are brought to the reader's attention in such a way as to subvert their own supposed function, much as the recounting of the dropped pen earlier in the poem prevented the poem from recounting anything else. In both cases, the attention directed towards representation, whether by way of form in the first canto or of process in the second, effectively disables it.

The Middle East: "impossible à décrire"

The speaker's apparent discomfort with the conventions of literary representation reaches its peak at the start of canto 3. He begins with a disingenuous assertion of his goal:

> Je jure devant Dieu que mon unique envie
> Était de raconter une histoire suivie.
> Le sujet de ce conte avait quelque douceur,
> Et mon héros peut-être eût su plaire au lecteur. (3.1)
>
> [I swear before God that my only wish / Was to tell a coherent story. / The subject of this tale had such tenderness, / And my hero might have known how to please the reader.]

But in the next stanza he admits that his plan has gone awry:

> Dans tout ce que je fais j'ai la triple vertu
> D'être à la fois trop court, trop long, et décousu.
> Le poème et le plan, les héros et la fable,
> Tout s'en va de travers, comme sur une table
> Un plat cuit d'un côté, pendant que l'autre est cru. (3.2)
>
> [In everything I do I have the triple virtue / Of being at once too short, too long, and rambling. / The poem and the plan, the heroes and the fable, / Everything goes on awry, as on a table / A cooked dish on one hand and a raw one on the other.]

The situation seems unsalvageable:

> Mes amis à présent me conseillent d'en rire,
> De couper sous l'archet les cordes de ma lyre,
> Et de remettre au vert Hassan et Namouna.
> Mais j'ai dit que l'histoire existait, — la voilà.
> Puisqu'en son temps et lieu je n'ai pas pu l'écrire,
> Je vais la raconter; l'écrira qui voudra. (3.4)

> [My friends now advise me to laugh about it, / To cut the strings of my lyre under its crossbar, / And to put Hassan and Namouna back out to pasture. / But I have said that the story would exist — there it is. / Since I could not write it in its time and place, / I will tell it; let write it whoever wishes.]

And here the speaker finally begins to tell the story of Namouna, but only after he stages a resignation, taking on the pose of oral storyteller ("raconter") and abandoning that of writer ("écrire"). As has already been demonstrated, the poem emphasizes the textuality of the "conte oriental" as a genre, despite its origins in the (originally oral) *1001 Nights*. Only a writer can engage in it, and now the speaker/poet is no longer posing as a writer.

On the other hand, this self-conscious gesture of resignation is also one of the most orientalist of "Namouna." After all, Shahrazad, the speaker inscribed in the *1001 Nights*, and therefore the quintessential creator of oriental narrative, was a storyteller, a raconteuse, not a writer. If the speaker of "Namouna" is laying claim to the status of storyteller, he is also allying himself with Shahrazad. This shift of self-identification also constitutes a substitution of an oriental(ist) mode of representation for a conventional or classical one.[104] Thus after two long cantos in which conventional literary representation is teased apart and eventually disabled, here in canto 3 Musset seems finally to be offering an alternative, revisiting (albeit from a different perspective) Hugo's opposition between mimesis and orientalism so as to propose orientalism as a successor to mimesis.

Because of the nature of Namouna's story as told in the third canto, however, this proposal is but momentarily plausible. The actual story of Namouna is the only uninterrupted part of the narrative, yet it is also the only portion of the poem supposedly delivered by the orientalist raconteur rather than the writer. Moreover, narrative progression is presented in the rest of the poem as a conventional trait; it is odd, then, that narrative progress is restored after conventional representational writing has been laid open to challenge. So if "Namouna" is offering orientalism as an alternative to conventional literary representation, it is doing so only after orientalism has suddenly begun to

---

[104] The poem's exaggerated spontaneity and apparent lack of revision also support this impression of orality.

resemble strongly the very conventionality to which it has thus far been opposed. Rather than suggest orientalism as a solution to the problems of conventional literary representation, "Namouna" seems instead to poke fun at those (including Hugo) who would adopt such an opinion, seeking in a oriental(ist) mode some relief from the tedious limitations of conventional literary textual production.

As a whole, "Namouna" is interested principally in the way in which oriental(ized) subject matter facilitates exploration of the potential of the imagination.[105] The speaker has scorned the researched orientalism of the dictionary and of d'Herbelot's *Bibliothèque orientale* and has exhibited instead the powers of literary invention. The Orient's importance is not as a geographical or cultural entity but instead as a locus for the action of the imagination. The local color that accompanies reality-driven (albeit fantasized) portrayals of the Orient is inappropriate to such a context, and Musset makes a point of avoiding it:

> Si d'un coup de pinceau je vous avais bâti
> Quelque ville *aux toits bleus*, quelque *blanche* mosquée,
> Quelque tirade en vers, d'or et d'argent plaquée,
> Quelque description de minarets flanquée,
> Avec l'horizon *rouge* et le ciel assorti,
> M'auriez-vous répondu: "Vous en avez menti!"
>
> (1.24; emphasis his.)

[If with a brush stroke I had constructed for you / Some city *with blue roofs*, some *white* mosque, / Some passage in verse, plated with gold and silver, / Some description of minarets side-by-side, / With a *red* horizon and a matching sky, / You would have answered me: "You have lied!"]

The speaker bluntly refuses to follow in the path of orientalists who claim to depict the reality or truth of the Orient, yet he claims to base his refusal on his respect for truth. Musset is indirectly alleging that Hugo's use of local color (literally) in *Les Orientales* constitutes just such an untruth, even though, like Hugo, he accepts the Orient as a space of fantasy.[106] More to the point, Musset turns a challenge to one of Hugo's tactics (use of local color) into a disavowal of the validity of the strategy of representation (a literary act in a particular authentic relationship with reality).

---

[105] Seyhan sees a similar tendency among certain German romantic writers on India, arguing that their "India constitutes the recovery and reinvention of an occulted system of representation that gives Western imagination access to an alternative and unexplored path of signification" (*Representation and Its Discontents* 77–8).

[106] Both Maurice Allem and Patrick Berthier identify this stanza as a direct critique of *Les Orientales*; see Musset, *Poésies complètes*, ed. Allem, p. 698, n. 9, and *Premières poésies*, ed. Berthier, p. 455, n. 4.

This challenge goes far beyond Shelley's claim of disinterest in "Mahometan manners" and their "minute delineation." Shelley is merely disinclined, seeing such a sociological portrayal as peripheral to his universalist moral aims. Musset, on the other hand, suggests that the whole project is fundamentally invalid in that there can be no genuine representation of the Orient. As he says of his poem's orientalized hero, "Hassan était un être impossible à décrire" [Hassan was a being impossible to describe] (1.26). But Hassan is a Frenchman; by identifying Hassan's French origins, Musset also suggests the extent to which the Orient as customarily represented in orientalist literature is actually, as Said explains in *Orientalism*, a European creation. Musset seems to understand that the represented Orient is also a repository for European fantasies, that the typical orientalist's Orient is as much invented as his own pointedly fabricated Orient, and perhaps even that the stereotypical figure of the oversexed sultan is as much a fiction as his own Hassan.

Moreover, if the fantastic, stereotyped Orient that Hassan symbolizes is nonetheless "impossible à décrire" [impossible to describe], then perhaps, in Musset's view, referentiality itself (the meontic) is as unlikely as representation (the mimetic). "Namouna" is, then, more about the literary representation of the Middle East than about the Middle East itself. But by casting doubt on the ability of literature to represent a (conventionally) quintessentially representable referent — the Middle East — Musset is inevitably also questioning the whole enterprise of representation. For Musset, then, to "represent" the Orient is also to explore alternatives to representation, ways of producing poetry that neither depend so heavily upon mimetic representation of an actual or presumptive reality nor indeed assume that such a representation is truly possible.

This skepticism clearly distinguishes Musset's poetics from Hugo's and Byron's. Although Byron lays out the inadequacies of mimesis in *Don Juan*, he maintains it as a privileged mode. Hugo casts aside his amimetic experiments to realign himself with the status quo, limiting his demands for poetic autonomy to the choice of subject matter. Musset, on the other hand, uses his orientalist experiment to show how impossible the whole endeavor of mimesis is, how no literary representation can imitate reality. A return to mimesis would seem only foolish.

Chapter 3

Orientalist poetics and the nature of the Middle East

Thus far, this book has been concerned mainly with orientalism's Orient as an arena for poetic experimentation, especially experimentation at the boundaries of mimesis. The current chapter, in contrast, probes the qualities that enabled the Orient to serve this important purpose throughout the nineteenth century and thereby to displace nature as a poetic origin. Specifically, I will argue that the Orient's perceived unnaturalness is the crucial feature that produces the Orient as an amimetic locus. In this respect, my argument will diverge from that of Saree Makdisi, who sees nature (chiefly defined as the outdoor environment) and the Orient as instances of "anti-modern otherness" — "self-enclosed and self-referential enclaves of the anti-modern" — that operate in parallel as places of shelter from the anxieties of modernization.[1] Although there is no doubt that both the Orient and nature stand apart from modernity and its processes, it is also important to take into account the interaction between these two entities. As this chapter will show, nature and the East function in opposition to one another aesthetically, even if, as Makdisi proposes, they are at the same time working in tandem as counterpoints to the modern. Although the Orient and nature are each capable of serving as a poetic origin, they generate disparate poetics. Using William Wordsworth's articulation of the oppositional relationship between European nature and Middle Eastern nature as a point of departure, I will show how a range of nineteenth-century poets — Felicia Hemans, Charles Leconte de Lisle, Théophile Gautier, Matthew Arnold, and Alfred Tennyson — develop this relationship, often as the basis for an alternative to mimesis.

The question of the Orient's relationship with nature is especially significant if one considers that the concept of nature is central to Western aesthetics. When E.J. Chételat and his anonymous correspondent complain of Victor Hugo's failure to imitate nature, they are calling upon a tradition of criticism rooted in the philosophy of Plato and Aristotle. That tradition has not, of course, been stable through the centuries; as M.H. Abrams explains in his classic study of romantic-period criticism, *The Mirror and the Lamp*, poets'

---

[1] Makdisi, *Romantic Imperialism* 10, 12.

and critics' understanding of both the value and constitution of "nature" have varied dramatically.[2] Opinions on the aesthetic significance of nature have also been far from uniform. Still, nature — however variously constituted and evaluated — remains vital to any formulation of nineteenth-century French and British poetics.

Most critics have generally accepted Abrams's contention that in the early nineteenth century, English poets started to value poetry more for its expression of poets' feelings and emotions than for what Chételat's correspondent praises as the faithful imitation of nature.[3] As my analysis of Hugo's *Les Orientales* suggests, French poetry follows a similar developmental course despite its slightly later starting point. Abrams explains that the old concern with accuracy undergoes a metamorphosis: "the first-order criterion now becomes the relation of a poem to the feeling and state of the mind of the poet; and the demand that poetry be 'true' [...] gives way to the demand that poetry be 'spontaneous,' 'genuine,' and 'sincere.'"[4] More recently, some critics have complicated Abrams's now-conventional interpretation. Frederick Burwick, for example, suggests that Abrams overemphasizes "the shift from art as imitation to art as expression" while neglecting "the interplay of imitation and expression" in romantic poetry.[5]

Yet even within the more limited delineation espoused by Abrams, nature continues to serve as a fundamental source of poetic inspiration. Indeed, elevated by what James Heffernan labels "the Wordsworthian doctrine that rural experience alone can teach the heart how to feel,"[6] nature actually assumes a new importance as higher status is granted to the poet's emotional reaction to the contemplation of nature. Nature's function as a standard of

---

[2] Abrams, *The Mirror and the Lamp: Romantic Theory and the Critical Tradition* (Oxford: Oxford UP, 1953) esp. chs. 1, 10. See also Joseph Beach, *The Concept of Nature in Nineteenth-Century English Poetry* (New York: Pageant, 1956) esp. ch. 1. For a more recent overview of nineteenth- and twentieth-century critical thinking on nature and Romantic poetry, see Paul H. Fry, "Green to the Very Door? The Natural Wordsworth," *Studies in Romanticism* 35.4 (1996): 535–43.

[3] Chételat, ed., *Les Occidentales* 10.

[4] Abrams, *The Mirror and the Lamp* 298.

[5] Burwick, "The Romantic Concept of Mimesis" 179. Other critics who have questioned Abrams's formulation include Thomas McFarland, who relies upon Kant and the German romantics (to whom both Abrams and Beach also allude) to argue that art's imitation of nature does indeed remain paramount in romanticism, but as part of a distinctly romantic "doctrine of organic form"; see McFarland, *Romanticism and the Forms of Ruin* 36–43. Numerous critics have also countered Abrams by stressing the heterogeneity of Romanticism. See for example Butler, "Romanticism in England," *Romanticism in National Context*, ed. Roy Porter and Mikulas Teich (Cambridge: Cambridge UP, 1988) 37–67; and Mary A. Favret and Nicola J. Watson, eds., *At the Limits of Romanticism: Essays in Cultural, Feminist, and Materialist Criticism* (Bloomington: Indiana UP, 1994).

[6] James A.W. Heffernan, "Wordsworth's London: The Imperial Monster," *Studies in Romanticism* 37.3 (1998): 429.

moral and aesthetic rightness also remains essential.[7] When, for instance, Marilyn Butler says of Wordsworth that "his vision of nature represented England as still a pastoral society, which was comforting," she is calling on nature both as an object of contemplation and as a standard of rightness.[8] Paul Fry explains that "[b]y Wordsworth's time, 'nature' was a 'technical term' [...], referring to the laws and operations of the physical world." He adds, however, that "[t]here is also the ontology of nature: its mode of being, its status as beings or as a being, its relation to human being, and the being of its being."[9] Yet even in this expansive ontological sense, and even granted "the almost inevitable confusion anyone is likely to feel when trying to say what nature *is*," the basis for the nineteenth-century British and French concept of nature is inevitably nature as known in Europe.[10] The Orient functions as nature's other, placing it at the center of nineteenth-century aesthetics.

William Wordsworth and the nature of the Middle East

Wordsworth's later contemporary Thomas Love Peacock (1785–1866) assumes that the East is incompatible with a European ideal of nature. This assumption forms the foundation of his proposal that orientalism itself obstructs the proper relationship between poetry and nature. In his famous 1820 critical essay "The Four Ages of Poetry," Peacock singles out "that egregious confraternity of rhymesters, known by the name of the Lake Poets," whose "return to nature" he finds simplistic and hypocritical. They appear, he says sarcastically,

> to have ratiocinated much in the following manner: "Poetical genius is the finest of all things, and we feel that we have more of it than any one ever had. The way to bring it to perfection is to cultivate poetical impressions exclusively. Poetical impressions can be received only among natural scenes: for all that is artificial is anti-poetical. Society is artificial, therefore we will live out of society. The mountains are natural, therefore we will live in the

---

[7] For a summary of influences on and origins of this development, see Arthur O. Lovejoy, "On the Discrimination of Romanticisms" *English Romantic Poets: Modern Essays in Criticism*, ed. M.H. Abrams (New York: Oxford UP, 1960) 3–5. See also Christopher Thacker, *The Wildness Pleases: The Origins of Romanticism* (New York: St. Martin's, 1983) 1–3, 12, 192, 235.

[8] Butler, "Repossessing the Past" 68.

[9] Fry, "Green to the Very Door?" 538, 539.

[10] Fry, "Green to the Very Door?" 537; emphasis his. In arguing that Wordsworth is indeed a "nature poet," Fry implies but never problematizes the European basis for the concept; for example, in asking (tongue in cheek) "whether the nature poetry of Wordsworth is green [for trees] or *gray* [for rocks and stones]," he leaves no place for non-European landscape forms such as deserts, steppes, or prairies (548; emphasis his).

mountains. There we shall be shining models of purity and virtue, passing the whole day in the innocent and amiable occupation of going up and down hill, receiving poetical impressions, and communicating them in immortal verse to admiring generations."[11]

Despite this supposed devotion to nature, however, even "Mr. Wordsworth, the great leader of the returners to nature, cannot describe a scene under his own eyes without putting into it [...] some [...] phantastical parturition of the moods of his own mind."[12] To meet the demands of current fashion, poets busy themselves "wallowing in the rubbish of departed ignorance, and raking up the ashes of dead savages to find gewgaws and rattles for the grown babies of the age."[13] Peacock's contention is that "barbaric manners and supernatural interventions" — such as those Southey incorporates into *Thalaba* — are the essential factors destroying the legitimacy of the return to nature.[14] Given that, as we have seen, both barbarism (foreignness, difference, otherness) and the supernatural are among the Orient's dominant characteristics in English and French poetry, Peacock could accept neither the Orient as a subject nor the possibility of orientalism as an aesthetic approach.

Peacock proceeds to list the offending poets: Walter Scott, George Gordon Byron, Robert Southey, William Wordsworth, Samuel Taylor Coleridge, Thomas Moore, and Thomas Campbell. Southey and Moore are cited explicitly for their orientalism. Byron and Campbell are charged with other types of exoticism, but both (like Scott and Coleridge) would have been recognized by contemporary readers for their orientalist endeavors as well. Of the seven poets on Peacock's list, Wordsworth is the only one not criticized for exoticism. Indeed, Wordsworth is among those romantic poets least attracted to the Islamic Orient. He has no poems devoted entirely to Middle Eastern subjects, and only a handful — including "Septimi Gades," which I will discuss in detail shortly — that even make reference to the Middle East. Aside from the famous Dream of the Arab episode in book 5 of *The Prelude*, the best known of these poems is "The Solitary Reaper" (1807), which strongly resembles "Septimi Gades" in its use of the Arabian desert as the unnatural counterpart of a European outdoor scene.[15] In both poems, the stature of the natural European

---

[11] Peacock, "The Four Ages of Poetry," *Memoirs of Shelley and Other Essays and Reviews*, ed. Howard Mills (London: Rupert Hart-Davis, 1970) 127.
[12] Peacock, "The Four Ages of Poetry" 128.
[13] Peacock, "The Four Ages of Poetry" 128.
[14] Peacock, "The Four Ages of Poetry" 128.
[15] Four lines of "The Solitary Reaper" are relevant here:

No Nightingale did ever chaunt
More welcome notes to weary bands
Of travellers in some shady haunt,
Among Arabian sands. (9–12)

landscape is enhanced by comparison with the desert, and the value of the European figure's intimacy with the natural setting is increased by the desert travelers' inability to emulate it. Thus despite its rarity, Wordsworth's use of the Islamic Orient as a subject, and especially of an unnatural Eastern nature juxtaposed to the European landscape, is important in the context of an aesthetic philosophy and a body of work that depend so heavily on a certain conception of nature.[16]

Since European nature remains the undisputed standard in poems such as "The Solitary Reaper" and "Septimi Gades," one could fairly propose that any environment that did not share Europe's physical characteristics would be judged unnatural and even morally deficient. Thomas McFarland offers an analysis along these lines, in his reading of the Georgian landscape in Wordsworth's "Ruth" (1800), for example.[17] Such an argument for the essential similarity of all "exotic" sites is pursued even further by Alan Bewell, who shows how, in the Enlightenment tradition to which Wordsworth is heir, the various "'savage' peoples," including Arabs, along with Indians, Eskimos, and Hottentots, are united in their original difference from Europeans.[18] Even Bewell, however, remarks on the specificity of the Enlightenment's — and Wordsworth's — assumptions about Arabs and about the Middle Eastern environment. Bewell argues that "the popular representation of the desert wastes of the Middle East indicated [...] the enormous power of despotic governments or 'destructive nations' to lay waste nature."[19] In making this argument, Bewell proposes a link between a political morality familiar from our reading of Percy Shelley's *The Revolt of Islam* and the natural environment of the Middle East ("desert wastes"). Further, as Bewell suggests in his reading of the Dream of the Arab, the Arabian desert is "no ordinary landscape" not merely because of its physical characteristics but also because it is "a world

---

Beer addresses briefly the orientalism of both "The Solitary Reaper" and the Dream of the Arab episode; see "Fragmentations and Ironies" 262–3. Other Wordsworth poems with orientalist components include a sonnet beginning "The fairest, brightest, hues of ether fade" (1815) and a poem on the Crusades, "The Armenian Lady's Love" (1835).

[16] Heffernan makes a similar argument for the importance of London in the development of Wordsworth's approach to nature; see "Wordsworth's London" 423. The aesthetic implications of Wordsworth's orientalism will be addressed more fully in chapter 4.

[17] McFarland, "Green Savannahs: Wordsworth and the Moral Bonding with Nature" *European Romantic Review* 3.1 (1992): esp. 53.

[18] Bewell, *Wordsworth and the Enlightenment: Nature, Man, and Society in the Experimental Poetry* (New Haven: Yale UP, 1989) 21–2. Along the same lines, Heffernan concludes that "[b]y 1800 wild beasts and non-Caucasian racial groups [...] had become equally exotic and almost interchangeable" (Heffernan, "Wordsworth's London" 436).

[19] Bewell, *Wordsworth and the Enlightenment* 241. Bewell's examples are Volney's *Ruins of Empires* and Shelley's "Ozymandias."

where human life has made little difference."[20]

There are at least two factors, then, that give the environment of the Middle East (and the desert particularly) special significance, making it exemplary as no other area of the nineteenth-century world.[21] First, the desert's physical traits remain important. Its dryness, heat, and desolation, the extraordinary contrast between it and its oases, the total absence of familiar vegetation or scenery, all contribute to an impression of unnaturalness that seems unparalleled in Wordsworth's depictions of other types of landscape, even those equally lacking in what McFarland calls the "criteria of the sublime."[22] Second, the peculiarities of the Middle Eastern landscape are irrevocably tied to assumptions about human connections with that landscape, and ultimately to claims about the human relationship with nature in general.

While acknowledging the important, substantive differences among romantic poets even within England alone, we can at least follow Abrams in presuming that, for the romantics, the natural environment's great purpose is to inspire some human feeling that can be transmuted into poetry. Wordsworth, who is Abrams's prime example here, goes so far as to make nature the "cardinal standard of poetic value."[23] Typically, nature in this context is rural and sparsely inhabited by simple people. These simple people who live in nature are superior, and their habits and characteristics comprise the norm of what is societally "natural."[24] For Wordsworth in particular, then, the adoption of nature as a moral standard is inseparable from the concept of nature as environment.[25] In other words, when we think of nature in Wordsworthian

---

[20] Bewell, *Wordsworth and the Enlightenment* 258. See also Donald Wesling, *Wordsworth and the Adequacy of Landscape* (London: Routledge and Kegan Paul, 1970) esp. 18, 59, 75, for discussion of the high status Wordsworth accords to the inclusion of the human in depictions of nature.

[21] One might compare the Middle East's role in the nineteenth century with that of Tahiti in the eighteenth. While Tahiti's exemplary function had more to do with sexual freedom than with political repression, Tahiti's natural environment was as much interconnected with its symbolic identity as the Middle East's was. For further discussion, see Thacker, *The Wildness Pleases* ch. 9.

[22] McFarland, "Green Savannahs" 53. Compare Graeme Stones's argument that the desert does in fact constitute a sublime place, but nonetheless an "un-Wordsworthian" one (Stones, "'Upon a dromedary mounted high,'" *Charles Lamb Bulletin* 104 [1998]: 150).

[23] Abrams, *The Mirror and the Lamp* 105.

[24] See Abrams, *The Mirror and the Lamp* 105. For a summary of precedents for this view, see Beach, *The Concept of Nature* 18–19; and Thacker, *The Wildness Pleases* 29–30.

[25] For further background and elaboration, see Beach, *The Concept of Nature* 13, 187–9, 199–203. Alan Bewell points out the historical underpinnings of this view, as well as the complex relationship between nature and human agency in Wordsworth's thinking; see *Wordsworth and the Enlightenment* 239–42. The intricacy of Wordsworth's treatment of nature in its real and moral aspects is further discussed in Mark Jones, "Double Economics: Ambivalence in Wordsworth's Pastoral," *PMLA* 108.5 (1993): esp. 1108. See also Dan Latimer, "Real Culture and Unreal Nature: Wordsworth's Kingdom of Dissimilitude," *New Orleans Review* 14.1 (1987): 45–54, for a reinterpretation of Wordsworth's views on culture and nature in light of Schiller's philosophy.

romanticism, we need to think of two coexisting and interconnected phenomena, one mainly environmental (mountains, valleys, streams, vegetation), and the other human and social, a norm of feelings, behaviors, and moral sentiments.

When European romantic poets write about the Middle East, though, they must confront the fact that nature in the conventionalized Middle East does not look like nature in France or Britain. Nor is Middle Eastern nature an environment amenable to the cozy yet exalted relationship with people that is assumed by Wordsworth and his like-minded colleagues. This difference becomes very clear in Wordsworth's "Septimi Gades," which foregrounds the contrast between nature in Europe and nature in the Middle East.[26] The assumptions about nature and about human interaction with nature that underlie Wordsworth's other attempts at exotic settings, such as the Georgian savannah of "Ruth," are evidently already well formed in "Septimi Gades," written when Wordsworth was only twenty. Thus even at this extremely early point in Wordsworth's career, the Middle East has already become an archetypal setting within which he proposes and elaborates the notions that emerge later at the center of his poetics.

The first natural landscape depicted in "Septimi Gades" is that of the Rhone region in France; the second is the area around Grasmere, England. The two scenes share their crucial elements: a rural dwelling ("humble shed," "lone grey cots" [13, 22]), sharp inclines ("mountains," "purple slopes [...] and pastoral steeps" [15, 20–2]), and a body of water ("streamlet," "deeps" [16, 23]). Despite the fact that the English scene is initially offered as a counterpoint to the French one, the poem's speaker presents the two places as functionally interchangeable, explaining that "if the wayward fates deny" (19) him the opportunity to revisit the Rhone, then his "willing voice shall hail" (21) Grasmere. As a result, the two locations are in effect conflated into a single image of a fertile, mountainous area, well watered but sparsely populated. This is exactly the type of setting that Butler describes as Wordsworth's ideal: "it is an aesthetic landscape, empty of people."[27]

This image has little in common with the one presented next, that of Arabia. Where England and France have "orchard blooms," "purple slopes," and "azure sky" (17, 20), Arabia is merely "pale" (26). There is no topographical

---

[26] "Septimi Gades" was composed about 1790 but was not published in the poet's lifetime. The title quotes the first two words of Horace's Ode II.vi, upon which Wordsworth's poem is loosely based. "Septimi" is a form of the name of the friend to whom Horace addresses his poem; "Gades" ("Gadis" in Horace) is Latin for Cadiz. Although the English poem as a whole is rather derivative, its reference to the Arabian desert is Wordsworth's own.

My source for Wordsworth's poetry is the 1977 *Poems*, edited by John O. Hayden. For more information on the text and context of the poem, see Wordsworth, *Early Poems and Fragments, 1785–1797*, ed. Carol Landon and Jared Curtis (Ithaca: Cornell UP, 1997) 264, 760–7.

[27] Butler, "Romanticism in England" 54.

elevation and no water, since the landscape consists only of flat, "thirsty sands" (26). Although in both cases the human inhabitants are few, the position of human beings in the two sets of landscapes differs sharply. In the European settings, people (whether the speaker or the presumed inhabitants of the "lone grey cots") are comfortably, albeit passively, situated in their surroundings. Even in the poem's last stanza, which depicts the harshness of a European winter, the nasty weather outside simply accentuates the coziness inside, and the storm "rock[s]" (75) the speaker's home as if it were rocking some sort of cradle. One senses no antagonism whatever between humans and nature. In contrast, the "faint and heartless" (25) traveler through the Arabian desert stands in an oppositional relationship with his environment. Even as he recollects his last stop at an oasis, where his physical needs were met, there is no emotional bond comparable to that of the speaker with his environment. As the use of the present tense verb "seems" (27) shows, any emotional connection between the traveler and the oasis environment is purely retrospective, nostalgic. As he stands "heartless," having lost courage in the face of the extremes of nature that assault him, it seems impossible that his experience of the desert environment could yield the sort of inspiration and comfort that the poem's speaker anticipates finding at Grasmere.

Since the traveler's identity (national or otherwise) is never specified, we can only conclude that his experience of nature differs from the speaker's principally because of the difference in the environment that each encounters.[28] On the European landscape, Wordsworth says, nature

> Has showered her various wealth;
> There Temperance and Truth abide
> And Toil with Leisure at his side,
> And Cheerfulness and Health (45–8)

But the desert has no such moral attributes and stands instead as nature devoid of virtue: an unnatural nature. This is as true of the oasis as it is of the desert, for the bounty of the oasis is as intemperate as the desert's barrenness. The oasis is a place of relief from mortal suffering more than one of "Cheerfulness" or "Health." It is all "Leisure," just as the desert is all "Toil." Thus not only is the Middle Eastern environment presented as physically dissimilar to European nature, but it is also lacking in the moral qualities that make nature central to romanticism.[29]

---

[28] Such a conclusion runs counter to Bewell's view that Enlightenment anthropology (and, with certain qualifications, Wordsworth's approach as well) sought to "emphasize [...] and accentuate [peoples'] difference" (*Wordsworth and the Enlightenment* 29), even while attempting to explore universal human questions. Also significant here is the fact that Wordsworth includes the traveler simply as a figure for the speaker, not to create any symbolic antagonism between the two or to suggest one's inferiority to the other.

[29] Makdisi observes a more polarized articulation of this contrast in early-nineteenth-century rhetoric on India: "the region becomes [...] a degenerate and perverse — sick —

Comparing Jane Austen's representations of landscape with Wordsworth's, John Rieder doubts that "Wordsworth's exalted faith in nature can be understood unless it is held next to the still viable association of land ownership with classical virtue and paternalistic order in Austen."[30] This linkage of nature with land ownership is inapplicable to the Orient as Wordsworth knew it; indeed, Norman Daniel argues convincingly that the Islamic Middle East's lack of a landed gentry was one of the essential factors in Western discomfort with the Ottoman world.[31] Although Wordsworth's speaker does not aspire to the grandeur that Austen's characters do, his depiction of European nature in "Septimi Gades" strongly implies the presence of "a solid, self-justifying social order" of the sort Rieder finds in Austen's *Pride and Prejudice* (1813).[32] In contrast, Wordsworth's Middle Eastern landscape exists without either the social structures or the natural features that allow spiritual and aesthetic engagement with the outdoor environment.

Felicia Hemans's ambivalence

If Wordsworth uses the Orient mainly as a counterpoint by which to clarify humanity's relationship with European nature, Felicia Hemans (1793–1835) assumes a less pragmatic, more ambivalent approach to the nature of the Orient, in both its environmental and moral senses. Hemans also writes far more often than Wordsworth on foreign topics. Her collection *Lays of Many Lands* (1825) is composed almost entirely of poems with various foreign settings and includes two poems on Middle Eastern subjects.[33] The subject matter of her *Records of Woman* (1828) is mainly foreign as well.[34] In addition, oriental allusions — Middle Eastern and even more commonly Indian

---

version of Europe, plagued with all the [...] associations of European 'illnesses' and 'weaknesses'" (Makdisi, *Romantic Imperialism* 115).

[30] Rieder, "Wordsworth and Romanticism in the Academy," *At the Limits of Romanticism: Essays in Cultural, Feminist, and Materialist Criticism*, Ed. Mary A. Favret and Nicola J. Watson (Bloomington: Indiana UP, 1994) 35.

[31] Daniel, *Islam, Europe and Empire* 11.

[32] Rieder, "Wordsworth and Romanticism" 35.

[33] These are "Moorish Bridal Song," the first poem in the collection, and "The Suliote Mother." The remaining poems may be categorized as follows: seven European, five Greek, three ancient Briton, two North American, one Brazilian, and one Indian. Poems of note in other collections include: "The Crusader's Return" (Levant/Italy), "The Mourner for the Barmecides" (Baghdad), "The Captive Knight" (Levant), "The Palm Tree" (unspecified East), "The Sleeper on Marathon" (Persia/Greece), and "An Hour of Romance" (Levant). I will discuss "The Mourner for the Barmecides" and "An Hour of Romance" in chapter 4.

My source for Hemans's poems is *The Poetical Works of Felicia Dorothea Hemans* (Oxford: Oxford UP, 1914).

[34] Ten of these poems are set in continental Europe, four in Britain, three in North America, one in Greece, and one in India. No Middle Easterners are included, although the Indian poem does have Muslim characters ("The Indian City").

— are frequent in her poems, regardless of their setting.

Typical of Hemans's orientalism is her poem "The Traveller at the Source of the Nile" (1826), which chronicles Scottish explorer James Bruce's arrival at what he supposed to be the source of the Nile.[35] "The Traveller" takes Middle Eastern nature — the Nile specifically — as its starting point. The landscape is intensely attractive, even sublime:

> In sunset's light o'er Afric thrown,
> A wanderer proudly stood
> Beside the well-spring, deep and lone,
> Of Egypt's awful flood. (1–4)

Bruce is inspired by the scene: "his heart beat high" (11), "The rapture of a conqueror's mood / Rush'd burning through his frame" (13–14). As night falls, though, he begins to experience an anticlimax. "[*A*]*nd is this all?*" (24; emphasis hers) he asks in a panic, and then answers his own question, becoming more despondent by the moment:

> No more than this! — what seem'd it *now*
> First by that spring to stand?
> A thousand streams of lovelier flow
> Bathed his own mountain land!
> Whence, far o'er waste and ocean track,
> Their wild, sweet voices call'd him back. (25–30; emphasis hers)

After another stanza elaborating on the nostalgic appeal of the Scottish landscape, Hemans sharpens the contrast between Bruce's current surroundings and his memories:

> But, darkly mingling with the thought
> Of each familiar scene,
> Rose up a fearful vision, fraught
> With all that lay between;
> The Arab's lance, the desert's gloom,
> The whirling sands, the red simoom! (37–42)[36]

---

[35] In 1770, Bruce (1730–1794) came upon the source of the Blue Nile, which he misidentified at the time as the true Nile. As Hemans acknowledges in a brief note following the poem, "The Traveller" (first published in the *Monthly Magazine, or British Register*) is based on Bruce's record of his adventures. Bruce, a Scot educated in London, published his account, *Travels to Discover the Source of the Nile, In the Years 1768, 1769, 1770, 1771, 1772 & 1773*, in 1790 (London: G.G.J. and J. Robinson). Other major editions appeared in 1805 and 1813, along with at least four abridgments between 1790 and 1826. Hemans might have used any of these, since the abridgments tend to preserve this climactic scene more or less entirely.

[36] A simoom is a violent sandstorm, by this time a common trope in British orientalist literature.

Bruce then bursts into tears, and the poem ends primly with the moral: "— Oh, happiness! how far we flee / Thine own sweet paths in search of thee!" (53–4).[37]

"The Traveller" presents European nature not only as Bruce's literal point of departure but also metaphorically as the basic standard by which experience is to be judged. Although the landscape at issue in the poem is the Scotland of Bruce's childhood, Hemans identifies it only ambiguously as "mountain land" (28).[38] Because she does not specify a nationality, she appears to be generalizing the opposition between the Nile region and its European counterpart. The Middle East is an alternative to Europe, a site of exploration, but in the end its difference alienates rather than attracts. As is the case for the speaker of Wordsworth's "Septimi Gades," there is no substitute for the recollected European landscape as the origin of the protagonist's satisfaction, but that landscape's irreplaceability is confirmed only by contrast with the East. The unnaturalness of the East is produced in turn both by comparison with idyllic European nature and by its own characteristics. The poem's depiction of the desert is essential to this development; the desert is "a fearful vision," typified by violence — the Arab has a lance, the sand is whirling, the sandstorm is red. Yet even the first stanza's apparently sublime description of the Nile's source foreshadows the denaturalization of the environment; the stark contrasts and a sense of anxiety ("deep and lone," "awful flood") have little in common with the calmness and hospitality ascribed to the European landscape in this poem or in "Septimi Gades."

At no point, moreover, is Bruce's relationship with the Middle Eastern environment anything but oppositional. Both his confidently imperialist "conqueror's mood" and the terrified despair to which it gives way are grounded in an unquestioned antagonism towards the landscape. In contrast, the poem stresses the mutual affection between Bruce and the Scottish scenes he remembers. The Scottish landscape is portrayed as actually yearning for him as much as he for it; three times it "call'd him back" (30, 31, 35). The poem never raises even the possibility of such an attachment between the explorer and the landscape near the Nile. The poem's only other human figure, the Arab with the lance, is so completely integrated into his surroundings that it makes no sense to speak of an attachment between distinct entities. This

---

[37] Here Hemans makes her only substantial departures from Bruce's account. Bruce does not admit to weeping. And far from resolving on a domestic happiness, he reaffirms the value of his project, mainly in imperialist terms. For a related reading of Hemans's poem in light of the intersection between imperialism and domesticity, see my "Florence Nightingale, Felicia Hemans and James Bruce's 'Fountains of the Nile,'" *Journal of African Travel Writing* 5 (1998): 53–69.

[38] In his own account, Bruce emphasizes the Scottishness of his recollections by mentioning Scottish rivers by name before listing several other European rivers whose beauty also rivaled the Nile's.

effectively marks both him and his environment as unnatural. The natural and proper (romantic) role of a human being is to experience nature, not to participate in it as if on a par with climatic phenomena like sandstorms. Correspondingly, nature is to stand apart from human beings so as to sustain or inspire them, not to assimilate them as the desert has done to the Arab. Even if we read this scene from a culturally relativistic perspective, granting that, like Bruce, the Arab evidently enjoys an intimacy with his native environment, we cannot deny the inability of the desert — and by extension of the Middle East as a whole — to function within the romantic parameters of the natural.

In both "Septimi Gades" and "The Traveller at the Source of the Nile," then, the Middle East is unnatural as a physical environment and as a moral matrix. To adopt Fry's terminology, it is ontologically unnatural where Europe is ontologically natural, however marred Europe may be by increasing urbanization and modernization.[39] European landscape remains not only primary but distinctly preferred, both for its own attributes and for the type of relationship with humans that it offers, and even for the type of humanness it enables. Wordsworth's oriental references serve chiefly to clarify the status of nature and of the human-nature relationship in Europe; in a classic orientalist move, they define the natural by juxtaposing it with its unnatural other. Hemans joins Wordsworth in his rejection of the Orient, and specifically of oriental nature, as an alternative to the European standard. But "The Traveller" also engages in an understated metacommentary on orientalism. The poem is, in effect, a chronicle of European attraction to, and ultimate disenchantment with, orientalism. The Nile region, including the desert, stands in for the entire Orient, and Bruce for the orientalist, whose devotion to his subject falls away into despair.[40] By the end of "The Traveller," the Orient is an alternative that fails to deliver despite its glorious promises and that is to be supplanted — as at the end of Hugo's "Novembre" — by a domestic vision that is its counterpart from the outset.

---

[39] See Fry, "Green to the Very Door?" 539.

[40] The degree to which Hemans is self-critical, or critical of her age, has been debated, with some claiming that her poetry is superficial, and others answering that it is merely "superficially superficial"; see Anne Mack, J.J. Rome, and Georg Mannejc, "Literary History, Romanticism, and Felicia Hemans," *Modern Language Quarterly* 54.2 (1993): 225–31. There may be strong justification for reading "The Traveller" much as Mack reads Hemans's 1827 "The Homes of England": "Hemans's is a poetry of quotation, a conscious elevation of various inherited and signifying signs. [...] Hemans executes a remarkable critique of the ideology of cultural endurance, a critique all the more stunning for its domesticity and lack of pretension" (230). For comparable arguments, see Diego Saglia, "Epic or Domestic?: Felicia Hemans's Heroic Poetry and the Myth of the Victorian Poetess," *Rivista di Studi Vittoriani* 2.4 (1997): 129, 146–7; and Susan J. Wolfson "'Domestic Affections' and 'the spear of Minerva': Felicia Hemans and the Dilemma of Gender," *Re-Visioning Romanticism: British Women Writers, 1776–1837*, Ed. Carol Shiner Wilson and Joel Haefner (Philadelphia: U of Pennsylvania P, 1994) 130.

Truth in illustrating Robert Southey and Thomas Moore

Following Raymond Schwab, Saree Makdisi proposes that as Europeans expanded their knowledge of Eastern literatures, they "benefit[ed] from the discovery and commodification of [...] new sources of inspiration or versification. And yet, [...] the great value of such an intellectual commodity lies not merely in its beauty, its inspiration, its charm, but in its sheer difference from the standard European classics."[41] In other words, the East contributed a valuable and previously lacking "sense of alterity."[42] As we have seen, Wordsworth and Hemans enlist alterity to reinforce the borders of the culturally defined self. Robert Southey, on the other hand, engages the alterity of the Orient with evident enthusiasm — rather like Bruce during his conquerer's high. For all three poets, as for many of their contemporaries, the Orient's pervasive unnaturalness is the determining element of its otherness, but whereas Hemans's and Wordsworth's poems reveal a discomfort with that unnaturalness, Southey's *Thalaba* exploits it consistently.

For Southey, the Orient's unnaturalness is an essential source both of its appeal and of its aesthetic value. Because the Orient is always already unnatural, it readily supports his mingling of natural and supernatural, and of materials from disparate or even conflicting sources. But these are only instances of a greater, general benefit: in an epistemological world where nature remains the cardinal standard of truth, orientalism frees Southey from the confinement of this standard of truth.[43] Even where *Thalaba* claims to be offering authentic portrayals of Middle Eastern nature, its readers would lack an empirical basis for judging the accuracy of its depictions. The commandment to imitate nature has little force where obedience to it cannot be verified. Similarly, orientalism shields Southey from the early-nineteenth-century version of authenticity that shifts the standard for truth in poetry away from external nature and towards the poet's inner feelings. Because an orientalist poem such as *Thalaba* does not pretend to express any particular emotion on the part of the poet, this gauge of truth cannot pertain to it. As a result, the new, romantic emphasis on the sincere expression of feelings proves to be as ineffective a measure of truth as the old standard of external nature

---

[41] Makdisi, *Romantic Imperialism* 108.
[42] Makdisi, *Romantic Imperialism* 108.
[43] Here I would disagree with Mohammed Sharafuddin, who argues that in *Thalaba* Southey "seeks [...] the disclosure of the right relationship between man and nature. [...] Nature is not only pure in itself, but it can help man gain virtue and purity. The Arabian desert thus forms an appropriate setting for a moral epic" (Sharafuddin, *Islam and Romantic Orientalism* 107). Sharafuddin is right to recognize the importance of the "relationship between man and nature," and also to understand the great extent to which Middle Eastern nature stands in contrast to its "pastoral" European counterpart. But he interprets the natural environment of the Middle East as merely another kind of nature and so fails to perceive its essential unnaturalness and the important moral and aesthetic implications of that unnaturalness.

Fig. 1 *Thalaba the Destroyer* (1846)

mimetically represented. In effect, then, the use of the Orient as a subject provides a third course in addition to these two, one that allows poets to step outside the presumed linkage between poetry and truth, whether based on external nature or on an expression of human nature. At the same time, it offers them an extraordinary opportunity to create and represent a new "truth," a truth that benefits from a presumption of authenticity but that is, paradoxically, unverifiable by definition.

I suggested in chapter 1 that this peculiar dance of authenticity and verifiability is played out in the text of *Thalaba,* as Southey's tremendous footnotes form an elaborate apparatus of authentication that turns the impulse towards verification always inwards in the direction of (more) text, rather than outwards in the direction of any empirical Middle Eastern reality. But I would like to turn now instead to a Victorian-era illustration of *Thalaba* in which the odd relationship between authenticity and verifiability emerges with a different twist (see fig. 1). This illustration, from an 1846 edition of his works, is meant to depict a scene from Thalaba's idyllic youth with his foster sister and future wife Oneiza; the caption reads: "How happily the days / Of Thalaba went by!"[44] The fit between the illustration and the poem is not good. The lush, almost junglelike surroundings are not consistent with the text, which mentions a stream but emphasizes the desert environment of Arabia. Thalaba is both too pudgy and too richly dressed to be the athletic foster son of an average bedouin, as he is described in the poem. While the quiver of arrows lying next to him might be plausible, the European gentleman's hat is not, nor are the Egyptian pyramid and the North American tepee in the background. The impression left is that of a conglomeration of primitivist elements, not a natural landscape in the customary sense.[45]

If we compare this illustration with one from the 1839 edition of Thomas Moore's *Lalla Rookh,* we see that it is a different version of the same image (see fig. 2).[46] In this case, it represents a deathbed scene rather than an idyllic

---

[44] Southey, *The Complete Poetical Works* 247.

[45] Of course, nonorientalist poems are also afflicted with incongruous illustrations in nineteenth-century editions. Carl Woodring notes, for instance, that the mood of illustrations to Wordsworth often conflicts with the sense of the poems, as when "The boy who commits ravage in the poem *Nutting* gazes naively in the engraving toward a picturesque tree" (Woodring, "Wordsworth and the Victorians," *The Age of William Wordsworth: Critical Essays on the Romantic Tradition,* ed. Kenneth R. Johnston and Gene W. Ruoff [New Brunswick, NJ: Rutgers UP, 1987] 268–9). Similarly, Thacker mentions more than one instance of confusion between different categories of the exotic in painting; see Thacker, *The Wildness Pleases* 182. Still, this image of tepee and pyramids in the jungle seems an extreme misconstruction.

[46] Thomas Moore (1779–1852) was an Irish poet active in London. Although the main story of his remarkably successful *Lalla Rookh* is set in India, the poem contains embedded tales set elsewhere in the East. The tale illustrated by this image is set in Egypt. The illustration appears in Moore, *Lalla Rookh, An Oriental Romance* (London: Longman, Orme, Brown, Green and Longmans; and Philadelphia: Lea and Blanchard, 1839).

Fig. 2 *Lalla Rookh* (1839)

childhood; the illustration is captioned: "Nay, turn not from me that dear face — / Am I not thine — thy own lov'd bride — / The one, the chosen one, whose place / In life or death is by thy side?"[47] The arrows and the tepee are missing, and a peri has appeared to care for the souls of the departed. The costumes of the two figures are quite compatible with the story. Even the pyramid is plausible, given the poem's Egyptian setting. The plentiful vegetation hardly resembles the "fresh and springing bower" of orange trees described in the poem, but at least the text does indicate fertile surroundings. Moreover, the human import of the scene is much more consistent with this poem than with *Thalaba*. The two sad-looking figures are posed to suggest a death scene; the man's hand is contorted as he sinks back in weakness, with the woman supporting his lolling head.

While it is impossible to determine on purely technical grounds which of these two illustrations is the original, the image's greater compatibility with the Moore poem certainly suggests that it began its life with *Lalla Rookh* rather than *Thalaba*.[48] The Southey edition's appropriation of the picture was probably motivated by financial considerations; it would have been much cheaper to have a plate made from an existing drawing than to commission a new drawing. However, we may safely speculate that there was also an aesthetic justification — or at least an excuse — for the reuse of the drawing. Whoever was responsible for selecting illustrations (almost certainly not Southey himself) would have been seeking an image of a young couple in an oriental setting. Defined in these terms, the adoption of the *Lalla Rookh* picture seems absolutely reasonable, but it also reveals the great extent to which the criterion of orientalism was allowed to override all others. The result is an illustration that misrepresents both the physical details and the emotional content of the text. Regardless, its blatant orientalism obviates the need to verify its relation either with Southey's text or with the Middle Eastern scene it purports to depict.

The origin of this paradoxically unverifiable authenticity may be found in the notion of the Orient as unnatural. Nature in the orientalist Middle East is functionally absent because the natural environment of the Orient is not perceived or presented as being in the same category as the nature upon which

---

[47] Moore, *Lalla Rookh* 164.

[48] Print Curator Marjorie B. Cohn informs me that the Southey illustration is an engraving, while the Moore is an etching. The two were definitely made from different plates. She conjectures that the Southey image is a pirated one based on the same drawing that had been etched for the Moore volume. (Personal conversation with Marjorie B. Cohn, Fogg Art Museum, Harvard University; June 19, 1995.) Cohn's view is supported by the presence of acknowledgments in the London and Philadelphia edition of *Lalla Rookh*. There is a second title page which adds: "From the nineteenth London edition"; and the illustration's caption is followed by: "London. Published by Longman, Orme, Brown, Green & Longmans. Paternoster Row / and Lea and Blanchard, Philadelphia." A pirate user would be unlikely to make such acknowledgments.

the classical connection between truth and nature is based. The Orient's undifferentiated unnaturalness, ontological as well as visual, means that one oriental image will do as well as any other. The recycling of *Lalla Rookh*'s illustration in *Thalaba* and Southey's use of the incongruous or implausible both derive from the same conception of the Middle East. The assumption of oriental unnaturalness authorizes both the poet and the pirate press to neglect mimeticism's doctrine of the faithful imitation of nature.

Leconte de Lisle: "Le Désert," "le désert du monde"

Middle Eastern (un)nature is once again central to the orientalist poetry of Charles Leconte de Lisle (1818–1894). Leconte de Lisle's intellectual roots were in the romanticism of Victor Hugo, but he later became a leader in the Parnassian movement. Although Parnassian poets as a group tended to rely on chronologically and geographically distant settings, Leconte de Lisle was especially attracted to exotic subjects from the beginning of his career. His opus includes numerous orientalist poems; there are five poems with explicitly Middle Eastern subjects or settings in his *Poèmes barbares* [*Barbarian Poems*] alone.[49] His Creole family background and his birthplace on the southeast African island of Réunion (also his home for extended periods) opened the possibility of a more intimate connection with the exotic than any other nineteenth-century orientalist poet could have shared. Within his poems, however, his affiliation with the French literary tradition seems largely to have outweighed his personal associations with the exotic. It would be difficult to detect any consistent or substantive linkage between his poetic use of the Orient and his own status as an "exotic."

While Leconte de Lisle's attachment to the exotic is inclusive, he finds the Orient especially inspirational, noting late in his life that his first reading of Hugo's *Les Orientales* had caused him to have a "vision d'un monde plein de

---

[49] These are: "La Vérandah" ["The Veranda"], "Le Désert" ["The Desert"], "La Fille de l'Emyr" ["The Emir's Daughter"], "Le Sommeil de Leïlah" ["Leïla's Sleep"], and "L'Oasis" ["The Oasis"] (1872 edition). This collection also contains poems set in ancient Egypt, the biblical Levant, and India, as well as many on other exotic but not oriental subjects. *Poèmes tragiques* [*Tragic Poems*] (1886 edition) includes "L'Apothéose de Mouça-al-Kébyr" ["The Apotheosis of Mouça-al-Kébyr"] (the first poem of the collection), "Le Suaire de Mohammed ben-Amer-al-Mançour" ["The Shroud of Mohammed ben-Amer-al-Mançour"], and "Les Roses d'Ispahan" ["The Roses of Ispahan"] as well as several other poems with Eastern subjects. "L'Orient" ["The Orient"], which I discuss in chapter 4, is the second poem in the posthumous *Derniers poèmes* [*Last Poems*]. Of Leconte de Lisle's four major collections, only *Poèmes antiques* [*Ancient Poems*] (1881 edition) has no Middle Eastern poems, its oriental poems being mainly Indian.

My source for Leconte de Lisle's poems is *Oeuvres de Leconte de Lisle*, ed. Edgard Pich, 4 vols. (Paris: Société d'édition "Les belles lettres," 1976).

lumière. [...] Ce fut comme une immense et brusque clarté" [vision of a world full of light. ... It was like an immense and sudden brightness].[50] Although his movement away from romantic moralism and towards the Parnassian vision of art for art's sake is motivated by a broad aesthetic and spiritual idealism, he expresses it in his poems mainly through the representation of exotic places and times. As I will show through a detailed reading of his "Le Désert" ["The Desert"], the unnatural nature of the Islamic Orient becomes the basis for a generalized vision of the human condition, and thereby also for the poetics formulated around this vision.

"Le Désert" begins by setting the scene and introducing the poem's bedouin protagonist.[51] The framework for this introduction is a lengthy question, reminiscent of Hugo's "La Douleur du pacha" in its inclusion of relatively unmotivated and plentiful local color:

> Quand le Bédouin qui va de l'Horeb en Syrie
> Lie au tronc du dattier sa cavale amaigrie,
> Et, sous l'ombre poudreuse où sèche le fruit mort,
> Dans son rude manteau s'enveloppe et s'endort,
> Revoit-il, faisant trêve aux ardentes fatigues,
> La lointaine oasis où rougissent les figues,
> Et l'étroite vallée où campe sa tribu,
> Et la source courante où ses lèvres ont bu,
> Et les brebis bêlant, et les boeufs à leurs crèches,
> Et les femmes causant près des citernes fraîches,
> Ou, sur le sable, en rond, les chameliers assis,
> Aux lueurs de la lune écoutant les récits? (1–12)

[When the bedouin who is going from Horeb to Syria / Ties his emaciated mare to the trunk of a date palm / And, in the dusty shade where the dead fruit withers, / Wraps himself in his rough cloak and falls asleep, / Does he see again, for a respite in his scorching toils, / The distant oasis where figs ripen, / And the narrow valley where his tribe camps, / And the flowing spring where his lips have drunk, / And the bleating ewes, and the oxen at

---

[50] *Discours de réception à l'Académie Française* [*Acceptance Speech at the French Academy*], delivered on March 31, 1887; cited in Alison Fairlie, *Leconte de Lisle's Poems on the Barbarian Races* (Cambridge: Cambridge UP, 1947) 5. Leconte de Lisle would have been about twenty at the time he describes. Schwab's general analysis of Leconte de Lisle's orientalism is useful in this context; see *The Oriental Renaissance* 404–6, 418–20.

[51] "Le Désert" appeared originally in Leconte de Lisle's *Poèmes et poésies* [*Poems and Poetry*] of 1855 and was later included in the 1872 edition of *Poèmes barbares*, his most noted collection. The 1855 version was reprinted in 1857 and 1858. "Le Désert" was not included at all in the first edition of *Poèmes barbares* in 1862. When it appeared there in 1872 and thereafter, it was missing its final eight lines; the difference between the two versions will be discussed below. For further information, see *Oeuvres de Leconte de Lisle*, ed. Edgard Pich, 2: viii–xiii, 125. For a discussion of the reception of *Poèmes barbares*, see Joseph Vianey, *Les Poèmes barbares de Leconte de Lisle* (Paris: Nizet, 1955) ch. 13.

their mangers, / And the women chatting near the cool cisterns, / Or, on the sand, the camel drivers sitting in a ring, / Listening to tales in the gleam of the moon?]

There are two distinct environments here, both stereotypical of orientalist depictions of Middle Eastern nature. The first is the desert, dry and harsh, with a date palm as its only vegetation. Much like the desert in Wordsworth's "Septimi Gades," this desert world is antagonistic to its inhabitants, the exhausted bedouin and his skinny horse. The other environment represented is that of the oasis, which is situated as a kind of hypothetical recollection, a memory that the bedouin could be having but is not. Like Wordsworth's oasis, this is a fertile place, with ripening figs and plenty of fresh water. While less exaggeratedly lush than Wordsworth's, it still offers a sharp contrast with the image of the desert, both physically and in terms of human beings' interaction with it. The desert's unnaturalness is accentuated by contrast with the relatively temperate environment of the oasis.

In turn, despite its distinctive vegetation, the oasis appears to approximate the rural European outdoors. The women chatting next to a reservoir and the camel drivers sitting on the sand seem to have a very comfortable relationship with the natural environment around them. However, if we examine the structure of this passage, a more complicated situation emerges. The heart of the passage consists of four lines beginning with "Et" [And] plus the definite article. The first of these locates the tribe's camp; the construction of this line parallels the preceding one, which creates a conceptually appropriate linkage between "La lointaine oasis" [The distant oasis] and "l'étroite vallée" [the narrow valley] at the beginning of each line. The second halves of the lines appear mismatched, though, since "où rougissent les figues" [where figs ripen] corresponds with "où campe sa tribu" [where his tribe camps]. This puts the camping of the tribe into the same category as the ripening of the figs, as if both were equally part of the processes of nature. This striking incorporation of the human into nature recurs in the subsequent lines. The flowing stream, bleating ewes, and chatting women are presented as syntactic equals, each following its own "Et" without any acknowledgement of the women's humanity.

It is possible to interpret these bedouins as fully integrated into their natural environment, as if enacting the Wordsworthian ideal of, in McFarland's words, "[f]ull humanity" achieved "where person and nature are symbolically conceived as interpenetrating one another."[52] But other factors suggest a significant divergence from Wordsworth's vision. First, "Le Désert" seems to move beyond a "symbolic interpenetration"; the human figures are presented as if actually part of the oasis's natural environment. As a result, they stand to

---

[52] McFarland, "Green Savannahs" 42.

lose much of their human status. Such a loss is definitely not part of Wordsworth's ideal, which requires that the human being remain a separate, independent consciousness able to experience nature. Leconte de Lisle gives no indication of such an experiential relationship between his bedouins and their surroundings. Both the women and the camel drivers seem to use natural features (the reservoir, the sand) as outdoor furniture more than as objects of conscious contemplation. In turn, the poem's presentation of the bedouins as if they themselves were features of the landscape contaminates nature with the human, in effect "denaturing" it.[53]

While this integration of human beings into the Middle Eastern environment may reflect a racist inability to accept the bedouins as truly human,[54] I would propose instead that "Le Désert" is moving towards a different ideal of human interaction with the natural environment, one that aspires to the unselfconsciousness of Eden more than the deliberative engagement with nature to which the romantics subscribed. In this context, the Middle East's difference from Europe allows it to serve Leconte de Lisle as a kind of test case; the conventionally unnatural nature of the Middle East gives him the opportunity to experiment with an alternative, counterromantic relationship between humans and their environment.[55]

The next section of the poem, in which the speaker answers the question asked in the first dozen lines, emphasizes the Middle East's unnaturalness as well, but this time in relation to supernatural and mythological phenomena. The bedouin protagonist, wrapped up asleep in his cloak, does not dream of the hypothetical oasis just described, but instead experiences a distinctly Islamic vision in which he is carried to Paradise. His mount is the same miraculous creature who bore Muḥammad on his nighttime journey to Jerusalem and to the seven heavens:

---

[53] It is interesting to compare this literary depiction of humans in nature with visual portrayals of humans in oriental architectural spaces. In an 1840s image of the Alhambra reproduced by Rae Beth Gordon, for instance, a man and a boy stand in an elaborately decorated archway that frames a symmetrical series of additional archways receding from view (see Gordon, *Ornament, Fantasy, and Desire* 9). Another man (like the first two, in Middle Eastern dress) is seated between the second and third archways. While the first two figures are clearly interacting with one another, the third appears silent and abstracted. His pose mirrors that of the archway behind him, such that his body completes the curve of the arch in reverse. He seems very much part of the massive yet delicate architecture surrounding him. This figure's absorption into his surroundings corresponds in many respects with that of Leconte de Lisle's bedouins into their environment.

[54] See Said, *Orientalism* 102, 108, 161 for comments on such racist tendencies.

[55] Robert O. Steele approaches this problem from a complementary perspective, arguing that in general, Leconte de Lisle "denied the notion that Nature could have any direct relationship to Man" ("The Avant-gardism of Leconte de Lisle," *Nineteenth-Century French Studies* 17.3–4 [1989]: 322). Certainly, "Le Désert" presumes nature's absolute indifference to human beings.

> Non, par delà de cours des heures éphémères,
> Son âme est en voyage au pays des chimères.
> Il rêve qu'Al-Borak, le cheval glorieux,
> L'emporte en hennissant dans la hauteur des cieux;
> Il tressaille, et croit voir, par les nuits enflammées,
> Les filles de Djennet à ses côtés pâmées.
> De leurs cheveux plus noirs que la nuit de l'enfer
> Monte un âcre parfum qui lui brûle la chair;
> Il crie, il veut saisir, presser sur sa poitrine,
> Entre ses bras tendus, sa vision divine. (13–22)

> [No, as the ephemeral hours pass, / His soul is traveling to the land of myths. / He dreams that Al-Borak, the glorious horse, / Carries him neighing into the heights of the heavens; / He trembles, and believes he sees, in the blazing night, / The girls of Paradise swooned at his sides. / From their hair, blacker than the night in Hell, / Rises a pungent perfume that burns his flesh; / He cries out, he wants to seize, to press against his chest, / Between his outstretched arms, his divine vision.]

Inevitably, the bedouin is denied fulfillment as his dream slips away:

> Mais sur la dune au loin le chacal a hurlé,
> Sa cavale piétine, et son rêve est troublé;
> Plus de Djennet, partout la flamme et le silence,
> Et le grand ciel cuivré sur l'étendue immense! (23–6)

> [But on the dune far away the jackal howled, / His mare stamps, and his dream is disturbed; / No more Paradise, everywhere the heat and the silence, / And the high coppery heavens over the immense expanse!]

The poem's narrative scheme establishes this (lost) Paradise as a correlate of the (never recalled) oasis. Not only are Paradise and the oasis alternate answers to the same questions (Of what does the napping bedouin dream?), but certain details of the oasis reappear transformed in Paradise. "Les filles de Djennet" [The girls of Paradise] stand in the stead of the oasis's chatting women. Swooning at the bedouin's sides, they form a circle of bodies that resembles the group of camel drivers sitting "en rond" [in a ring] in the sand of the oasis. The description of the oasis is dominated by the concluding nighttime image, which absorbs two lines while no other detail is granted more than one. Night is the prevailing motif in the description of Paradise as well; "nuit(s)" is the only noun used more than once in the entire ten-line passage. Night is also at the center of the passage's only explicitly figurative moment, in which the girls' hair is said to be "plus noirs que la nuit de l'enfer" [blacker than the night in Hell].

Yet despite these significant links between the oasis and Paradise, equally important connections may be drawn between Paradise and the desert. Horses are significant in the descriptions of both the desert (the bedouin's mare) and Paradise (Al-Borak, although the equine identity of this creature is not undisputed in Islamic tradition). With the pungent perfume of the girls' hair, Paradise burns much as the desert scorches and desiccates. Moreover, while "nuit" is the only noun shared between the oasis and Paradise, several essential words recur from desert to Paradise: "rêve," "flamme"/"enflammées," "ciel"/"cieux." "Ciel" [Heaven] is the most crucial of these, since it characterizes both the exalted location of the bedouin's vision ("la hauteur des cieux") and the harshness of the desert to which he returns ("le grand ciel cuivré"). Finally, the very first line of the poem explains that the bedouin protagonist is on a journey from Horeb (Mt. Sinai) to Syria; in line 14, his soul is described in the same way, as being "en voyage." The bedouin's trip from Horeb (in the south of the Sinai Peninsula) to Syria parallels on a smaller scale that of Muḥammad from Mecca (in the western part of the Arabian peninsula) to Jerusalem. Both are south-to-north journeys with a destination in the Levant. Each journey is in turn associated with an ascension (mi'râj) to the heavens.[56] Thus the bedouin's journey on the ground becomes fundamentally inseparable from his soul's dream journey, as well as from Muḥammad's own legendary journey, which has become the poem's emblem of Islamic culture.

While "Le Désert" depicts three disparate environments — the desert, an oasis, and Paradise — there is in the end no firm boundary between them. The desert and the oasis remain physically distinct from one another, but they are joined through the bedouin's supernatural vision of Paradise. The parallel between his earthly journey and his dream journey symbolically allows traveling through the desert to become equated with traveling to Paradise, and the oasis (possible earthly destination) with Paradise (actual dream destination). These multiple connections act to subvert the original opposition between oasis and desert. Both are in the end closely tied to Paradise, and to a paradise that is not only supernatural but also unquestionably Islamic, from its name (Djennet) to its mode of transportation (Al-Borak) and its female inhabitants (the houris). The result is a circular situation, in which the Middle East is characterized by its unnaturalness (climatic extremes, peculiar relationship between human beings and the environment, susceptibility to visions and the supernatural), but each instance of unnaturalness is itself

---

[56] The legend of Muḥammad's trip to Jerusalem and ascension into the heavens is based on a very scant reference in Sura 17 of the Qur'an. In subsequent traditions and in literature, the basic story and its spiritual significance become much elaborated. See R. Paret, "Al-Burāk," *The Encyclopedia of Islam*, 2nd ed. (Leiden: E.J. Brill, 1958–); B. Schrieke, J. Horovitz, and J.E. Bencheikh, "Mi'rādj," *The Encyclopedia of Islam*, 2nd ed.; W. Montgomery Watt, *Muhammad: Prophet and Statesman* (Oxford: Oxford UP, 1961) 81; and Annemarie Schimmel, *Mystical Dimensions of Islam* (Chapel Hill: U of North Carolina P, 1975) 27, 41, 48, 148, 204, 218.

constructed as Middle Eastern, and as Islamic in particular.

In its later versions, "Le Désert" ends here, having created a symbolically laden composite of the unnatural Middle East. The strength of this composite is reinforced by the title itself, which gathers both of the nondesert environments (the oasis and Paradise) into the category of desert. In the original version of the poem, however, the title is given a more culturally universal twist by eight additional lines:

> Dans sa halte d'un jour, sous l'arbre desséché,
> Tout rêveur, haletant de vivre, s'est couché,
> Et comme le Bédouin, ployé de lassitude,
> A dormi ton sommeil, ô morne solitude!
> Oublieux de la terre, et d'un coeur irrité,
> Il veut saisir l'amour dans son éternité;
> Et toujours il renaît à la vie inféconde
> Pâle et désespéré dans le désert du monde. (27–34)

[In his day's resting place, under the parched tree, / Every dreamer has lain down, worn out with living, / And like the bedouin, yielding to weariness, / Has slept your sleep, oh dreary solitude! / Unmindful of the earth, and of an angered heart, / He wants to seize love in its eternity; / And always he rises to barren life / Pale and desperate in the desert of the world.]

In these lines the desert acquires a metaphorical significance that exceeds the bounds of the Middle East, Islam, and even external nature.[57] The desert is not simply what one encounters between Mt. Sinai and Syria; it is "le désert du monde" [the desert of the world], and by extension the Middle East now stands for the sorry condition of the whole world. The Islamic Orient offers a context for the dreamer's dejection, much as it provided a counterpoint for the speaker's confidence in Wordsworth's "Septimi Gades." As in Wordsworth's poem, this tactic is effective only because of the Middle East's predetermined unnaturalness. The failure of the desert (including the oasis and Paradise) to find a place along the continuum of the natural enables it to represent the dreamer's extraordinary state of mind. Although the rhetorical impact of the desert as an emotional point of reference continues to derive from its implied contrast with the standard European vision of nature, that traditional, domestic standard is nowhere evident in "Le Désert." It has been effectively supplanted by the alternative to it: the desert and oriental unnature. Thus the Orient has displaced nature from this poem.

Rather than seek an ideal in nature, as Wordsworth, Hugo, and even Hemans do, Leconte de Lisle seems to look for his "Paradise" in the Orient.

---

[57] Pich discusses this ending but reads the entire poem as an expression of hopeless love; see *Leconte de Lisle et sa création poétique: Poèmes antiques et Poèmes barbares, 1852–1874* (Paris: Chirat, 1975) 219–21.

The ideal he proposes is that of the oasis and the Islamic "Djennet," places in which relations between the individual and the world are uncomplicated by consciousness. It is a paradigm that Wordsworth, Hugo, and Hemans would find discomfiting, reliant as they are on the ability of consciousness to organize experience. Unlike his predecessors' ideals, which are envisioned as existing within empirical reality, Leconte de Lisle's Paradise never leaves the realm of the imagination. When it is vested in the oasis, it is a hypothetical memory, not a genuine recollection. When it is vested in the Islamic heaven, it is a dream, part of the bedouin's "vision divine." This forced intimacy between Paradise and the imagination suggests an equally forced, but also significant, intimacy between the Islamic Orient (locus of both oasis and Paradise/"Djennet") and the imagination, such that the Orient appears as a product of the imagination, while at the same time the Orient becomes the sole domain of the imagination.[58]

The source of this formulation may be sought in Hugo's idea of the East as the locus of "pure poésie." However, as we saw in chapter 2, Hugo ultimately directs his imagination outside the East, whereas for Leconte de Lisle in this poem, the imagination seems to remain bound to the Orient. Leconte de Lisle evidently shares some of Hugo's final disappointment in the Orient; the Middle Eastern desert is after all the model for "le désert du monde." But instead of resorting once again to Europe and mimesis, as Hugo does, Leconte de Lisle stays with the Orient. From it he creates a totalized, universalized figure for both the idealism and the despair of the human condition. Mimesis too is distanced, as each apparently mimetic move is filtered to dispel any sense of concrete reality; however clearly depicted, the bedouin's stay in the oasis is a false memory, his trip to Paradise is a fading dream, and he himself is (especially in the longer version of the poem) more archetypal than real.

Théophile Gautier: the composite desert

In a career that, like Leconte de Lisle's, moved away from romanticism and towards a Parnassian aesthetic, Théophile Gautier (1811–1872) shared his contemporary's long-standing devotion to oriental subjects. The impact of Hugo's *Les Orientales* was as powerful for him as for Leconte de Lisle.[59] Like Leconte de Lisle, whom he influenced, Gautier tended to see the Orient as free of the perversions of modern life, a place where humankind might regain a

---

[58] As I will discuss in chapter 4, the exclusive connection between the Orient and the imagination proves fundamental to the evolution of the idea of art for art's sake.
[59] See Tennant, *Théophile Gautier* 39, 40, 45, 106; and Joanna Richardson, *Théophile Gautier: His Life and Times* (London: Max Reinhardt, 1958) 20.

more ideal state of being.[60] Although he is now recognized primarily as a prose writer, Gautier's numerous orientalist poems are of significant interest.[61] He was one of several major nineteenth-century French writers, including François-René de Chateaubriand, Gustave Flaubert, and Gerard de Nerval, to have visited the Middle East, but he was perhaps the only one to have fancied himself a kind of switched-at-birth Middle Easterner.[62] Partly because of this feeling of personal affiliation with the exotic (pretended in his case), but mainly because of his intense engagement with the evolving French literary tradition, his sensibilities appear very like Leconte de Lisle's.

It will be no surprise, then, that Gautier's 1838 sonnet "La Caravane" ["The Caravan"] relies on virtually the same figurative use of the unnatural desert as the longer version of Leconte de Lisle's "Le Desert," which may have been influenced by it.[63]

---

[60] See Tennant, *Théophile Gautier* (London: Athlone, 1975) 17; and Denise Brahimi, *Théophile et Judith vont en Orient* (Paris: La Boîte à Documents, 1990) 91.

[61] For a summary of orientalism in Gautier's poetry, see Jacques Lardoux, "L'Orient dans les poésies de Théophile Gautier" *L'Orient de Théophile Gautier*, vol. 1 (Proc. of International Colloquium, May 1990, Monte Cristo) 213–29. Gautier's poems on Middle Eastern subjects include: "Les Souhaits" (1830; see chapter 4); "La Caravane" and "Le Nuage" (1838); "Le Cheik" and "A l'Alhambra moresque" (c. 1840); "In deserto" (1842); "La Fuite," "Gazhel," and "Sultan Mahmoud" (1845); "Le Bedouin et la mer" (1846); "Nostalgies d'obelisques" (1851); "La Fellah" (1861); "L'Esclave noir" (1863); and "L'Odalisque à Paris" (1867) ["The Wishes," "The Caravan," "The Cloud," "The Sheikh," "At the Moorish Al-Hambra," "In deserto," "The Flight," "Ghazal," "Sultan Mahmoud," "The Bedouin and the Sea," "Nostalgia for Obelisques," "The Fellah," "The Black Slave," "The Odalisque in Paris"]. Among Gautier's works of orientalist fiction are: "Une nuit de Cléopâtre" (1838), "Le Pied de momie" (1840), "La Mille et deuxième nuit" (1857), and *Le Roman de la momie* (1857) ["A Night of Cleopatra," "The Mummy's Foot," "The Thousand and Second Night," *The Novel of the Mummy*]. Gautier also composed an orientalist ballet, *La Péri* [*The Peri*], in 1843.

My source for Gautier's poetry is René Jasinski's 1970 edition of *Poésies complètes de Théophile Gautier*.

[62] Several biographers mention Gautier's tendency to see himself as a Middle Easterner, in sexual and spiritual matters particularly; see for instance Brahimi, *Théophile et Judith* 17–18, 115; and Richardson, *Théophile Gautier* 23, 37–8, 51, 111–2. Gautier's travels in the region were extensive. Following a visit to Spain in 1840, he traveled to Algeria in 1845, Turkey in 1852, and Egypt and Algeria in 1869. His stay in Turkey yielded a complete travel account (*Constantinople*, 1853); the first Algerian trip was the source for numerous pieces, collected in 1865 as *Voyage pittoresque en Algérie* [*Picturesque Travels in Algeria*]. He wrote several articles about his journey to Egypt, now reprinted along with other materials as *Voyage en Egypte* [*Travels in Egypt*] (ed. Paolo Tortonese [Paris: La Boîte à Documents, 1991]). This reconstructed *Voyage* contains the second volume of an 1877 prose collection entitled *L'Orient* (2 vols. [Paris: Charpentier]). The first volume of this collection gathers various pieces written by Gautier about the Orient, defined very broadly; only a minority have to do with the Middle East. For further information about Gautier's travel and travel writing, see Tortonese's introduction to *Voyage en Egypte*; and Brahimi, *Théophile et Judith* 7–115.

[63] "La Caravane" first appeared in Gautier's collection *La Comédie de la mort* [*The Comedy of Death*]. Editor René Jasinski notes that the poem is a "pessimistic reply to the 'human caravan' of *Jocelyn*" (Alphonse de Lamartine's 1836 work; see *Poésies complètes de Théophile Gautier* 1: lvii).

> La caravane humaine au Sahara du monde,
> Par ce chemin des ans qui n'a pas de retour,
> S'en va traînant le pied, brûlée aux feux du jour,
> Et buvant sur ses bras la sueur qui l'inonde.
>
> Le grand lion rugit et la tempête gronde;
> A l'horizon fuyard, ni minaret, ni tour;
> La seule ombre qu'on ait, c'est l'ombre du vautour,
> Qui traverse le ciel cherchant sa proie immonde.
>
> L'on avance toujours, et voici que l'on voit
> Quelque chose de vert que l'on se montre au doigt:
> C'est un bois de cyprès, semé de blanches pierres.
>
> Dieu, pour vous reposer, dans le désert du temps,
> Comme des oasis, a mis les cimetières:
> Couchez-vous et dormez, voyageurs haletants.

[The human caravan in the Sahara of the world, / Along that track of years that makes no return, / Disappears dragging its feet, burned by the fires of day, / And drinking on its arms the sweat which drenches it.

The big lion roars and the storm rumbles; / On the fleeing horizon, neither minaret nor tower, / The only shade one has is the shade of a vulture, / Which crosses the sky looking for its filthy prey.

One moves always forward, and here one sees / Something green that one points out with a finger: / It is a cypress wood, strewn with white stones.

To refresh you, in the desert of time, God / Has put cemeteries like oases: / Lie down and sleep, worn travelers.]

The desert depicted in this poem conforms in its key respects to deserts portrayed in the other poems discussed thus far. It is a hot, dry, harsh environment through which any travel is grueling and dangerous.[64] Human interaction with the desert is inevitably adversarial, never spiritually privileged as it is with the European nature envisioned by Wordsworth, Hemans, and Hugo. Moreover, what might at first seem to offer relief from the desert ultimately disappoints as well. Here the cypress wood turns out to be strewn with stones; the poem's final stanza figures it as a cemetery rather than as the expected oasis. Like the oases of "Septimi Gades," "The Traveller at the Source of the Nile," and "Le Désert," this (anti)oasis fails to provide relief. Its

---

[64] Similarly desolate deserts appear in Gautier's short story "Une nuit de Cléopâtre" (written in the same year as "La Caravane") and in his 1840 travel account, *Voyage en Espagne* [*Travels in Spain*].

betrayal is also compounded at the level of signification. The "Quelque chose de vert que l'on se montre au doigt" [Something green that one points out with a finger] appears at first to be a sign whose referent is an oasis. But the "real" referent turns out to be the cemetery of cypress trees interspersed with white stones.[65] This bait and switch becomes a metaphor of the Orient's subversion of mimesis. The desert oasis, a quintessentially unnatural Middle Eastern environment, resists a straightforward linkage of sign with referent just as, in other contexts, the Orient resists a solid connection between representation and reality.

The lack of description in "La Caravane" also carries an antimimetic function. The desert is described as if already visualized, so that only certain identifying reference points need be noted. For example, the declaration that neither minaret nor tower is visible presupposes that minarets and towers are to be expected on the horizon at the edge of a desert. The desert's heat is similarly taken for granted; its effects (fatigue, perspiration) are emphasized, but the heat itself is named only indirectly, in the phrase "feux de jour" [fires of day]. Finally, the transformation of the cypress wood from a potential oasis into a cemetery relies upon a conventionalized vision of the relationship between deserts and oases, such that a glimpse of green off in the distance must of course be an oasis. Thus Gautier's approach here runs counter to mimesis both in its reluctance to represent directly and in its unstated incorporation of the (un)natural landscape into a fundamentally textual universe, that of orientalist allusion. Grant Crichfield's comments on Gautier's *Constantinople* clearly apply to "La Caravane" as well: "Gautier rarely speaks of the East without anchoring his discourse in an Occidental system of allusions. It is virtually impossible for him to write Asia in its own terms; his text on Turkey becomes a set of references primarily to European representation and knowledge."[66] Nor is Gautier concerned with such porousness of boundaries between text and empirical reality. As he says of his visit to Egypt, "La scène qui allait se passer devant nous réellement, nous l'avions imaginée et décrite par avance dans la *Roman de la momie*" [the scene that was about to pass before us in reality we had already imagined and described in the *Novel of the Mummy*].[67]

---

[65] Cypress trees seem to have a morbid or funereal connotation during this period.

[66] Grant Crichfield, "Decamps, Orientalist Intertext, and Counter-Discourse in Gautier's *Constantinople*," *Nineteenth-Century French Studies* 21.3–4 (1993): 306. Kubilay Aktulum's argument is similar; see Aktulum, "Les Stéréotypes dans *Constantinople*" 40–5. Both Aktulum and Crichfield are following Said's line of argument.

[67] Gautier, "Egypte — Vue générale," *L'Orient* 99. Compare Thomas Moore's boast that "Although I have never been in the East myself, yet every one who *has* been there declares that nothing can be more perfect than my representations of it, its people, and life, in 'Lalla Rookh'" (cited in C. Edmund Bosworth, "Arabic Influences in the Literature of Nineteenth and Early Twentieth Century Britain," *Tradition and Modernity in Arabic Language and Literature*, ed. J.R. Smart [Richmond, UK: Curzon P, 1996] 159; his emphasis).

In "La Caravane," the various conventional details of desert portrayal are combined to create an impression of "desert." But this is a composite, not a portrait of a physically plausible desert; in a real desert, for example, sweat would probably evaporate before it could be drunk. This composite desert image becomes a model of disappointment, despair, and death. Missing from Gautier's rendition is the possibility of idealism entailed in the oasis and dreamed Paradise of Leconte de Lisle's "Le Désert." Elements of "Le Désert"'s environment at least hold out hope for the nourishment of the human spirit typically provided by European nature, even though Middle Eastern nature as depicted by Leconte de Lisle does not meet European specifications overall. Gautier's desert is instead a metaphor for mortality. Thus, as in "Le Désert," the Middle East functions as a totalized figure for the human condition, with the difference that Gautier's view of that condition is uniformly cynical.[68]

There is no place for nature in Gautier's paradigmatic, composite desert. Yet, like the landscape of Leconte de Lisle's "Le Desert," Gautier's natureless desert plays virtually the same role that romantic poetics assigns to European nature. Gautier uses his desert to gain access to and to express an inner emotion (desolation), much as a romantic poet such as Wordsworth might do with a European outdoor scene. However, Gautier positions himself at an ironic distance from the romantic model. The landscape he depicts is far removed from both the uplifting sublime and the comfortable domesticity of romanticism. It is by no means the uncontaminated object of contemplation

---

[68] In this sense, Gautier's poem can be seen as a precursor of Charles Baudelaire's second "Spleen" poem (1857), which ends:

> L'ennui, fruit de la morne incuriosité,
> Prend les proportions de l'immortalité.
> — Désormais tu n'es plus, ô matière vivante!
> Qu'un granit entouré d'une vague épouvante,
> Assoupi dans le fond d'un Sahara brumeux;
> Un vieux sphinx ignoré du monde insoucieux,
> Oublié sur la carte, et dont l'humeur farouche,
> Ne chante qu'aux rayons du soleil qui se couche.

> [Ennui, fruit of dreary incuriosity, / Assumes the proportions of immortality. / — Henceforth you are no more, oh living matter! / Only a piece of granite surrounded by a vague horror, / Stifled in the depths of a somber Sahara, / An old sphinx ignored by the heedless world, / Forgotten on the map, with a fierce mood which / Sings only to the rays of the setting sun.]

(Baudelaire, *Oeuvres complètes*, ed. Marcel A. Ruff [Paris: Éditions du Seuil, 1968] 85.) For a general analysis of Baudelaire's reactions to Gautier's orientalism, see Luc Vives, "Les Poèmes de la momie: influence de l'imaginaire orientaliste et égyptisant de Théophile Gautier dans l'oeuvre de Charles Baudelaire," *Bulletin de la Société Théophile Gautier* 21 (1999): 53–70.

idealized by the romantics, nor does the speaker of the poem ever locate himself in the act of contemplating the landscape he describes. Gautier has dispensed entirely with the notion of a mimetic (or even consistently verisimilar) representation of nature. Instead, he puts forward an oriental landscape that is from the beginning firmly embedded in metaphor and textuality, but that is able to perform the same poetic function as its natural, European counterpart.

"In deserto": European nature in absentia

Gautier's poem "In deserto" (1842) follows a different course towards much the same end.[69] As Michael Riffaterre says, the poem "represents something that is not the desert to which the description is [...] referring."[70] On the other hand, the description of the desert environment in "In deserto" remains intensely invested in the minute details of the landscape. The poem begins by delineating the landscape's large geological landmarks:

> Les pitons des sierras, les dunes du désert,
> Où ne pousse jamais un seul brin d'herbe vert;
> Les monts aux flancs zébrés de tuf, d'ocre et de marne,
> Et que l'éboulement de jour en jour décharne;
> Le grès plein de micas papillotant aux yeux,
> Le sable sans profit buvant les pleurs des cieux,
> Le rocher refrogné dans sa barbe de ronce,
> L'ardente solfatare avec la pierre-ponce (1–8)

> [The peaks of the sierras, the dunes of the desert, / Where not a single blade of green grass ever grows; / The mountains with flanks zebra-striped in tuff, ochre, and marl, / And which landslides strip day by day; / The sandstone full of mica flashing before the eyes, / The sand vainly drinking the heavens' tears, / The crag frowning in its beard of thorns, / The fiery sulfer vent with the pumice stone]

This long description ends at last in an intersection with the speaker's hardened emotional state. All these features of the desert, he declares,

> Sont moins secs et moins morts aux végétations
> Que le roc de mon coeur ne l'est aux passions.
> Le soleil de midi, sur le sommet aride,
> Répand à flots plombés sa lumière livide,

---

[69] One of a number of poems based on Gautier's trip to Spain in 1840, "In deserto" appeared first in the *Revue de Paris* and was then included in Gautier's 1845 *Poésies nouvelles*.

[70] Riffaterre, *Semiotics of Poetry* (Bloomington: Indiana UP, 1978) 10.

Et rien n'est plus lugubre et désolant à voir
Que ce grand jour frappant sur ce grand désespoir. (9–14)

[Are less dry and less dead to vegetation / Than the rock of my heart is to passion. / The noonday sun on the arid summit / Pours out its livid light in leaden waves, / And nothing is more lugubrious and desolate to see / Than that great day striking that great despair.]

Riffaterre sees this shift from landscape to emotion as the beginning of a transition from mimesis to semiosis.[71] As in Wordsworth's "Septimi Gades," the desert is offered as a standard against which the speaker's own emotional status may be expressed and quantified. The mainly figurative function of the desert, though, corresponds more closely to that of the longer "Le Désert" and "La Caravane." As in the latter, the metaphoric function of the landscape overwhelms its function as setting.

Once the relationship between the two functions is established, the speaker goes on to delineate the smaller-scale characteristics of this now-figurative landscape:

Le lézard pâmé bâille, et parmi l'herbe cuite
On entend résonner les vipères en fuite.
Là, point de marguerite au coeur étoilé d'or,
Point de muguet prodigue égrenant son trésor;
Là, point de violette ignorée et charmante,
Dans l'ombre se cachant comme une pâle amante:
Mais la broussaille rousse et le tronc d'arbre mort,
Que le genou du vent comme un arc plie et tord;
Là, pas d'oiseau chanteur, ni d'abeille en voyage,
Pas de ramier plaintif déplorant son veuvage:
Mais bien quelque vautour, quelque aigle montagnard,
Sur le disque enflammé fixant son oeil hagard,
Et qui, du haut du pic où son pied prend racine,
Dans l'or fauve du soir durement se dessine. (15–28)

[The fainting lizard yawns, and in the burned grass / One hears echo the fleeing vipers. / There, no daisy with the starry golden heart, / No lavish lily of the valley letting go its treasure; / There, no ignored and charming violet, / Hiding itself in the shade like a pale lover: / But [instead] reddish underbrush and the trunk of a dead tree / That the wind's knee twists and bends like a bow; / There, no singing bird, nor traveling bee, / No plaintive dove deploring its widowhood: / But indeed some vulture, some highland eagle, / Fixing its haggard eye on the fiery disk, / And who, from the peak's height where its foot takes root, / Stands out boldly in the evening's tawny gold.]

---

[71] Riffaterre, *Semiotics of Poetry* 7–8.

Although this description is minutely detailed, its terms emphasize absent as well as actually perceived traits. We learn almost as much about what the desert landscape does not contain (five lines) as about what it does (eight lines).[72] In addition, the poet's choice of these absent features is significant for their specific association with European nature. The daisies, lilies of the valley, violets, songbirds, bees, and doves are (at least by convention) not to be expected in the desert, but they are (just as conventionally) part of a European image of nature that is grounded in the pastoral tradition and assimilated by the romantics.[73] The poem clearly portrays the desert environment in terms set by its European counterpart; the desert is thereby constituted as unnatural. Yet the two environments turn out to share certain characteristics. For instance, at the very beginning of Gautier's list of absent traits is the "marguerite au coeur étoilé d'or" [daisy with the starry golden heart]; in the last line of the section, gold appears once again, but this time in the desert landscape, as "l'or fauve du soir" [the evening's tawny gold]. In addition, all of the desert's missing European features are either plants or winged creatures. The passage's final image of the desert combines these two categories when the highland eagle's foot takes root as if the bird were a plant.

The presence of these few shared characteristics suggests once again the interchangeability that enables the desert, while in opposition to an implied Europe, to substitute for Europe in the speaker's figurative framework. As in Leconte de Lisle's "Le Désert" and in Gautier's "La Caravane," the desert is cast in nature's role as a medium for expression. The impenetrable, inhospitable "roc de mon coeur" [rock of my heart] finds its metaphoric counterpart in the oriental desert. The abnormal, unhealthy state of the speaker's feelings matches the unnatural, unwholesome environment of the desert, just as European nature might correlate with healthier emotional conditions. This match supports a more fundamental correspondence at an aesthetic and philosophical level, as the Middle Eastern environment takes the generative place of European nature without reproducing it.

To say that oriental (un)nature can displace European nature within poetic practice is not, of course, to imply a binary opposition between the two such that the one appears as a reflection of the other. This becomes clear in "In deserto" when one considers the perspective from which the desert landscape is presented. Whereas in a poem such as Wordsworth's famous one beginning "I wandered lonely as a cloud" (1807), which depicts a landscape very much as an observer might experience it, the physical characteristics of Gautier's desert could not possibly be experienced as they are presented. It is unlikely that a single observer could notice, simultaneously or even in quick succession, all of

---

[72] Gautier's tactic of emphasizing the absent/negative rather than the present/positive strongly resembles Hugo's in "La Douleur du pacha."
[73] Riffaterre comments particularly on the absence of flowers; see *Semiotics of Poetry* 59.

the features to which the first eight lines of the poem allude: peaks, dunes, mountainsides, thorns, sulfur vents, etc. Even if one made the dubious assumption that each individual element of the depicted landscape were accurately represented as a natural phenomenon, the image of the desert that emerges is a hypothetical, totalized one, quintessential rather than documentary. The effect here is desertness, not a desert. As Riffaterre observes, such "details [...] are contradictory only as descriptions, only if we keep trying to interpret them as mimesis; they cease to be unacceptable when we see them as the logical and cogent consequences of the positivization of the desert code."[74]

The final section of the poem reinforces this idea of the desert as quintessence rather than topography, but it also gives this quintessence an emphatically Middle Eastern value:

> Tel était le rocher que Moïse, au désert,
> Toucha de sa baguette, et dont le flanc ouvert,
> Tressaillant tout à coup, fit jaillir en arcade
> Sur les lèvres du peuple une fraîche cascade.
> Ah! s'il venait à moi, dans mon aridité,
> Quelque reine des coeurs, quelque divinité,
> Une magicienne, un Moïse femelle,
> Traînant dans le désert les peuples après elle,
> Qui frappât le rocher dans mon coeur endurci,
> Comme de l'autre roche, on en verrait aussi
> Sortir en jets d'argent des eaux étincelantes,
> Où viendraient s'abreuver les racines des plantes;
> Où les pâtres errants conduiraient leurs troupeaux,
> Pour se coucher à l'ombre et prendre le repos;
> Où, comme en un vivier, les cigognes fidèles
> Plongeraient leurs grands becs et laveraient leurs ailes. (29–44)

> [Such was the crag that Moses, in the desert, / Touched with his rod (so that) its exposed flank, / Trembling suddenly, let spout forth in an arc / A cool cascade onto the lips of the people. / Ah! If there came to me in my aridity / Some queen of hearts, some divinity, / A magician, a female Moses, / Dragging the people after her into the desert, / Who would strike the crag in my hardened heart, / One would see, as from that other boulder, / Gush out sparkling waters in jets of silver, / Where plants' roots would

---

[74] Riffaterre, *Semiotics of Poetry* 11; he is speaking of the final passage of the poem, but his comment is equally applicable here. Constance Gosselin Schick's analysis of Gautier's description in *Venice* suggests a complementary reading: "With each added detail, with each added bit of supposedly precise, exact visual notation, Gautier's descriptions effect a move away from that kind of mimesis or *effet de réel* which seeks to make itself forgotten as medium, transparent as mediation and moves towards the hyperbolic and self-gratifyingly poetic" (Schick, "A Case Study of Descriptive Perversion: Théophile Gautier's Travel Literature," *Romanic Review* 78.3 [1987]: 364).

come to drink; / Where wandering shepherds would drive their herds / To lie down in the shade and rest; / Where, as in a fishpond, faithful storks / Would dip their great bills and clean their wings.

The composite and quintessential character of the desert is reinforced in these lines by the introduction of Moses, which allows the Spanish desert depicted to assume the figurative value of the conventional Middle Eastern desert.[75] The link between the hypothetical female Moses and the desert is affirmed by the poem's syntax. The final, defining view of the desert is that of the highland eagle discussed above; the female Moses is introduced in almost exactly the same terms: "quelque vautour, quelque aigle montagnard" [some vulture, some highland eagle] versus "Quelque reine de coeurs, quelque divinité" [Some queen of hearts, some divinity]. By relating the female Moses to this eagle who exemplifies the union of bird and plant motifs in the poem, Gautier firmly establishes the orientalized Spanish desert as the correlate of European nature. The remainder of the poem confirms the desert's ability to fill the place of nature, again through the use of bird and plant motifs. Gautier begins with "les racines des plantes" [plants' roots], a formulation that cements the link between the eagle (described earlier as rooted) and the flowers absent from the desert. He ends the poem with another bird image, that of storks grooming their wings in the flood of the speaker's released emotions. The

---

[75] The association between Spain and the Orient is not Gautier's invention; once again, he relies upon convention rather than creating a new relationship among elements in his poem. As Michael Cotsell says, "the East began in Spain" (Cotsell, ed., *Creditable Warriors, 1830–1876* [Atlantic Highlands, NJ: Ashfield, 1990] 34). Nor is Gautier's depiction of a Spanish desert as if it were Middle Eastern unique to this poem. For instance, another of his poems, "L'Escurial" (1840), describes its Spanish setting in terms of a Middle Eastern standard, which it meets easily:

Jamais vieux Pharaon, au flanc d'un mont d'Egypte,
Ne fit pour sa momie une plus noire crypte;
Jamais sphinx au désert n'a gardé plus d'ennui (7–9)

[Never did an old pharaoh, on the flank of an Egyptian mountain, / Make a blacker crypt for his mummy; / Never did a desert sphinx keep watch over more ennui]

During the visit to Spain that prompted "In deserto," Gautier seems to have been especially attracted to Spain's Moorish relics (see Richardson, *Théophile Gautier* 45–7). Both Brahimi and Kathleen Bulgin cite Gautier's *Voyage en Espagne* in this regard: "L'Espagne [...] n'est pas faite pour les moeurs européennes. Le génie de l'Orient y perce sous toute les formes, et il est fâcheux peut-être qu'elle ne soit pas restée moresque ou mahométane" [Spain is not made for European customs. The genius of the Orient pierces it in all its forms, and it is perhaps unfortunate that it has not remained Moorish or Mohammedan] (Brahimi, *Théophile et Judith* 24; and Bulgin, "L'Appel de l'Orient au voyageur en Espagne," *L'Orient de Théophile Gautier*, vol. 1 [Proc. of International Colloquium, May 1990, Monte Cristo] 155). For further discussion, see Brahimi, *Théophile et Judith* 23–7; and Bulgin, "L'Appel de l'Orient" 153–60.

speaker's movement from despair to the possibility of psychological health is accompanied by a transformation in the desert environment. The arrival of water and storks signals the naturalization of a landscape whose unnaturalness had been marked by the absence of both water and birds (other than the eagle). The fidelity of storks is a European stereotype; that these storks are faithful ("cigognes fidèles") implies a concomitant Europeanization of the landscape. But whether barren or newly fertile, Middle Eastern nature is as able as the conventionally fertile European version of nature to prompt or to organize human emotions.

Given the thematic centrality of human emotion, the absence of actual humans or human activity in this scene is striking. As already discussed, the observer implied at the beginning of the poem cannot reasonably be a single human being. Nor does the first-person speaker ever position himself within the scene. Moses is introduced in a simile that interprets the scene rather than being part of it, and he is in any case too legendary to count as a real person. The female Moses is both hypothetical and supernatural. The shepherds and the female Moses's followers are human, but they form undifferentiated, hypothetical groups altogether lacking in psychological development. Indeed, Gautier seems even to have idealized such a human-free desert. In comments on Eugène Fromentin's *Un été au Sahara* [*A Summer in the Sahara*], for instance, Gautier concludes: "Aussi notre idéal est-il celui de M. Fromentin — un ciel sans nuage sur le désert sans ombre! Le désert! — 'c'est Dieu sans les hommes'" [Thus our ideal is that of Mr. Fromentin — a cloudless sky over the unshaded desert! The desert — "it is God without men"].[76]

Although Gautier's praise for such an antimodern, depopulated, aesthetic landscape appears oddly Wordsworthian, Wordsworth would not perceive the desert as a possible manifestation of his ideal landscape.[77] Gautier's exclusion of human beings also contrasts with Leconte de Lisle's depiction of a Middle Eastern environment in which humans and nature are unnaturally indistinguishable. Yet the two views are similar in a couple of key respects. First, both present a relationship between nature and human beings that differs profoundly from the conventional, romantic (Wordsworthian, Hugoesque) one. Second, despite its very different relationship with human beings, the desert is, in each case, able to fulfill the aesthetic function conventionally assigned to European nature: to inspire and structure experience and its expression. In neither case is the desert able to do this because it, like a forest or a glade, is a natural phenomenon. Rather, the desert is useful to Gautier and Leconte de

---

[76] Gautier, "Le Sahara," *L'Orient*, 2: 372; this was probably written in 1854 or shortly thereafter.

[77] See for comparison Marcel Voisin's argument that Gautier's privileging of the Orient "represents his continuous flight from the modern ugliness and surliness born of industrialization and triumphal capitalism" (Voisin, "La Pensée de Théophile Gautier," *Relire Théophile Gautier: le plaisir du texte*, ed. Freeman G. Henry [Amsterdam: Rodopi, 1998] 81).

Lisle precisely because it is unnatural. In their poems, the protagonists' affiliation with the Orient, that place of desolation, unnaturalness, abnormality, and barbarism, is also a rejection of the optimism, emotional engagement, and domesticity of romanticism.

Riffaterre offers Gautier's "In deserto" as an example of an apparently descriptive poem that "ceases to be descriptive, ceases to be a sequence of mimetic signs, and becomes a single sign, perceived from the end back to its given as a harmonious whole, wherein nothing is loose, wherein every word refers to one symbolic focus."[78] His analysis traces the poem's progression from apparent mimesis to semiosis, a state in which "the text is no longer attempting to establish the credibility of a description."[79] However, Riffaterre does not acknowledge orientalism's crucial contribution towards the poem's antimimetic trend. As my reading shows, it is as impossible to segregate the oriental from the unnatural as it is to disengage the unnatural from the antimimetic.

Out of the desert: Byron's "Turkish Tales"

Nineteenth-century orientalist poems tend to concentrate the Islamic Middle East's unnaturalness in its deserts, as we have seen. However, unnaturalness is evident even in oriental landscapes whose physical or visual difference from a European standard is far less pronounced. The rest of this chapter will consider two such landscapes: first, the varied rural scenery of Byron's *The Bride of Abydos* (1813), *The Giaour* (1813), and *The Corsair* (1814); and second, the urban settings of poems by Matthew Arnold and Alfred Tennyson. In each case, the environment is, like the desert, clearly differentiated from its European counterpart. None of these environments attains a relationship with people comparable to that of the rural European landscape as depicted by Wordsworth or Hemans. Nonetheless, each of these oriental settings shares with the Middle Eastern desert the capacity to displace nature by usurping its poetic function.

The settings of Byron's so-called Turkish Tales are typically more lush than those discussed thus far.[80] Seascapes are common, as are fertile inland landscapes. *The Bride of Abydos*, for instance, begins:

---

[78] Riffaterre, *Semiotics of Poetry* 12.
[79] Riffaterre, *Semiotics of Poetry* 10.
[80] A number of critics supply more comprehensive analyses of orientalism in Byron's "Turkish Tales" than mine. See especially Butler, "The Orientalism of Byron's *Giaour*," *Byron and the Limits of Fiction*, ed. Bernard Beatty and Vincent Newey (Totowa, NJ: Barnes and Noble, 1988) 78–96; Leask, *British Romantic Writers and the East* ch. 1; and Sharafuddin, *Islam and Romantic Orientalism* ch. 4.

> Know ye the land where the cypress and myrtle
>   Are emblems of deeds that are done in their clime,
> Where the rage of the vulture — the love of the turtle —
>   Now melt into sorrow — now madden to crime? —
> Know ye the land of the cedar and vine?
> Where the flowers ever blossom, the beams ever shine,
> Where the light wings of Zephyr, oppressed with perfume,
> Wax faint o'er the gardens of Gúl in her bloom;[81]
> Where the citron and olive are fairest of fruit,
> And the voice of the nightingale never is mute;
> Where the tints of the earth, and the hues of the sky,
> In colour though varied, in beauty may vie,
> And the purple of Ocean is deepest in die;
> Where the virgins are soft as the roses they twine,
> And all, save the spirit of man, is divine —
> 'Tis the clime of the East — 'tis the land of the Sun —
> Can he smile on such deeds as his children have done? (1.1–17)

Like Gautier's desert scenes, this landscape is clearly a composite of conventional traits. Although its fertility and variety distinguish it from the desert, its paradoxical relationship with human beings is not the one glorified by Wordsworthian romanticism. On the one hand, the speaker presents the landscape as a figure for human emotions and actions ("the cypress and myrtle / Are emblems of deeds that are done in their clime"). On the other, he implies a fundamental disjunction between the beautiful outdoor landscape and the violent "spirit of man" that inhabits it. Neither of these positions approximates the one Wordsworth and Hemans idealize.

The ending of *The Bride of Abydos* confirms the difficulty of postulating a fulfilling relationship with the outdoor environment of the Orient. Selim, the poem's rebellious "hero," is killed in a battle at the seacoast. As he expires,

> Fast from his breast the blood is bubbling,
> The whiteness of the sea-foam troubling;
> If aught his lips essayed to groan
> The rushing billows choked the tone! (2.579–82)

After Selim's death, his body lies on the shoreline so that he is

> shaken on his restless pillow,
> His head heaves with the heaving billow —
> That hand — whose motion is not life —
> Yet feebly seems to menace strife —
> Flung by the tossing tide on high,
>   Then levell'd with the wave —

---

[81] Byron footnotes "Gúl" as "the rose"; the word is Persian. My source for the "Turkish Tales" is *The Complete Poetical Works*, ed. Jerome McGann, vol. 3 (Oxford: Clarendon, 1981); reprinted by permission of Oxford University Press.

>   What recks it? though that corse shall lie
>   Within a living grave? (2.605–12)

As his corpse becomes carrion for scavenging birds, Selim is united with nature in a highly practical but unsavory fashion that has nothing in common with the spiritual and intellectual engagement applauded by Byron's more Wordsworthian contemporaries in their nonorientalist poetry. The failure of such an engagement is made explicit in the "rushing billows" that choke off anything that Selim's "lips essay'd to groan." Thus although this coastal setting is physically dissimilar to the desert, its deleterious effects upon Selim suggest a functional correspondence between the two environments. That correspondence is implied earlier by Selim himself when he compares "My tent on shore" with "my galley on the sea" (2.390). He casts the two in equivalent roles: "Borne by my steed, or wafted by my sail, / Across the desart, or before the gale, / Bound where thou wilt, my barb! or glide, my prow" (2.392–4). Even in this moment of (false) confidence, however, Selim's attitude towards both sea and desert suggests dominance rather than receptivity to inspiration or even comfortable coexistence.[82]

When Selim attempts a more typically romantic interaction with the outdoors, he is unsuccessful, although the blame is perhaps due as much to his own lack of sensitivity as to the deficiencies of the landscape. At one point, he looks out "o'er the dark blue water, / That swiftly glides and gently swells," but he is too distracted to appreciate it: "he saw nor sea nor strand" (1.242–3, 245). On another occasion, he complains that

>   to view alone
>   The fairest scenes of land and deep,
>   With none to listen and reply
>   To thoughts with which my heart beat high
>   Were irksome (1.59–63)

Neither Selim's difficulty concentrating nor his need for a human interlocutor finds any parallel in the focused and mutually sufficient relationship between natural scenery and human beings that Wordsworth and Hemans propose for their poems' protagonists. Whereas Hemans's Bruce hears clearly the summons of the Scottish highlands, Selim is oblivious to the outdoor environment's efforts to communicate with him. In the first lines of canto 2, for example, "rising gale," "breaking foam," "shrieking sea-birds," "clouds," and "tides" all warn him not to go, but "He could not see, he would not hear" (2.8–12).

Like *The Bride of Abydos*, *The Giaour* and *The Corsair* present Middle Eastern nature as an attractive, productive environment whose unnaturalness consists chiefly in its excess and in its conflicted relationship with people. The

---

[82] See 2.345–8 for a further example of Selim's attitude of domination.

setting of *The Giaour* is a "Fair clime" (7), one of the "Edens of the eastern wave" (15), a region

> where Nature lov'd to trace,
> As if for Gods, a dwelling-place,
> And every charm and grace hath mixed
> Within the paradise she fixed (46–9)[83]

Far from appreciating this wondrous place, "man, enamour'd of distress" has "mar[red] it into wilderness" (50–1). Moreover, nature too can kill, in the form of "the Simoom, / [...] / Beneath whose widely-wasting breath / The very cypress droops to death" (282–5). Even if the potential for destruction is balanced, it ensures a mutual antagonism between human beings and their outdoor surroundings. Communion between the setting and the characters exists only in that the scene correlates with the emotional makeup of its population. As the title character confesses, "The cold in clime are cold in blood, / [...] / But mine was like the lava flood / That boils in Aetna's breast of flame" (1099–102). However, climate and region are tropes; there is no psychological or spiritual linkage between them and the speaker of these lines.

Such a linkage seems possible at first for *The Corsair*'s Conrad, who displays a close attachment to his home, a "lone, but lovely dwelling on the steep" (1.509) reminiscent of the rural habitations in Wordsworth's "Septimi Gades." But unlike the speaker of that earlier poem, Conrad must turn away from the sight of his home in order to maintain his emotional stability: he "shrunk whene'er the windings of his way / Forced on his eye what he would not survey" (1.507–8). When the landscape appears to speak with him as the Scottish mountains do with Bruce, it speaks treacherously, for the rocks, dolphins, and sea bird can offer only a false welcome in the absence of his beloved Medora (3.555–88). Finally, *The Corsair* also participates with its fellow "Turkish Tales" in the aestheticization of the explicitly oriental landscape. For instance, the extended description of sunset that opens canto 3 frankly distinguishes this extraordinary sight from any European version; the sinking sun is

> Not, as in Northern climes, obscurely bright,
> But one unclouded blaze of living light!
> O'er the hush'd deep the yellow beam he throws,
> Gilds the green wave, that trembles as it glows. (3.3–6)

Despite its beauty, the scenery does not offer its human observers the intellectual and spiritual benefits readily provided by European natural

---

[83] A similarly idyllic landscape description occurs in lines 388–97. For comments on the paradisic associations of Byron's Orient, see Makdisi, *Romantic Imperialism* 132; and Sharafuddin, *Islam and Romantic Orientalism* 231.

settings. Although Makdisi is right to point out that Byron is drawn to such landscapes precisely for their otherness, that otherness seems inevitably to dislocate characters from setting at least as much as it promotes what Makdisi describes as "the desire (however chimerical) to experience the East 'as such.'"[84] In other words, the denaturalization of nature in the East may emblematize the experience of otherness, but that experience comes with a price.

The Middle Eastern landscape's function as a manifestation of nature is compromised further in *The Corsair* by the inclusion of elaborate architectural elements into the scenery. A description of nightfall, for example, lists columns, a minaret, a mosque, a turret, and a kiosk alongside moonbeams and olive, cypress, and palm trees (3.37–46). There is no distinction made between natural and constructed components of the scene. *The Giaour* includes a similar nighttime scene in which the title character "looks […] o'er the olive wood" but sees a mosque with crescent and lighted lamps (221–3).[85] The apparently unproblematic intrusion of the built environment into otherwise rural, natural scenery accentuates the Orient's unnaturalness. In *The Bride of Abydos*, this process is neatly encapsulated in the reference to a "pictured roof" (1.272), accompanied by Byron's note that "The ceiling and wainscots, or rather walls, of the Mussulman apartments are generally Painted, in great houses, with one eternal and highly coloured view of Constantinople."[86] This decoration of interior space with outdoor images collapses the distinction between scenery and design, and with it the possibility of the Islamic Middle East as a place where nature can exist as a discrete and independent entity.

In all three of these poems, the abundantly described Middle Eastern settings clearly define the subject matter's essential difference. Like the other poems of this chapter, the "Turkish Tales" display this difference as unnaturalness. Because Byron's Orient is rarely a desert, that unnaturalness is less immediately physical, but it remains evident in the exaggerated beauty of the poems' composite landscapes and in the dysfunctional relationships between characters and their surroundings. The Orient's unnaturalness thus extends beyond the features of its physical environment to encompass the social structure of the Islamic Middle East, as is apparent as well from the political critique advanced in poems such as *The Bride of Abydos*. Rather as the desert of Gautier's "In deserto," the unnatural surroundings of Byron's "Turkish Tales" are able to organize the experience of the characters they contain. This function is virtually indistinguishable from that of European nature in Wordsworthian romanticism, although the experience at issue is quite

---

[84] Makdisi, *Romantic Imperialism* 120, 133.
[85] See *The Giaour* 449–52 and *The Corsair* 1.598 for additional descriptions of illuminated mosques.
[86] Byron, *The Complete Poetical Works* 3: 438.

distinct from that favored by Wordsworth. In this important respect, oriental unnature acts in the same capacity as European nature, thereby displacing it as a poetic origin.

The excessiveness inherent in the aestheticization (and occasionally the demonization) of oriental unnature in these poems disqualifies it as the basis for a mimetic approach to representation. There can be no empirically verifiable referent for *The Giaour*'s "Edens," for example, yet that poem is plentifully supplied with authenticating footnotes. The notes add both another layer of discourse (as Diego Saglia argues in the case of Southey's *Roderick*)[87] and another level of narrative disjunction, compounding the discontinuities already inherent in the fragmentary structure of *The Giaour*, and to a lesser extent of the other "Turkish Tales." As I explain in chapter 2, the fragment as a form tends to work outside of mimesis. Here, the fragment's relationship with mimesis is further strained by the gap between the compulsive mimeticism of the footnotes' descriptions and the clearly antimimetic excess of the poems' descriptions. Oriental unnature necessitates both: mimeticism because the oriental oddity must be documented, and antimimeticism because the unnatural is not subject to representation as an experientially available referent would be.[88] Thus it is in the relationship between (fragmentary) poetic text and documentary footnote that the Orient as unnatural becomes most obviously central to the poetics of the "Turkish Tales."

Matthew Arnold in Bukhara: nature in the Middle Eastern city

Matthew Arnold (1822–1888) envisions a contentious and unstable relationship between nature and humanity and finds nature itself an unreliable source of guidance and inspiration. Like the other poets of this chapter, he uses the Islamic Middle East as an arena in which to elaborate his views of nature and its relations with both poetry and humanity. He too sees the relationship between people and nature as especially awkward in the Orient, but he does

---

[87] See Saglia, "Nationalist Texts and Counter-Texts" 444.
[88] Both Makdisi and Sharafuddin argue that Byron's Orient is in fact experientially available. Although both acknowledge the continuing influence of literary orientalism, Sharafuddin characterizes Byron's orientalism as "realistic" (Sharafuddin, *Islam and Romantic Orientalism* 214); Makdisi suggests that "Byron's Orient seems to be the Orient's Orient — the real Orient 'out there,' and not some vaguely-realistic figurative landscape produced by a Western imagination" (Makdisi, *Romantic Imperialism* 133). Byron's comparatively extensive travels in the region no doubt counteracted to a significant degree whatever received ideas he may have had about the East. However, in presenting the Orient as Edenic, for example, he makes an unmistakable move away from realism and into the realm of the imagination. Inevitably, this move entails a shift from mimesis as the representation of the empirically knowable and towards a kind of referentiality in which the referent is not securely derived from reality.

not assume that the conventionally natural environment of Europe automatically enables human beings' productive engagement with their outdoor surroundings. In this respect, his approach has more in common with his French contemporaries (Gautier, Leconte de Lisle) than with his British predecessors (Wordsworth, Hemans, Byron). Arnold has a reputation as a Victorian with an atypically non-Anglocentric, even multicultural view; this may play a role in his willingness to look skeptically at his own cultural inheritance, although it is important to recall that Arnold's intellectual range is, for the most part, limited to Europe.[89] In any case, Arnold produced a small but significant corpus of Middle Eastern poems, including "The Sick King in Bokhara" (1849), to which I will turn shortly.[90] I will begin for the sake of comparison with Arnold's "In Harmony with Nature," a nonorientalist sonnet published in the same year as "The Sick King."[91]

"In Harmony with Nature" explores humanity's rapport with nature in a nonorientalist context. The speaker of the poem strongly criticizes the advice alluded to by the poem's original title: "To an Independent Preacher, who

---

[89] Park Honan emphasizes Arnold's "Europeanism" in this context; see Honan, "Matthew Arnold: Europeanism and England," *Creditable Warriors, 1830–1876*, ed. Michael Cotsell (Atlantic Highlands, NJ: Ashfield, 1990) 143–57. Isobel Armstrong's comments on "cultural boundaries" and "territorial margin[s]" in Arnold's poetry are also useful in this context; see Armstrong, *Victorian Poetry: Poetry, Poetics and Politics* (London: Routledge, 1993) 207. For further information on Arnold's work on non-European topics, see Honan, *Matthew Arnold: A Life* (New York: McGraw-Hill, 1981) 291, 313, 367. Arnold's 1871 lecture on "A Persian Passion Play" (to which Honan refers briefly) is an especially interesting example. The bulk of the lecture offers an extremely favorable assessment of the Persian genre, yet Arnold ends by asserting that the Islamic play's message is a "strong [...] testimony to Christianity" (Arnold, *Essays in Criticism: First Series*, ed. Thomas Marion Hoctor, S.S.J. [Chicago: U of Chicago P, 1968] 157). John D. Yohannan comments perceptively on the mix of spiritual attraction, imperialism, and racism that characterizes Arnold's orientalism; see Yohannan, *Persian Poetry in England and America: A 200-Year History* (Delmar, NY: Caravan, 1977) ch. 8, esp. pp. 78–80.

[90] Arnold's other major orientalist poem is *Sohrab and Rustum* (1853). Related poems include "A Summer Night" (1861); "East and West" (1867); and two items of juvenilia, "Inspired by Julia Pardoe's *The City of the Sultan*" and "Constantinople."

My source for Arnold's poetry is *The Poems of Matthew Arnold*, Ed. Kenneth Allott and Miriam Allott (London: Longman, 1979).

[91] "In Harmony with Nature" was probably composed 1844–47, and "The Sick King of Bokhara" 1847–48. See *The Poems of Matthew Arnold*, Ed. Allott and Allott, 44, 79. "In Harmony" is a popular poem among Arnold's twentieth-century interpreters and critics. See Beach, *The Concept of Nature* 398–9; William E. Buckler, *On the Poetry of Matthew Arnold: Essays in Critical Reconstruction* (New York: New York UP, 1982) 40–2; Honan, *Matthew Arnold* 322; Thaïs E. Morgan, "Rereading Nature: Wordsworth between Swinburne and Arnold" *Victorian Poetry* 24.4 (1986): 430–1, 433; Alan Roper, *Arnold's Poetic Landscapes* (Baltimore: Johns Hopkins UP, 1969) 116, 118, 188, 193, 200; Sylvia Bailey Shurbutt, "The Poetry of Matthew Arnold: Nature and the Oriental Wisdom," *University of Dayton Review* 17.3 (1985–86): 42; William Thesing, "Matthew Arnold and the Possibilities of the Nineteenth-Century City," *CLA Journal* 24.3 (1981): 290; and Woodring, "Wordsworth and the Victorians" 270.

preached that we should be 'In Harmony with Nature.'" He lectures this "restless fool" (1) of a preacher:

> Know, man hath all which Nature hath, but more,
> And in that *more* lie all his hopes of good.
> Nature is cruel, man is sick of blood;
> Nature is stubborn, man would fain adore;
>
> Nature is fickle, man hath need of rest;
> Nature forgives no debt, and fears no grave;
> Man would be mild, and with safe conscience blest.
>
> Man must begin, know this, where Nature ends;
> Nature and man can never be fast friends.
> Fool, if thou canst not pass her, rest her slave!
> (5–14; emphasis his)

Arnold follows the romantics and their classical forebears in acknowledging nature as the fundamental standard from which human moral development must depart, yet he argues against basing human standards on natural ones. Instead, he presents his speaker as a man in search of a new (and as yet undefined) relationship with nature. The speaker recognizes not only the "impossibility" of being truly in harmony with nature but also the undesirability of such a goal. "Nature and man can never be fast friends," he concludes.

The alternatives are as he sets them out in the poem's final line: either remain subordinate to nature or surpass her, presumably in a spirit of greater moral advancement. However, although Arnold writes here of "pass[ing]" nature, the body of the poem advocates a more adversarial relationship. Even while "man" can be cruel and unforgiving, the speaker emphasizes human mildness, even weakness; nature, on the other hand, shows no such capacity for gentleness. In juxtaposing humankind and nature in these lines, he is undoubtedly implying that whatever hope there is for human beings lies more in their divergence from nature than in their ability to "pass" nature on the same track. This ambiguity of message is irresolvable within the text, but the basic philosophical question underlying it is nonetheless clear: what, the poem asks, is the proper relationship between nature and humankind? Romanticism has already replied to that question; by raising it again, Arnold suggests dissatisfaction with romanticism's answer.[92]

---

[92] Useful comments on Arnold's view of nature and his relationship with romanticism may be found in: Beach, *The Concept of Nature* ch. 14; Buckler, *On the Poetry of Matthew Arnold* 12–17, 90–102, 180–2; A. Dwight Culler, *Imaginative Reason: The Poetry of Matthew Arnold* (New Haven: Yale UP, 1966) 1–17; Pauline Fletcher, *Gardens and Grim Ravines: The Language of Landscape in Victorian Poetry* (Princeton: Princeton UP, 1983) ch. 3; Morgan,

Arnold returns once again to the same question in "The Sick King in Bokhara."[93] This longer poem (232 lines) tells the story of a "Moollah" who presents himself to the king as his own accuser, claiming to have cursed his own mother and demanding to be put to death according to Islamic law. Twice the king rejects his plea and has him driven out as a madman. On the third occasion, the king is forced to turn the case over to the "Ulemas," who sentence the mullah to death by stoning. The king orders the sentence carried out, but charges that the man be allowed to escape if he attempts to do so. The man does not, and is killed; the king then has the body brought to him, and he begins to prepare it for burial in his own royal tomb. The poem, which takes the form of a conversation, begins with the court poet, Hussein, narrating the story for the king's vizier, who has been ill and is unaware of the situation. As the body is carried in, the vizier and the king then debate the appropriateness of the king's grief for the dead mullah.

Editors Kenneth Allott and Miriam Allott state that "[t]he subject interested [Arnold] for its suggestion that the moral law may transcend rational expediency and yet be sanctioned by the individual conscience."[94] However, this formulation should be investigated further, especially in light of the moral uncertainty of "In Harmony with Nature." Superficially, the moral law here is the law of Islam, the law that requires (all extenuating circumstances aside) the death of a son who curses his mother. But if we compare this notion of law to that of "nature" in the preceding poem, we find a strong parallel, one that suggests that the law portrayed in "The Sick King" is relevant beyond the narrow bounds of (supposed) Muslim doctrine. Nature in "In Harmony with Nature" is "cruel" (7), "stubborn" (8), unforgiving, fearless, and harsh. Law in "The Sick King" could easily be described in precisely the same terms.

Moreover, the relationship postulated between nature and human beings in "In Harmony" very much resembles the relationship that develops between the king and the law in "The Sick King." "In Harmony" announces that "man is sick of blood" (7), "man hath need of rest [...] and fears [the] grave" (9–10), and "Man would be mild, and with safe conscience blest" (11). This composite picture of "man" closely matches the more detailed (though still somewhat generic) portrait of the king. The king's struggles with the law can easily be predicted on the basis of this correspondence; his decision about the mullah's fate should be, must be, "in harmony" with the law, yet his own moral bent strongly opposes such a decision. If the mullah who yearned for compliance

---

"Rereading Nature"; and Shurbutt, "Matthew Arnold's Concept of Nature: A Synthesist's View," *Victorian Poetry* 23.1 (1985): 97–104.

[93] See *The Poems of Matthew Arnold*, Ed. Allott and Allott, pp. 79–80, for information on Arnold's sources for this poem. Bokhara (modern spelling "Bukhara") is located to the northeast of Iran in Uzbekistan; in Arnold's time, the city was the capital of the Bukhara Khanate, a state that became a Russian protectorate in 1868.

[94] *The Poems of Matthew Arnold*, Ed. Allott and Allott, p. 80.

with the law is a "fool" (40) and a "madman" (91), such compliance is, in the king's view, equally foolish and equally mad — but also unavoidable.[95] Nature and law appear, then, to be filling the same slot in Arnold's moral universe. Both nature and law lack pity, that essential human quality which Arnold presents both in this poem and in "In Harmony" as humankind's only saving grace. Neither law nor nature offers a suitable guide for human behavior.

The virtual interchangeability of law and nature in this context is reinforced by the relative absence of outdoor scenery from "The Sick King in Bokhara." The only natural scene described is that of a tiny pool, which the mullah is delighted to find during a time of drought:

> Now I at nightfall had gone forth
> Alone, and in a darksome place
> Under some mulberry-trees I found
> A little pool; and in short space,
> With all the water that was there
> I filled my pitcher, and stole home
> Unseen (65–71)

This little pool fills the role customarily assigned in orientalist literature to an oasis, providing water to the needy. Like oases in other nineteenth-century poems I have discussed, this mini-oasis is depicted as clearly separate and distinct from its surroundings. Unlike its counterparts, though, this place is almost threatening; it is "darksome," and the mullah, who is obviously apprehensive about being there, shows none of the desire to linger that is so characteristic of visitors to other literary oases. The place becomes yet another example of the motif of the unsatisfying oasis as the plot of the poem reveals that this pool is in fact the source of the mullah's current predicament. Had he not found the pool, he would not have had extra water to hide at home. He would then have had no reason to curse his mother when she drank the precious water.

While the pool is the immediate cause of the mullah's difficulty, the climate and geographic location of Bukhara bear the real blame. The mullah explains the circumstances:

> Thou know'st, how fierce
> In these last days the sun hath burned;
> That the green water in the tanks
> Is to a putrid puddle turned;

---

[95] For discussion of "The Sick King"'s moral position, see Allott and Allott, "Arnold the Poet: (ii) Narrative and Dramatic Poems," *Matthew Arnold*, ed. Kenneth Allott (Athens: Ohio UP, 1976) 75, 82, 84–8; Buckler, *On the Poetry of Matthew Arnold* 34–7; Culler, *Imaginative Reason* 105–13; Honan, *Matthew Arnold* 175–6; John Woolford, "The Sick King in Bokhara: Arnold and the Sublime of Suffering," *Matthew Arnold: Between Two Worlds*, ed. Robert Giddings (London: Vision, 1986) esp. 113–4.

> And the canal, which from the stream
> Of Samarcand is brought this way,
> Wastes, and runs thinner every day. (58–64)

Nature is presented much as in "In Harmony with Nature," but here "In Harmony"'s generalities (cruelty, harshness, etc.) are given a concrete — and specifically oriental — manifestation. Arnold's city of Bukhara becomes a version of the conventional Middle Eastern desert, within which the pool serves as an oasis. The heat and dryness of Bukhara are emphasized in the succeeding lines, to the exclusion of other characteristics.[96] Thus while the outdoor environment may appear not to have a prominent place in this poem, it is at the very root of the mullah's problem, and therefore of the king's moral dilemma as well. This version of nature is, as I have shown, distinctly Middle Eastern. The same is true of law; the poem's central moral deliberation depends upon the supposed inflexibility and unforgiving character of Islamic law. In effect, unnatural Middle Eastern nature forms a conceptual complex with Islamic law in "The Sick King," a complex that corresponds closely to European nature as depicted in "In Harmony" but not to the conventional romantic vision of nature.

In the European context (romantic or not), nature is presumed to be an external force, a phenomenon largely independent of human beings even when they interact with it. However, this boundary is not cleanly maintained when law substitutes for nature. Although law may be understood to originate outside of humankind (in this poem, God is the source), the law — unlike nature — cannot function without human beings; indeed, the poem's moral dilemma devolves precisely from this fact. Moreover, the limited and compromised depiction of nature in "The Sick King" is further removed from a European model by the mingling of purely natural elements with those bearing a human stamp; this is the same tactic we have already observed in Byron's orientalist poetry, but it is pursued far more consistently here. For instance, the most sustained portrayal of nature in this poem is the description of the pool, yet references to the mullah's house (its roof, a door) are interspersed throughout the description. And the natural phenomenon of the pool is incorporated into a very explicitly urban setting, thereby once again smudging the line between nature and human design. Like Byron's "Turkish Tales" and Shelley's *The Revolt of Islam*, "The Sick King" explores universal political and

---

[96] This poem contains a few other references to natural phenomena, but the hot, dry environment retains its dominance. See lines 193–204, in which the king describes his various attempts to counteract this environment, with sherbets and orchards and cisterns — and all, he says, "in vain." See also the king's description of his tomb (222–3), which is on a hill near a stand of apricot trees; again, however, this more benign version of nature appears to be helpless, associated with death rather than life.

moral problems within an explicitly Islamic Middle Eastern setting,[97] but Arnold's complex deployment of law adds a conceptual dimension lacking in his predecessors' work.

"The Sick King" shows the interlocking of the human and the natural in two ways: by positioning law (which requires human implementation) as nature (which does not), and by presenting a totalized environmental image in which the products of nature are inseparable from those of human activity. This image has little to do with mainstream romanticism's model of pure, European nature. The skeptical attitude towards nature that Arnold expressed in "In Harmony with Nature" comes to fruition here, mediated by oriental (un)nature. Like Leconte de Lisle and Gautier, he sees the East as a place of moral desolation. As they do, he uses this image of the Orient not only to articulate and explore an emotional crisis, but also to reflect upon an aesthetic crisis in his relationship with his romantic forbears.[98]

Alfred Tennyson's Basra: natural phenomena and urban construction

Alfred Tennyson's concern with the poetic function of nature and with the relationship between humans and nature is, like Arnold's, revealed through his portrayal of a Middle Eastern city. Tennyson (1809–1892) also joins Arnold in using the conventions of orientalism to establish his own aesthetic position vis-à-vis romanticism. Tennyson's "Written by an Exile of Bassorah, while sailing down the Euphrates" (1827), one of a number of Middle Eastern poems clustered in the early part of his long career, depicts the obstacles to a fulfilling relationship between the landscape and its inhabitants. The unnatural urban environment of the East informs the poem's stance much as rural nature informed that of Wordsworth's "Septimi Gades," but the resulting poetics diverge sharply from Wordsworth's.[99]

---

[97] Shelley's poem calls upon the Middle East's reputation for the tyranny of kings and of religion very much as Arnold's does. On the other hand, Arnold appears cognizant of, and interested in, the sorts of moral ambiguities and complexities that Shelley's polarized approach tends to elide. Rather than preach like *The Revolt of Islam*, "The Sick King" queries, explores, and debates. The law remains paramount, but there are many ways of responding to its demands.

[98] See for comparison James Najarian's comments on Arnold's "anti-romantic aims" in *Sohrab and Rustum* (Najarian, "'Curled minion, dancer, coiner of sweet words': Keats, Dandyism, and Sexual Indeterminacy in *Sohrab and Rustum*," *Victorian Poetry* 35.1 (1997): 23–4.

[99] Tennyson set a number of poems in India, Africa, and pharaonic Egypt, as well as the biblical Levant. "Persia" (1827), "The Expedition of Nadir Shah into Hindostan" (1827), "Recollections of the Arabian Nights" (1830; see chapter 4), and "Fatima" (1832) are especially noteworthy. Also of great interest is "Locksley Hall" (1842), which does not have a Middle Eastern setting but is patterned after the Muʻallaqa of Imru' al-Qays, perhaps the most famous poem in Arabic literature. Tennyson traveled widely within Europe, but never to the Orient, although he expressed the desire to do so; see Susan Shatto, "The Strange Charm of 'Far, Far Away': Tennyson, the Continent, and the Empire," *Creditable Warriors, 1830–1876*,

Tennyson's "On a Mourner," which depicts European nature without reference to the Orient, offers a useful point of comparison for "Written by an Exile."[100] Although "On a Mourner" takes a less wary view of nature than Arnold's "In Harmony with Nature," the two poems share the assumption that nature is external to and independent from humankind — not, as in the oriental context of "The Sick King," inseparably linked with it. "On a Mourner" begins by giving nature divine status, proclaiming its glories:

I
Nature, so far as in her lies,
  Imitates God, and turns her face
To every land beneath the skies,
  Counts nothing that she meets with base,
  But lives and loves in every place;

II
Fills out the homely quickset-screens,
  And makes the purple lilac ripe,
Steps from her airy hill, and greens
  The swamp, where hummed the dropping snipe,
  With moss and braided marish-pipe;

III
And on thy heart a finger lays,
  Saying, 'Beat quicker, for the time
Is pleasant, and the woods and ways
  Are pleasant, and the beech and lime
  Put forth and feel a gladder clime.'

IV
And murmurs of a deeper voice,
  Going before to some far shrine,
Teach that sick heart the stronger choice,
  Till all thy life one way incline
  With one wide Will that closes thine. (1–20)

---

ed. Michael Cotsell (Atlantic Highlands, NJ: Ashfield, 1990) 113–4. While Shatto gives little attention to the Middle East per se, her discussion of Tennyson's approach to other non-European settings is useful. See also John McBratney, "Rebuilding Akbar's 'Fane': Tennyson's Reclamation of the East," *Victorian Poetry* 31.4 (1993): 411–7; Marion Shaw, "Tennyson's Dark Continent," *Victorian Poetry* 32.2 (1994): 157–79; and Yohannan, *Persian Poetry in England and America* ch. 9.

My source for Tennyson's poems is *The Poems of Tennyson* (1987), edited by Christopher Ricks.

[100] "On a Mourner" was written in 1833, just after the death of Tennyson's dear friend Arthur Hallam. It was not published until 1865, and then only with two of the poem's most intimate stanzas suppressed. See *The Poems of Tennyson* 1: 610; and Ricks, *Tennyson*, 2nd ed. (London: Macmillan, 1989) 111–3. I will discuss the 1865 version of "On a Mourner."

The remaining three stanzas continue this lesson, revealing nature as both comfort and inspiration to the "sick heart" of the mourner:

V
And when the zoning eve has died
  Where yon dark valleys wind forlorn,
Come Hope and Memory, spouse and bride,
  From out the borders of the morn,
  With that fair child betwixt them born.

VI
And when no mortal motion jars
  The blackness round the tombing sod,
Through silence and the trembling stars
  Comes Faith from tracts no feet have trod,
  And Virtue, like a household god

VII
Promising empire; such as those
  Once heard at dead of night to greet
Troy's wandering prince, so that he rose
  With sacrifice, while all the fleet
  Had rest by stony hills of Crete. (21–35)

Tennyson's vision of nature in "On a Mourner" diverges from Wordsworth's in two respects. First, much as the notion of art "imitating" nature diminishes art's stature, the poem's opening reference to nature "imitating" God places nature in a secondary rather than a primary position. Second, as in the Arnold poems just discussed, nature is assumed to be entirely independent of humans despite the great benefits it offers them. Otherwise, however, the poem's effect resembles that of Wordsworth's "Septimi Gades." "On a Mourner" presents nature as an outdoor phenomenon first and foremost, although it includes in this image some standard moral and mythological components. The poem's view of human engagement with nature is also much closer to the conventional romantic ideal than is Arnold's; Tennyson shows the mourner deriving comfort and direction from nature in a way that neither the foolish preacher nor the assorted characters in "The Sick King" are able to do.[101]

Like "On a Mourner," Tennyson's "Written by an Exile of Bassorah" frames an expression of grief in terms of the natural environment.[102] Although more melodramatic in tone, the first two stanzas do not diverge markedly from the standard of "On a Mourner:"

---

[101] For further analysis of Tennyson's view of nature, especially in the context of his reaction to romanticism, see esp. Timothy Peltason, "Tennyson, Nature, and Romantic Nature Poetry," *Philological Quarterly* 63.1 (1984): 75–93; and Fletcher, *Gardens and Grim Ravines*, ch. 1.

[102] Bassorah (modern spelling "Basra") is a city in southeastern Iraq, near the Persian Gulf.

> Thou land of the Lily! thy gay flowers are blooming
>   In joy on thine hills, but they bloom not for me;
> For a dark gulf of woe, all my fond hopes entombing,
>   Has rolled its black waves 'twixt this lone heart and thee.
>
> The far-distant hills, and the groves of my childhood,
>   Now stream in the light of the sun's setting ray;
> And the tall-waving palms of my own native wild-wood
>   In the blue haze of distance are melting away. (1–8)

The reference to "tall-waving palms" identifies this landscape as non-European, but the scene's relationship with the exile appears comparable to that described between nature and the mourner in the preceding poem. The natural environment exists unto itself in each case, despite its pronounced effect on human beings: solace for the mourner and anguish for the exile. The independence of nature from humankind appears even more emphatic in the exile's case; he laments, for example, that the flowers "bloom not for me."

On the other hand, the presence of this lament suggests the possibility of a more intimate relationship between nature and human beings than could be accommodated in "On a Mourner." This possibility is confirmed throughout the remaining stanzas:

> I see thee, Bassorah! in splendour retiring,
>   Where thy waves and thy walls in their majesty meet;
> I see the bright glory thy pinnacles firing,
>   And broad vassal river that rolls at thy feet.
>
> I see thee but faintly — thy tall towers are beaming
>   On the dusky horizon so far and so blue;
> And minaret and mosque in the distance are gleaming,
>   While the coast of the stranger expands on my view.
>
> I see thee no more: for the deep waves have parted
>   The land of my birth from her desolate son;
> And I am gone from thee, though half broken-hearted,
>   To wander through climes where thy name is unknown.
>
> Farewell to my harp, which I hung in my anguish
>   On the lonely palmetto that nods to the gale;
> For its sweet-breathing tones in forgetfulness languish,
>   And around it the ivy shall weave a green veil.
>
> Farewell to the days which so smoothly have glided
>   With the maiden whose look was like Cama's young glance,[103]
> And the sheen of whose eyes was the load-star which guided
>   My course on this earth through the storms of mischance! (9–28)

---

[103] By "Cama," Tennyson may have had in mind the Hindu god of love, although it is unlikely that many residents of Basra would have known of this deity.

The exile's spiritual closeness to the landscape before him may recall the mutuality of the romantic relationship between nature and human beings. However, the scene Tennyson describes here is not natural in the sense of Hemans's image of the Scottish highlands or Wordsworth's of the Rhone. The exile's depiction of the city of Basra mingles natural phenomena (the river, the horizon) with elements of the built environment (walls, towers, minaret and mosque), following the pattern set by Byron and retraced by Arnold.[104] Whereas European nature is typically defined in contradistinction to human productions like urban buildings, the environment of the exile of Basra does not maintain such a boundary. He perceives his beloved city as a composite of natural and constructed elements.[105] His devotion to it does not appear to be qualitatively different from his attachment to the strictly natural environment he describes in the first two stanzas. Moreover, the exile experiences the same acute separateness from the scene, regardless of the level of human contribution to the landscape.

While the poem, which is based upon the *1001 Nights* story of Nûr al-dîn's banishment to Baghdad, never spells out the reason for the speaker's exile, it certainly leaves the impression that his departure is not voluntary.[106] The exiled speaker's inability to remain in contact with the landscape makes a very unlikely scenario according to the standard romantic model, where nature is reliably present and available to be appreciated by those who desire to do so. Thus not only does the environment depicted in this poem not satisfy the usual romantic criteria because of its contamination by urban elements, but the poem's central human figure is unable to maintain his relationship with this environment, despite his desire for it. The poem's theme is his grief at this loss; in larger terms it also expresses dismay at the prospect of losing the handy, comfortable, inspirational romantic relationship with nature.

Pauline Fletcher argues that "[a]s he matured, Tennyson moved [...] toward landscapes that included or reflected human society."[107] "Written by an Exile"

---

[104] Fletcher emphasizes the importance of public gardens in the Victorian recognition of nature's presence in urban surroundings; see Fletcher, *Gardens and Grim Ravines* 98. The case here is quite different, however. Whereas the point of a public garden is its separateness from the industrial city that surrounds it, the effect of Tennyson's depiction of Basra (like Byron's and Arnold's) is to diminish, even eliminate, any such separateness between natural phenomena and urban, human construction.

[105] Tennyson's description of Iran in his 1827 poem "Persia" is, like that of Basra here, based on a combination of urban structures and natural features (hills, valleys, plains, rivers, vegetation). Although thematically the two poems bear little resemblance to one another, they make very similar use of their settings.

[106] See W.D. Paden, *Tennyson in Egypt: A Study of the Imagery in His Earlier Work* (Lawrence, KS: U of Kansas Publications, 1942) 130–1. According to Paden, Nûr al-dîn was banished from Basra for seducing a girl who was supposed to enter the king's harem. Tennyson's only reference to this element of the *1001 Nights*' story (the "maiden" of the final stanza) is remarkably chaste.

[107] Fletcher, *Gardens and Grim Ravines* 18.

is of course not at all a poem of Tennyson's maturity, yet it exhibits just such a landscape. Randy J. Fertel observes a similar movement away from a romantic vision of nature in Tennyson's late *Idylls of the King* (1862), in which he says that "Tennyson adopts an antipastoral strategy: the subtle subversion of pastoral conventions to illuminate pastoral's false idealism, hollow sentimentality, and vicious passivity."[108] Again, however, we find this same tendency in the very early "Written by an Exile," as the poem emphasizes both the corruption of the natural environment and the impossibility of a sustained engagement with nature. In short, at the very beginning of his career, Tennyson seems to be already experimenting with ideas that would blossom only years later, ideas that would define his place as a Victorian, rather than a romantic, poet. That he should choose a Middle Eastern subject for this experiment in poetics not only confirms the significance of orientalism in the evolution of Tennyson's poetics but also suggests once again orientalism's potency as an aesthetic alternative for nineteenth-century poets.

Orientalist poetics, Oscar Wilde

The seven poets of this chapter — Wordsworth, Hemans, Leconte de Lisle, Gautier, Byron, Arnold, and Tennyson — certainly do not form a unified group of like-minded individuals. Yet each writes poems in which the outdoor environment of the Middle East differs so significantly from European nature, in its features and in its relationship with human beings, that it is no longer fundamentally natural according to European standards. In each case, despite its difference, Middle Eastern nature can anchor a poem much as European nature does, but, because of its difference, the poem will not repeat the European pattern. The result is orientalist poetics, a theory and practice within which poets experiment with alternatives to the representation of nature.

Given the enormous significance of the concept of nature in the British and French poetic traditions, it is important to consider further what difference it makes to a poem to be grounded not in the representation of nature but instead in the representation of the Orient as an (unnatural) nature. The question to be answered is whether (or how) the resulting poem will reveal its differences from the romantic standard. Does the choice not to represent nature in its purer and more limited sense of "the natural world" have an impact on the poetic function of nature in its grander classic sense, in which mimesis is the representation or imitation of nature? In other words, how is the representational or mimetic character of poetry affected by the absence of nature as a solid aesthetic foundation?

---

[108] Randy Fertel, "Antipastoral and the Attack on Naturalism in Tennyson's *Idylls of the King*," *Victorian Poetry* 19.4 (1981): 337.

Writing near the end of the Victorian era, Oscar Wilde gestures towards an answer to this question. In "The Decay of Lying" (1889), an essay whose thesis is that nature and human life are properly the imitators of art (rather than vice versa, as is conventionally theorized), Wilde extols orientalism as a model for art that "break[s] from the prison-house of realism."[109] He outlines

> the struggle between Orientalism, with its frank rejection of imitation, its love of artistic convention, its dislike to the actual representation of any object in Nature, and our own imitative spirit. Wherever the former has been paramount, as in Byzantium, Sicily and Spain, by actual contact or in the rest of Europe by the influence of the Crusades, we have had beautiful and imaginative work in which the visible things of life are transmuted into artistic conventions, and the things that Life has not are invented and fashioned for her delight. But wherever we have returned to Life and Nature, our work has always become vulgar, common and uninteresting.[110]

Curtis Marez argues that for Wilde, "non-Western ornament could serve as raw material inspiring the artist-critic, but it could not itself be classified as art."[111] Even so, when Wilde volunteers "Orientalism" as an emancipator from the requirements of "Life and Nature," he is clearly promoting oriental artwork as an anti-mimetic ideal with the potential, as Marez says, to "inject […] new life into a moribund aesthetic tradition."[112] He expresses none of the regret that Arnold and Tennyson, and to a lesser degree Leconte de Lisle and Gautier, reveal at foregoing a romantic view of nature.[113] Wilde instead looks with pleasure to the Orient as the basis for an art liberated from the preoccupation

---

[109] Wilde, "The Decay of Lying" 981.

[110] Wilde, "The Decay of Lying" 979. This point belongs to Wilde's character Vivian, who is discussing the decorative arts, with reference as well to drama and the novel. Wilde's impression of "Orientalism" (he uses the term to connote the oriental rather than the orientalist) is drawn largely from stereotypes of Eastern art. Both Arabic script calligraphy and the Islamic prohibition on the representation of the human figure were well known in nineteenth-century Europe; both have repeatedly been held up as an example of oriental art's antimimetic bias.

[111] Curtis Marez, "The Other Addict: Reflections on Colonialism and Oscar Wilde's Opium Smoke Screen," *ELH* 64.1 (1997): 266.

[112] Marez, "The Other Addict" 279. Zhou Xiaoyi makes a very similar argument but emphasizes the importance of Japan as "an artistic Utopia" to the virtual exclusion of other oriental locations and artistic traditions ("Oscar Wilde's Orientalism and Late Nineteenth-Century European Consumer Culture," *Ariel: A Review of International English Literature* 28.4 [1997]: 52). Jeff Nunokawa's argument is comparable; see Nunokawa, "Oscar Wilde in Japan: Aestheticism, Orientalism and the Derealization of the Homosexual," *Oscar Wilde: A Collection of Critical Essays*, ed. Jonathan Freedman (Upper Saddle River, NJ: Prentice Hall, 1996) 153–7.

[113] For discussion of Wilde's aesthetic position as antiromantic, see Neil Sammells, "Wilde Nature," *Writing the Environment: Ecocriticism and Literature*, ed. Richard Kerridge and Neil Sammells (London: Zed, 1998) 125–6, 131.

with the representation of nature.[114] He differs from Thomas Love Peacock and E.J. Chételat only in his attitude; Wilde sees such freedom as highly desirable, while Peacock remains suspicious and Chételat hostile.

That Wilde should concur on this fundamental point with critics writing sixty and seventy years earlier is evidence of orientalism's role as the nineteenth century's predominant aesthetic other. Orientalism's distinctive and persistent presence as the embodiment of the unnatural is important to the evolution of poetics throughout the century. Orientalism functions as a medium for a succession of avant-garde poetic experiments, independent in varying degrees from the imitation of nature.

---

[114] Marez offers a more politicized reading of Wilde's stance, arguing that "Wilde in effect sustained his identification with the British Union and European culture by racializing ornamental otherness as a subsidiary adjunct to an Aesthetic Empire" (Marez, "The Other Addict" 258).

To a degree, William Jones's aesthetic philosophy prefigures Wilde's. Like Wilde, he looks to Asia for the rejuvenation of "our *European* poetry[, which has] subsisted too long on the perpetual repetition of the same images, and the incessant allusions to the same fables," as he explains in "An Essay on the Poetry of the Eastern Nations" (1772). But whereas Wilde, like the other nineteenth-century critics and poets I have discussed, sees an East valuable (or distasteful) for its movement away from nature as the ultimate aesthetic model, Jones finds instead in the Arabic, Persian, and Turkish literary traditions a laudable devotion to the representation of nature. For instance, Jones asks rhetorically "where can we find so much beauty as in the *Eastern* poems, which turn chiefly upon the loveliest objects in nature?" and he later praises the Persian epic poet Ferdûsî by saying that, like Homer, he "drew [his] images from nature herself" (Jones, *Works* 10:359, 332, 355; emphasis his). Thus despite his partial depriveleging of mimesis in his "Essay on the Arts, Commonly Called Imitative" (1772), it is Middle Eastern poetry's fidelity to nature that he offers as a remedy for neoclassicism's mannerist tendencies.

Chapter 4

The Orient's art, orienting art

When Oscar Wilde celebrates orientalism as a route to art's freedom from the representation of nature, he effectively encapsulates orientalism's most significant aesthetic function in the nineteenth century. The present chapter will show, through readings of poems by Wordsworth, Leconte de Lisle, Gautier, Landor, Moore, Hemans, and Tennyson, as well as Wilde, how the Orient's affiliation with the artful enables it to play a role approximating that which Wilde theorizes for it in retrospect. The Orient's crucial part in nineteenth-century poetics' movement away from an essentially romantic view of the purpose of literary art and towards aestheticism and the belief in the value of art for art's sake consistently depends upon the presumption that the Orient is characterized by unnaturalness, as discussed in the preceding chapter. Playing equally important roles, however, are the perception that the Orient is allied with art against nature and the assumption that Islamic Middle Eastern art is essentially antimimetic.

As this chapter will explain, orientalism provides a precious arena in which poets elaborate their attitudes towards art (per se and in contradistinction to nature). Orientalism also supplies poets with a variety of models, drawn from oriental textiles and architecture as well as literature, upon which to base a modified poetics. As orientalism comes increasingly to guide and structure the evolution of poetics, the particular characteristics stereotypical of the Orient — so important earlier in the century — begin to recede in significance; the luxuriance and obsession of romantic-period orientalist writing fades. What remains instead in the art for art's sake movements in both Britain (aestheticism) and France (Parnassianism) is an orientalism that is superficially suppressed yet fundamental to the poetics of the time.

A confederation of the Middle East and art: Wordsworth

Grudgingly and with skepticism, William Wordsworth's "The Haunted Tree" takes a first, essential step towards the destination Wilde announces seventy years later.[1] Wordsworth's unstated starting point is an assumed opposition

---

[1] Probably composed in 1819, "The Haunted Tree" was first published in 1820.

between nature and the East. To this he applies a second assumption, that of an affiliation between the East and art. The poem opens with praise for various features of a distinctly English landscape. The speaker mentions "rocks, fields, [and] woods" (5) before narrowing his focus to two types of vegetation heavily associated with England but not with the Orient: "the time-dismantled Oak" (7) and the "heath, which now, attired / In the whole fulness of its bloom" (8–9). Beneath the oak, the flowering heath "affords / Couch beautiful as e'er for earthly use / Was fashioned" (9–11). Although the pastoral scene described is eminently natural, beautiful couches can be fashioned either

> by the hand of Art,
> That eastern Sultan, amid flowers enwrought
> On silken tissue, might diffuse his limbs
> In languor; or, by Nature, for repose
> Of panting Wood-nymph, wearied with the chase. (11–15)

Wordsworth's figuring of art in the domain of an eastern sultan both confirms and capitalizes upon the association between the Middle East and art, while at the same time reinforcing the disjunction between the Middle East and nature. Wordsworth gives several clues to the unnaturalness of this sultan, who becomes a pivotal figure in the poem's aesthetics. The scene in which he appears, for instance, is clearly meant to be indoors, whereas nature is presented as an outdoor phenomenon throughout the remainder of the poem. Further, the sultan's languor appears unnatural, especially by comparison with the wood nymph's recent exertion, or even with the more stately exercise of the "Lady" who is the poem's true object of admiration. Although the wood nymph's mythical identity might seem at first to place her too in the category of the unnatural, she is closely affiliated with the European literary tradition in which the presence of such mythical figures is understood (paradoxically) to enhance the naturalness of a scene. Her participation in this tradition allows the poem to call upon nature not only as environment (as in the first eleven lines) but also as the premier standard of moral rightness — a standard that the languid sultan would be unlikely to meet.[2]

In "The Haunted Tree" and elsewhere, the alliance between the Orient and art is to a degree one of convenience: if both art and the Middle East are defined ontologically in terms of their opposition to nature, an association

---

[2] Wordsworth's choice of "languor" as the sultan's chief characteristic creates an additional point of contrast between the sultan and the nymph. Because "languor" is normally coded as feminine in English literature, Wordsworth's attribution of "languor" to the sultan feminizes him. A feminized sultan is a more unnatural one. Moreover, if there is no longer an absolute distinction of gender between the sultan and the nymph, the difference in the two figures' relations with the natural becomes all the more determinative of their identities, and the sultan's unnaturalness is thus brought even further into relief.

between them becomes inevitable.[3] The linkage of East and art is specified in "The Haunted Tree" in the image of the "flowers enwrought / On silken tissue." While the sultan is, like the speaker on the heath, surrounded by flowers, the sultan's flowers are not fresh, natural blossoms. Art's ability to make the silk bloom suggests the extent to which art in the Middle East usurps the place of nature, which is responsible for producing flowers elsewhere.[4] Art and the Middle East stand together in this poem, juxtaposed to nature, which is, in the guise of oak and heath, all "our human sense [doth] / Ask, for its pleasure" (5–6). This usurpation is quickly terminated as the poem proceeds to elide even the most innocuous aspects of the supernatural and instead casts the natural landscape as the self-sufficient observer both of the Lady and of its own beauties. By removing the speaker as observer, the poem posits the possibility of what Saree Makdisi terms in another context "a non-artistic form of natural poetry,"[5] a mode sharply divergent from that represented by the languid sultan in his ornamented surroundings. Thus nature's primacy is once again asserted, but only after the artful Orient's brief intrusion has played its key role in crystallizing the poem's aesthetic stance.

The Middle East as a source of art: Leconte de Lisle

While Wordsworth recognizes a connection between the Middle East and art, he rejects both rather than explore the potential this connection might have.[6] In contrast, when Leconte de Lisle describes nature in light of his own confederation of the Middle East and art, his poems reveal a consistent and

---

[3] Another poem in which Wordsworth relies upon an opposition between nature and art is his sonnet beginning "*A Poet!* He hath put his heart to school" (1842). This poem advocates a close relationship between poetry and nature. "Art" is presented as detrimental to poetry; let "[t]hy Art be Nature," he urges poets. The poem has no orientalist component.

Abrams would see the opposition of art to nature as characteristic of Wordsworth's critical philosophy. He argues that "'ornament' in Wordsworth's criticism becomes an entirely pejorative term," for "all art [...] was in his phrase 'the adversary of nature'" (Abrams, *The Correspondent Breeze: Essays on English Romanticism* [New York: Norton, 1984] 9, 12). Abrams does not acknowledge the oriental associations of either ornament or art, but they are more than clear in "The Haunted Tree." Other critics contest or complicate Abrams's view of Wordsworth's aesthetic devotion to nature; see for example Jones, "Double Economics"; Latimer, "Real Culture and Unreal Nature" esp. 46; and Makdisi, *Romantic Imperialism* 14–15.

[4] Byron's *The Bride of Abydos* depicts a similarly unnatural and artful interior scene; Zuleikha too has a "silken Ottoman," and "round her lamp of fretted gold / Bloom flowers in urns of China's mould" (2.64, 78–9).

[5] Makdisi, *Romantic Imperialism* 20.

[6] The Dream of the Arab episode of *The Prelude* (bk. 5) implies a somewhat more receptive attitude. Both the Arab's possession of books while traveling through a desert wasteland and his identification with a character from Cervantes suggest this figure's link with literary art. Still, the speaker welcomes the Arab, showing little of the hostility evident both in "The Haunted Tree" and thirty years earlier in "Septimi Gades" (see chapter 3).

significant appreciation of the resulting aesthetic possibilities. For Leconte de Lisle, the Orient's link with art positions it as an important source of inspiration; the artful East is a poetic origin for him, much as the pastoral landscape is for Wordsworth.

The centrality of the Orient to Leconte de Lisle's poetics becomes clear in analysis of two poems, both entitled "L'Orient" ["The Orient"] but written at opposite ends of his career.[7] Although the two poems share a single sensibility to a remarkable degree, the earlier one is more exuberant and more confident in its ability to reach the aesthetic ideal it projects:

> Comme un rubis superbe aux vives étincelles,
> Vous brillez aux regards, poétiques et belles,
>   O rives d'Orient!
> Sur vos sables dorés l'onde est bleuâtre et claire,
> Tous vos jours sont de feux et vos nuits de lumière,
>   Vous êtes le Levant.
>
> Vous êtes le Levant aux merveilles humaines,
> Aux vieux harems d'amour où la vie est sans peines,
>   Au splendide turban,
> Au costume idéal, au noble cimeterre,
> A l'arabe coursier volant dans la poussière
>   Aux combats du Croissant!
>
> O rives d'Orient, mon âme vous devine,
> Vous murmurez ainsi que l'onde crystalline
>   Qui coule en nos vallons,
> Vous êtes le doux vent qui fraîchit nos prairies
> Et fait couler au loin leurs surfaces fleuries
>   En de légers festons.
>
> Quand vient l'ombre du soir, comme une palme blanche
> Qui couronne vos bords, la vague qui s'épanche
>   Et rit sur votre sein,
> Semble, aux lueurs des cieux, une écharpe brodée,
> Sur votre humide cou négligemment jetée,
>   A replis de satin.
>
> Vous êtes le palais de brillante féerie,
> Vous êtes le seul vase où l'on puise la vie,
>   Et le droit de l'aimer;

---

[7] The first of these poems is of uncertain date (1836?), but was definitely composed early in Leconte de Lisle's life. It was not published until 1899, five years after his death. The second, written in 1886, was probably intended for his announced collection *Poèmes byzantins* [*Byzantine Poems*], which he did not live to complete. This later "L'Orient" first appeared in collection in the posthumous volume *Derniers poèmes* [*Last Poems*]. See for more information *Oeuvres de Leconte de Lisle* 3: xx, 228; 4: 21.

De l'empire d'amour vous êtes la richesse.
O rives d'Orient, le regard ne vous laisse
  Que pour vous rechercher!

[Like a superb ruby of vivid brilliance, / You sparkle on sight, poetic and beautiful, / Oh shores of Orient! / On your gilded sands the water is bluish and clear, / All your days are of fire and your nights of light, / You are the Levant.

You are the Levant of the human marvels, / Of the old harems of love where life is without cares, / Of the splendid turban, / Of the ideal costume, of the noble scimitar, / Of the Arab charger flying through the dust / To the battles of the Crescent!

Oh shores of Orient, my soul understands you, / You murmur just like the crystalline water / That flows in our vales, / You are the gentle wind that cools our meadows / And makes their flowered surfaces flow far and wide / In waving festoons.

When the shadow of evening comes, like a white palm tree / That crowns your edges, the wave that overflows / And smiles on your breast / Seems, in the heavens' gleam, an embroidered scarf, / Negligently tossed on your moist neck / In folds of satin.

You are the palace of sparkling enchantment, / You are the only vessel from which is drawn life / And the right to love it; / You are the wealth of the empire of love. / Oh shores of Orient, the gaze never leaves you / Except to seek you again.]

After delineating the stereotypical marvels of oriental nature, humanity, and splendor in the first two stanzas, the speaker demonstrates in the third stanza that the origin of beauty lies in the East. He begins with a simile ("O rives d'Orient [...] / Vous murmurez ainsi que l'onde crystalline / Qui coule en nos vallons" [Oh shores of Orient ... / You murmur just like the crystalline water / That flows in our valley]) that creates a parallel between the Orient and an almost Wordsworthian, rural, European landscape. Leconte de Lisle's speaker posits this correspondence with the absolute confidence of spiritual authority: "mon âme vous devine" [my soul understands you]. He then restates the Orient's role unmediated by any figure of speech: "Vous êtes le doux vent qui fraîchit nos prairies / Et fait couler au loin leurs surfaces fleuries / En de légers festons" [You are the gentle wind that cools our meadows / And makes their flowered surfaces flow far and wide / In waving festoons]. The Orient now becomes responsible for creating beauty from the raw material of the Occident. Without the gentle wind of the Orient, the meadows merely grow flowers; with it, they are festooned.

Leconte de Lisle's choice of this particular image is important. The flowery meadows would, of course, have natural beauty, but the oriental wind offers a different option, one that is artful rather than natural even while it enhances the natural beauty of the meadows. If Wordsworth's search for "a *non*-artistic form of natural poetry"[8] entails rejecting the East, Leconte de Lisle's vision of an artistic form of natural poetry requires welcoming and exploiting it. The aesthetic ideal Leconte de Lisle expresses in this poem corresponds in its essential respects with the position outlined by Jacques Derrida in discussion of Hegel: "artistic beauty is superior to natural beauty, as the mind that produces it is superior to nature. One must therefore say that absolute beauty, the *telos* or final essence of the beautiful, appears in art and not in nature as such."[9] In the context of this poem, the transformation from flowers to festoons indicates the creative power of the Orient, its ability to convert natural material into artificial, decorative structure.[10] Thus the oriental(ized), not the natural, assumes the role of the beautiful, and orientalism, as the producer of the beautiful, takes on the status of "the mind [...] superior to nature."

The subsequent stanza supplies another example of the Orient's transformative powers. The starting point is again a natural scene: a wave coming up over the shore's edge at evening. However, because the scene is set in the Orient, it connotes from the outset artistic as much as natural beauty. The wave is compared to a palm tree, that quintessential element of conventionalized Middle Eastern nature. This palm/wave "couronne" [crowns] the shores; the term alludes both to architecture and to the splendid ornaments of royalty. In either case, a presumably natural (and geographically generic) image of waves washing ashore has become not only specifically orientalized but also thereby reinterpreted through simile as a product of human art rather than of natural forces.[11]

To this already complex image, Leconte de Lisle adds yet another simile; the wave now "semble [...] une écharpe brodée, / Sur votre humide cou négligemment jetée, / A replis de satin" [seems ... an embroidered scarf, / Negligently tossed on your moist neck / In folds of satin]. Here again, the natural image is displaced through a comparison with a work of art: an embroidered scarf. Like the first simile, this one has a definitely oriental flavor; we might remember the "flowers enwrought / On silken tissue" with

---

[8] Makdisi, *Romantic Imperialism* 20; emphasis mine.

[9] Derrida, *The Truth in Painting* 25.

[10] For a technical discussion of festoons and of their connection with the arabesque, see Wilhelm Worringer, *Abstraction and Empathy: A Contribution to the Psychology of Style*, 1908, trans. Michael Bullock (New York: International Universities P, 1967) 73–6.

[11] Leconte de Lisle's approach here is comparable to that in another of his early poems, "Le Palmier" [The Palm Tree] (publ. 1899). Again, the Middle Eastern natural scene is construed as inherently artful: "Oriental, / Original, / Féérique même!" [Oriental, / Original, / Enchanting even!].

which Wordsworth surrounds his "eastern Sultan" in "The Haunted Tree," or the many nineteenth-century paintings of supposed odalisques, draped or surrounded with folds of cloth (no doubt "négligemment jetée" as well). Moreover, richly decorated clothwares such as this embroidered scarf are, like ornamented architectural details, classic representatives of oriental art.[12] The scarf supplements the previously described crowning so as to entirely overwhelm the initial natural image of the wave with a specifically oriental artfulness. In this context, the orient(al), including the Orient's natural environment, appears as fully and inherently artful.

"L'Orient" ends with an even grander assessment of the East's importance. The Orient is, the speaker concludes, "le seul vase où l'on puise la vie / Et le droit de l'aimer / De l'empire d'amour vous êtes la richesse" [the only vessel from which is drawn life / And the right to love it; / You are the wealth of the empire of love.][13] In short, it is the spiritual origin and destination of humankind.[14] Yet even this extraordinary status is grounded in the Orient's association with art; the Orient is "le palais de brillante féerie" [the palace of sparkling enchantment]. To identify the Orient as a palace inevitably recalls the poem's related earlier allusions: to ornamented architecture, to luxurious harems. A palace is, moreover, a work of art in itself. That this should be a palace of "sparkling enchantment" is only to be expected, for Leconte de Lisle's Orient is nothing if not sparkling, and enchantment too is an art. If, as the poem's final line says of the Orient, "le regard ne vous laisse / Que pour vous rechercher" [the gaze never leaves you / Except to seek you again], that is very much in keeping with the Orient's role as an aesthetic origin. It is, in effect, the point of reference to which the poet must always return.

Thus not only does this first "L'Orient" assume that art flourishes in and defines the East — two important suppositions in themselves — but it also gives the East a virtually unlimited sphere of influence. Once the Orient has been accepted as a source for art, it must also inform (if not actually dictate) the sort of art to which it gives rise. Leconte de Lisle implements this notion here in a supremely confident but relatively superficial fashion, embroidering

---

[12] Arnold, for instance, uses a similar reference to clothwares when he establishes the oriental setting at the beginning of "The Sick King in Bokhara." Gautier's inclusion of a cashmere scarf in his "Les Souhaits" (to be discussed shortly) offers yet another example.

[13] It is significant that Leconte de Lisle shifts from the "nous" [we] of stanza 3 to "on" [one] here. "Nous" implied an opposition between the Orient ("vous" [you]), and the Occident of "nos vallons" and "nos prairies" [our vales, our meadows]. The opposition between "vous" and "on" is much weaker and suggests at least the possibility of an occidental self being incorporated into the oriental; this possibility is very much in keeping with the poem's optimism about the speaker's relationship with the Orient.

[14] There is of course also a literal component of this idea of the Orient as origin, embedded particularly in the term "Levant." The Orient is the place of the rising sun, symbolically the birthplace of the world. The Christian mythology of a holy land in the Levant adds further depth to these classical associations.

his poem like the embroidered scarf of the fourth stanza. His second "L'Orient," a sonnet, adopts a more measured approach and reveals a greater awareness of orientalism's competitors, but it shares its predecessor's basic tenets, presenting the Orient as a spiritual and aesthetic source.

> Vénérable Berceau du monde, où l'Aigle d'or,
> Le soleil, du milieu des Roses éternelles,
> Dans l'espace ébloui qui sommeillait encor
> Ouvrit sur l'Univers la splendeur de ses ailes!
>
> Fleuves sacrés, forêts, mers aux flots radieux,
> Ame ardente des fleurs, neiges des vierges cimes,
> O très saint Orient, qui conçus tous les Dieux,
> Puissant évocateur des visions sublimes!
>
> Vainement, à l'étroit dans ton immensité,
> Flagellés du désir de l'occident mythique,
> En des siècles lointains nos pères t'ont quitté;
>
> Le vivant souvenir de la Patrie antique
> Fait toujours, dans notre ombre et nos rêves sans fin,
> Resplendir ta lumière à l'horizon divin.
>
> [Venerable cradle of the world, where the eagle of gold, / The sun, from the midst of the eternal roses, / In the dazzled space that was slumbering still, / Opened the splendor of its wings onto the Universe!
>
> Sacred rivers, forests, seas with shining waves, / Fiery soul of flowers, snows of untrodden peaks, / Oh most holy Orient, which conceived all the gods, / Powerful summoner of sublime visions!
>
> In vain, constricted within your immensity / Flagellated by desire for the mythic Occident, / In distant centuries our forefathers left you;
>
> The living memory of the ancient country / Always makes, in our shadow and our endless dreams / Your light resplendent on the divine horizon.]

Like its predecessor, this poem introduces the Orient in the context of an otherwise undistinguished natural image — in this case, the sunrise. Playing on the word "Orient"'s related meaning, "east," the speaker offers the Orient as the "vénérable Berceau du monde" [venerable cradle of the world], incorporating into his depiction conventional terminology such as "or" [gold] and "splendeur" [splendor].[15] This Edenic Orient then appears as a primary creative force: "O très saint Orient, qui conçus tous les Dieux, / Puissant évocateur des visions sublimes!" [Oh most holy Orient, which conceived all the gods, / Powerful summoner of sublime visions!]. The implicit linkage between the Orient and the idea of Paradise recalls Leconte de Lisle's "Le Désert" (discussed in chapter 3), but the Orient's aesthetic function here has more in common with that of the first "L'Orient." As there, the East is both a source for art and a persistent point of reference.

On the other hand, this poem's East is far more starkly and explicitly distinguished from the Occident than its predecessor's, in which there is no substantial discontinuity between the speaker's own occidental world and the Orient to which he looks with such admiration. When he proclaims that the Orient is the sole vessel in which life and love are possible, he does not appear to deny himself entry into that vessel. In contrast, the second "L'Orient" presents Orient and Occident as mutually exclusive alternatives. The speaker seems resigned to his ancestors' abandonment of the Orient in favor of "l'occident mythique" [the mythic occident] — an abandonment that Leconte de Lisle mirrors by choosing the strictly occidental sonnet form for this poem rather than the more expansive (and perhaps more orientalized) form of the first "L'Orient."

Leconte de Lisle also comes much closer in this poem to the conservative orientalism exemplified by Hugo's "Novembre" (discussed in chapter 2). Like Hugo, he indicates that memories and impressions of the Orient continue to guide aesthetic and spiritual life in the Occident, even while true participation in the world of the Orient seems beyond the speaker's reach.[16] However, "Novembre" lacks the sense of regret evident in this poem, which appears to long for the Orient rather than welcoming the return to the Occident. In the end, Leconte de Lisle presents the Orient as an origin from whose heights the Occident has fallen. Although the story of such a fall is of course fundamental to the history of Western culture (from the biblical Eden onwards), its particular aesthetic significance is foregrounded here through Leconte de Lisle's orientalism.

By resorting to the Orient, Leconte de Lisle articulates, in both poems, a specific and powerful aesthetic vision, in which the Orient assumes a formative role in both the genesis and development of art. That this conception of the Orient was useful to him at both ends of his career, despite evident changes in his aesthetic philosophy, suggests once again the potency of the East as a

---

[15] Leconte de Lisle's formulation here again reflects the convention of the Levant as the place of the rising sun and origin of the world.

[16] The fact that the speaker of the second "L'Orient" uses "tu" [you, familiar form] rather than "vous" [you, formal form] to address the East, despite the greater distance between speaker and Orient in this poem than in the first "L'Orient," suggests an intimacy unaffected by distance or inaccessibility.

standard in literary art. Whether this standard is attainable, as in his earlier poem, or not, as in his later one, the Orient continues to dominate Leconte de Lisle's poetics.

Middle Eastern art and Gautier's imagination

At the heart of the Orient's status as aesthetic source is the notion of the imagination, the ability to envision and express in artistic form what does not exist in empirical reality. Leconte de Lisle alludes to this in his second "L'Orient" when he calls the Orient "Puissant évocateur des visions sublimes" [Powerful summoner of sublime visions], but he does not devote particular attention to it. His colleague Théophile Gautier, on the other hand, places the imagination and its relationship with orientalism right at the center of his poem "Les Souhaits" ["The Wishes"] (1830).[17] This poem presents an imagination turned free to desire whatever it would; the result is a distinctly orientalized vision of art as well as of love.

"Les Souhaits" begins with a relatively generic fantasy:

> Si quelque jeune fée à l'aile de saphir,
>   Sous une sombre et fraîche arcade,
> Blanche comme un reflet de la perle d'Orphir,
> Surgissait à mes yeux, au doux bruit du zéphyr,
>   De l'écume de la cascade,
>
> Me disant: Que veux-tu? larges coffres pleins d'or,
>   Palais immenses, pierreries?
> Parle; mon art est grand: te faut-il plus encor?
> Je te le donnerai; je puis faire un trésor
>   D'un vil monceaux [sic] d'herbes flétries (1–10)

[If some young fairy with sapphire wings, / Under a somber, cool arcade, / White as a reflection of the pearl of Ophir, / Appeared before my eyes at the sweet sound of the breeze, / Of the waterfall's froth,

Saying to me: What do you want? Large chests full of gold, / Immense palaces, gems? / Speak; my art is great: what more do you need? / I will give it to you: I could make a treasure / From a worthless heap of withered grass]

---

[17] "Les Souhaits" was first published in Gautier's early collection *Poésies*.

Only the casual mention of Ophir identifies this fantasy of a wish-granting fairy as oriental.[18] The opulence of the wishes she proposes does conform to the stereotype of the oriental, and her position under an "arcade" could be construed as oriental since arches are commonly associated with Middle Eastern architecture, but neither of these elements has an explicitly oriental cast. However, the remainder of "Les Souhaits" is orientalist in the conventional nineteenth-century fashion. As the speaker answers his hypothetical fairy, he spins a broadly imperialist fantasy that presents the Orient in all its stereotyped glory:

> Je lui dirais: Je veux un ciel riant et pur
>   Réfléchi par un lac limpide,
> Je veux un beau soleil qui luise dans l'azur,
> Sans que jamais brouillard, vapeur, nuage obscur
>   Ne voilent son orbe splendide;
>
> Et pour bondir sous moi je veux un cheval blanc,
>   Enfant léger de l'Arabie,
> A la crinière longue, à l'oeil étincelant,
> Et, comme l'hippogriffe, en une heure volant
>   De la Norvège à la Nubie;
>
> Je veux un kiosque rouge, aux minarets dorés,
>   Aux minces colonnes d'albâtre,
> Aux fantasques arceaux d'oeufs pendants décorés,
> Aux murs de mosaïque, aux vitraux colorés
>   Par où se glisse un jour bleuâtre;
>
> Et quand il fera chaud, je veux un bois mouvant
>   De sycomores et d'yeuses,
> Qui me suive partout au souffle d'un doux vent,
> Comme un grand éventail sans cesse soulevant
>   Ses masses de feuilles soyeuses.
>
> Je veux une tartane avec ses matelots,
>   Ses cordages, ses blanches voiles
> Et son corset de cuivre où se brisent les flots,
> Qui me berce le long de verdoyants îlots
>   Aux molles lueurs des étoiles.
>
> Je veux soir et matin m'éveiller, m'endormir
>   Au son de voix italiennes,
> Et pendant tout le jour entendre au loin frémir
> Le murmure plaintif des eaux du Bendemir,
>   Ou des harpes éoliennes;

---

[18] Ophir is a place of unknown location in the biblical East; Solomon is supposed to have sought gold there.

Et je veux, les seins nus, une Almée agitant
  Son écharpe de cachemire
Au-dessus de son front de rubis éclatant,
Des spahis, un harem, comme un riche sultan
  Ou de Bagdad ou de Palmyre.

Je veux un sabre turc, un poignard indien
  Dont le manche de saphirs brille;
Mais surtout je voudrais un coeur fait pour le mien,
Qui le sentît, l'aimât, et qui le comprît bien,
  Un coeur naïf de jeune fille! (11–50)

[I would tell her: I want a pleasant, clear sky, / Reflected in a limpid lake, / I want a beautiful sun that shines on the azure, / Without fog, mist, (or) dark cloud ever / Veiling its splendid orb;

And to bound beneath me I want a white horse, / Fleet offspring of Arabia, / With a long mane, with brilliant eye, / And, like the hippogriff, flying in an hour / From Norway to Nubia;

I want a red kiosk, with gilded minarets, / With slender columns of alabaster, / With fantastic arches of hanging decorated eggs, / With walls of mosaic, with stained-glass windows / Through which the bluish daylight glides;

And when the weather is hot, I want a moving woodland / Of sycamores and ilexes / That follows me everywhere on the breath of a gentle wind, / Like a great fan ceaselessly raising / Its masses of silken leaves.

I want a tartan with its sailors, / Its rigging, its white sails, / And its copper hull where the waves are dashed, / That rocks me the length of verdant islets / By the feeble light of the stars.

I want to wake up and fall asleep, morning and evening, / To the sound of Italian voices, / And throughout the day to hear whispering far away / The plaintive murmur of the waters of Bendemir, / Or of Aeolian harps;

And I want, her breasts bare, an Almah waving / Her scarf of cashmere / Above her forehead sparkling with rubies, / Some spahis, a harem, like a rich sultan / Of either Baghdad or Palmyra.

I want a Turkish saber, an Indian dagger / Whose haft glitters with sapphires; / But above all I would like a heart made for mine, / That would be sensitive to it, love it, and understand it well, / A young girl's naïve heart!]

Although the speaker's fantasy includes substantial elements unrelated to the Orient, it is to the Orient that he returns time and again. Furthermore, the last two stanzas' focus on the East provides the framework for the speaker's final and supreme wish, even though the wish itself (for an innocent young female lover) appears universal rather than specifically Middle Eastern. As a result, the Orient emerges from "Les Souhaits" as the dominant force structuring the speaker's desires, a force that both supports and subsumes his other, nonoriental aspirations.

But ultimately the Orient is more than this, for "Les Souhaits" is about imagination and art as well as love and desire. Although the yearned-for "jeune fille" [young girl] is mentioned only in the poem's last line, she echoes strongly the "jeune fée" [young fairy] of the first line. Alliteration aside, both the "fée" and the "fille" are presented as hypothetical, archetypal figures, as is confirmed by the use of "quelque" [some] (for the fairy) and the indefinite article (for the girl). The girl's innocence is prefigured by the fairy's pearly whiteness. Most importantly, the girl's only named feature is her heart, which is "fait pour le mien, / Qui le sentît, l'aimât, et qui le comprît bien" [made for mine, / That would be sensitive to it, love it, and understand it well]. In other words, this is a girl who will understand his heart's desire — yet that is exactly what the fairy is now also able to do, thanks to the speaker's list of his desires. With the functions of the girl and the fairy essentially duplicating one another in this crucial respect, the speaker's professed desire for the girl becomes a restatement of his desire for the fairy, the same desire that leads him to postulate the fairy's existence in the first place. To use the terms of the poem's final stanza, what the speaker really wants most ("surtout je voudrais"), then, is the fairy. For him, the fairy represents the capacity not only to desire but also to conceive of what he desires: to imagine.[19]

Through the figure of the fairy, "Les Souhaits" defines this ability to imagine as oriental in origin and in character. Although, as noted above, the fairy's association with the Orient is initially slight, it becomes inevitable and potent in the context of the poem as a whole. The oblique orientalist suggestions of the first two stanzas are taken up and affirmed later in the poem. The reference to the arcade, for instance, is reflected and enhanced in the detailed description of Middle Eastern architecture in the fifth stanza. Similarly, the second stanza's allusion to opulent wealth becomes firmly grounded in the Middle East in the penultimate stanza as the speaker lists a rich sultan's possessions. Finally, as the speaker's desires are channeled through the fairy, they become concentrated around the Orient, suggesting a

---

[19] Brahimi says that for Gautier, "[t]he Orient is desire, desire is the Orient"; Lardoux claims that Gautier "makes of the Orient a veritable allegory of his desire" (Brahimi, *Théophile et Judith vont en Orient* 75; Lardoux, "L'Orient dans les poésies de Théophile Gautier" 215). Neither critic, however, notes the aesthetic dimension of this linkage between desire and the Orient.

specific link between the East and the fairy's identity.[20] Another version of this link appears in the speaker's subsequent request for an Arabian horse able to fly, "comme l'hippogriffe, en une heure [...] / De la Norvège à la Nubie" [like the hippogriff, ... in an hour / From Norway to Nubia].[21] Through its supernatural powers, the Arabian horse has very much the same empowering effect on the speaker as the fairy does. It can be no coincidence that the speaker wants the horse, like the fairy, to take him to the Middle East — and to a part of the Middle East (Nubia) that is about as far as one can get from Norway.[22]

Both the vehicle (the fairy) and the content of the speaker's imaginings are, then, fundamentally oriental. If we take as a premise that in claiming to desire a "jeune fille," the speaker is actually also restating his desire for a "jeune fée," we must conclude that the object of his desire is, at bottom, what the fairy represents — the ability to imagine — and further, that this ability is oriental in essence. "Les Souhaits" becomes, in this respect, a statement of aesthetics as much as of personal desire, reframing carnal desire as desire for imagination and then linking the gratification of the desire for imagination with the Orient.[23]

Further, in at least two instances, the poem suggests a connection between the Middle East and art in a more general sense. First, the fairy's opening speech describes her skill in terms of art: "mon art est grand" [my art is great]. This is the fairy's only definitive statement in a stanza that consists mostly of suggestions to the speaker; as a result, these four words acquire a status they might not otherwise. As evidence of her art's greatness, moreover, she explains that she is able to take the uninspiring material of nature and transform it into something of value and beauty: "je puis faire un trésor / D'un vil monceaux [sic] d'herbes flétries" [I could make a treasure / From a worthless heap of withered grass]. The fairy's depiction of her art conforms to the notion that art is to operate upon the raw material provided by nature. However, her view

---

[20] The association between "féerie" [enchantment] and the Orient is familiar from Leconte de Lisle's first "L'Orient," discussed above, and from his "Le Palmier," also noted above. Bulgin observes Gautier's repeated prose use of the term when describing the appeal of Arab Spain; see Bulgin, "L'Appel de l'Orient au voyageur en Espagne" 155.

[21] This steed bears more than a slight resemblance to "Al-Borak" of Leconte de Lisle's "Le Désert" (chapter 3).

[22] Nubia is an area of the Nile valley in southern Egypt and northern Sudan.

[23] Lisa Lowe cites a related example from Gustave Flaubert's *L'Éducation sentimentale* (1869). She describes the appearance of several oriental objects in the novel, arguing that "[t]he motifs are all heterogeneous fragments [...], incomplete allusions to disparate orientalisms, and their fragmentary qualities as motifs call attention to their importance as signifiers, and as marks of desire. Furthermore, the orientalist texts themselves, to which these motifs refer, also represent postures of incompletion, ultimately sentimental paradigms that constitute the invented Orient as a sublime ideal, a lost otherness, a time and space removed from the occidental world. The oriental motif [...] is an emblem of the desire to signify desire" (*Critical Terrains* 97).

rejects the imitation of nature and asserts instead the superiority of art. Thus not only does the fairy's brief statement identify the Middle East with imaginative art, but it also projects a vision of art highly consistent with avant-garde orientalist poetics.

Second, "Les Souhaits" reinforces the linkage of East and art in its elaborate description of the marvels of Middle Eastern architecture. It was, of course, not at all unusual for nineteenth-century Europeans to identify the Islamic Orient with its architecture, especially the arches, columns, domes, and minarets of its mosques. William Thackeray, for instance, says of Islam that "Never did a creed possess temples more elegant."[24] In poetry, as I have shown, the depiction of specifically Middle Eastern architectural forms plays an important role in defining the unnaturalness of oriental nature and in demonstrating the Orient's transmutation of nature into art.[25] "Les Souhaits" itself is only one of a number of Gautier's poems in which Middle Eastern architectural elements appear as a privileged motif.[26] The speaker of "Les Souhaits" grants Oriental architecture a prominent position by making architectural elements the first items he requests after (symbolically) arriving in the Middle East on the back of his Arabian horse. As the poem's first detailed and specific image of the Middle East, the speaker's depiction of Middle Eastern architecture here is in a position to define the terms of the poem's representation of the Middle East.

> Je veux un kiosque rouge, aux minarets dorés,
>   Aux minces colonnes d'albâtre,
> Aux fantasques arceaux d'oeufs pendants décorés,
>   Aux murs de mosaïque

---

[24] Cited in Cotsell, *Creditable Warriors* 36. A thorough discussion of the role of Islamic architecture in nineteenth-century European conceptions of and representations of the Islamic Middle East is provided by Çelik, *Displaying the Orient*. See also Jean-Claude Brunon, "Arabesque, baroque, caprice: essai sur la portée des *Grotesques* dans l'esthétique de Gautier," *L'Art et l'artiste*, vol. 2 (Proc. of International Colloquium, Sept. 1982, Montpellier) esp. 372–3, 377; Grossir, *L'Islam des Romantiques* 95–9; and MacKenzie, *Orientalism* ch. 4.

[25] This process is at odds with that preferred by more skeptical poets such as Wordsworth, whom Wesling describes in this context as having a "love of the assimilation of architecture to nature," rather than vice versa; see Wesling, *Wordsworth and the Adequacy of Landscape* 71.

[26] Distinctly Middle Eastern arches appear in Gautier's "La Jeune fille" (9), "La Basilique" (16–19), and "A l'Alhambra Moresque..." (1–4) ["The Young Girl," "The Basilica," "To the Moorish Alhambra..."]. Other Gautier poems that feature Middle Eastern architectural elements include "Moyen âge," "Ballade," "Portail," "Ce que disent les hirondelles," "L'Hirondelle," and "L'Amour" ["Middle Ages," "Ballad," "Portal," "What the Swallows Say," "The Swallow," "Love"]. Also worth noting is Gautier's prose work *Spirite* [*Spirit*] (written 1865), whose protagonist has an interest in Arab architecture; see Brahimi, *Théophile et Judith vont en Orient* 104. Elwood Hartman explores Gautier's fondness for architecture in general, but emphasizes the poet's preference for oriental architectural styles, both for their forms and for their decorations; see Hartman, *Three Nineteenth-Century French Writer/Artists and the Maghreb: The Literary and Artistic Depictions of North Africa by Théophile Gautier, Eugène Fromentin, and Pierre Loti* (Tübingen: Narr, 1994) esp. 17–19.

> [I want a red kiosk, with gilded minarets, / With slender columns of alabaster, / With fantastic arches of hanging decorated eggs, / With walls of mosaic]

No architectural element goes undecorated, and the decoration is absolutely Middle Eastern, even perhaps arabesque. The artful ornamentation on which Gautier insists in this passage is, moreover, inseparable from the major art form depicted here: the architecture itself. The speaker presents his Middle East as dominated and defined by ornamented architectural forms. His attention to architecture emphasizes not only the Orient's divergence from nature and natural forms but also the great extent to which such divergence is marked as specifically artful (rather than unnatural in the sense of supernatural, for instance). Further, by portraying every oriental architectural element as decorated, from the gilded minarets to the mosaic walls, he allows for a double and even triple artfulness. The architecture is an art form to which yet other art forms (gilding, eggs, mosaic) can be applied as ornamentation; in turn, the decoration applied to the eggs represents a third level of ornamentation.[27] The result has nothing to do with nature, nothing to do with the representation of nature, nothing to do with mimesis — but everything to do with beauty and with art existing unto itself and for its own sake. Rae Beth Gordon argues that "[w]hat Gautier [...] seek[s] in ornamental confusion is a second creation that will rival nature";[28] in "Les Souhaits," it seems, he attempts to materialize the object of this quest.

In the context of the poem as a whole, the fairy's dual allegiance to art and to the Middle East identifies the Middle East with art; the depiction of Middle Eastern architecture strengthens and specifies this connection. Such a connection is also consistent with the fact that the poem mentions no art that is not Middle Eastern in origin, beginning with architecture and following with dance and ornamented weaponry. By privileging architecture in particular, though, Gautier is able to offer a model for art as neither the art-less Occident, nor even the fairy, can do. Art appears exclusively attached to the East, and the

---

[27] Gordon observes that "Gautier admires Moslem invention for its figures that 'decompose ad infinitum in ever-new combinations and meanderings; they serve to express dreams of the infinite.' The intense interest in the Orient [...] prove[s] to be of great importance to the evolution of ornament in the realm of the Imaginary" (*Ornament, Fantasy, and Desire* 13; the Gautier citation is from 1852). See Hartman, *Three Nineteenth-Century French Writer/Artists* 19–20, for a brief analysis of Gautier's admiration for Islamic Arab art, particularly its "new colors and forms — ornaments and arabesques, as exemplified in calligraphy and embroidery." For a discussion of connections between visual and literary "arabesques" elsewhere in Gautier's work, see Jean-Claude Brunon, "Arabesque, Baroque, Caprice" 369–79.

[28] Gordon, *Ornament, Fantasy, and Desire* 16. For additional discussion of Gautier's rejection of nature in favor of art, see Pierre Laubriet, "Théophile Gautier, un annonciateur de l'esprit 'fin de siècle'?" *Bulletin de la Société Théophile Gautier* 13 (1991): 18–20; Schick, "A Case Study of Descriptive Perversion"; and Tennant, *Théophile Gautier* 20–3, 36, 103–4.

East aesthetically central as an origin of art. More significantly, through the beauty of its ornamented architecture, the Orient provides a way towards an art more purely a beautiful product of the imagination: l'art pour l'art, art for art's sake.

"Les Souhaits" was written early in Gautier's career, well before he had articulated a philosophy of "l'art pour l'art," which, like the Middle Eastern architecture he describes in this poem, prefers to dispense with the imitation of nature in favor of purer devotion to beauty and art. Yet it appears that the fundamental inclinations on which he would base this philosophy were, even at this early stage, remarkably secure. His notion of the Middle East as inherently artful allows it to emerge at the very heart of this developing aesthetic philosophy. His ideal of art for its own sake finds a source in the Orient, and specifically in the Islamic Middle East as a place defined by nonrepresentational art forms.

Nightingales and roses I: Walter Savage Landor and oriental literature

The idea of Middle Eastern art as a model for European artists is taken up by nineteenth-century poets in a variety of ways. Gautier's approach is at once among the grandest and the most subtly complex. At this stage of his career, however, Gautier gives little credit to Middle Eastern literature's potential as a model. He is attracted instead to a more generalized notion of art and to the plastic arts in particular. A number of English poems follow a different course, modeling themselves specifically upon Middle Eastern literature, which comes to serve as an important poetic source in its own right. My discussion of such poems begins with two based on the famous Persian trope of the nightingale's unrequited love for the rose: Walter Savage Landor's "The Nightingale and Rose," and Thomas Moore's "Beauty and Song."[29]

Landor's poem tells the story of a "maid" who is saddened by the tale of the besotted nightingale bleeding to death from the wounds inflicted by his beloved rose's thorns.[30] Landor carefully sets the scene before introducing the maid:

---

[29] As John D. Yohannan points out, this Persian story was well known in nineteenth-century England, with Byron, Tennyson, and Wilde making particular use of it; see Yohannan, *Persian Poetry in England and America* 67, 88–9, 97, 219.

[30] "The Nightingale and Rose" was published in Landor's *Works* in 1846; as most work on this edition was completed by 1840, the poem was probably composed by that date; see R.H. Super, *Walter Savage Landor: A Biography* (New York: New York UP, 1954) 289. Landor's engagement with the Middle East began more than four decades before this, with his influential long poem *Gebir* (1798; see chapter 1), and *Poems from the Arabic and Persian* (1800), which contains nine imitations. Landor also has a few orientalist prose works; for more information, see Smith, *Islam in English Literature* 168–71. For further discussion of these

> From immemorial time
>   The Rose and Nightingale
> Attune the Persian rhyme
>   And point the Arab tale:
> Nor will you ever meet
>   So barbarous a man,
> In any outer street
>   Of Balkh or Astracan,
> In any lonely creek
>   Along the Caspian shore,
> Or where the tiger sleek
>   Pants hard in hot Mysore,
> As never shall have heard
>   In tower or tent or grove
> Of the sweet flower's true bird,
>   The true bird's only love.
> They're known wherever shines
>   The crescent on the sword
> And guiltless are the vines
>   And Bacchus is abhorr'd. (1–20)[31]

Landor's approach here is conventional. He presents the Orient as a timeless place in which natural and man-made features are intermingled; the "street" (7) parallels the "creek" (9), and "tower," "tent," and "grove" are all placed in the same category (14). He asserts the area's Muslim identity with reference first to the crescent (18) and then to Islam's prohibition of wine (19–20).

While the diverse places he mentions in these lines are united by these stereotypical characteristics, they all share a more important trait as well: their inhabitants know the story of the nightingale and the rose.[32] The poem's first four lines declare the story's centrality to Middle Eastern literature — "the Persian rhyme," "the Arab tale" — but the rest of the speaker's introduction portrays the nightingale and the rose at the heart of Islamic culture as a whole. By so doing, Landor also grants literary art (of which the nightingale and rose story has become for this purpose the prime example) an exalted status within that culture. In turn, this move implicitly but forcefully characterizes Islamic

---

works, and of Landor's literary interest in the Middle East, see Sharafuddin, *Islam and Romantic Orientalism* ch. 1; and Super, *Walter Savage Landor* esp. 40–6, 48–51, 67–8.

My source for Landor's poetry is *The Poetical Works of Walter Savage Landor*, ed. Stephen Wheeler, 3 vols. (Oxford: Clarendon, 1937).

[31] Balkh is a town in northern Afghanistan. Astracan (mod. sp. "Astrakhan") is a city in eastern Russia near the Kazakh border. Mysore is a city in southern India.

[32] Landor's emphasis on the shared knowledge of this story blurs any functional distinctions among the various Eastern groups mentioned. As I noted in my discussion of Southey in chapter 1, such blurring is typical of nineteenth-century European poets, although it defies the careful efforts of prominent scholarly orientalists such as William Jones and, later, Edward Lane to delineate characteristics of specific groups.

culture in terms of its literary art, rather as Gautier's "Les Souhaits" does in terms of architecture.

Having thus established the story's oriental identity in the poem's frame, the speaker is ready to begin his narrative:[33]

> There was (we read) a maid,
>   The pride of Astrabad,
> Who heard what song-men said,
>   And, all that day, was sad.
> The moon hung large and round;
>   She gazed ere forth she went;
> [...]
> She hasten'd to the wood
>   Where idle bushes grew,
> The Rose above them stood,
>   There stood her lover too.
> Close were they, close as may
>   True lovers ever be! (21–6, 29–34)[34]

The complex position of empirical reality in these lines has substantial aesthetic consequences. Initially, there is no indication that "what song-men said" is anything but completely fictional. Yet when the maid goes outside that evening she finds that the "song-men" are describing a phenomenon that really exists. Thus not only does poetic or literary art characterize the world of the Islamic Orient, as suggested by the poem's introductory frame, but it also represents the reality of that world. In effect, then, there is no distinction between the Middle East's art and its reality: art is reality.

The interchangeability of art and reality is underpinned by the role of nature in this poem. Although nightingales and roses are both natural phenomena, the poem presents them first and foremost as deriving from literature rather than nature. When the maid goes out to the wood, they are then discovered in nature. This represents a nearly Wildean reversal of the classical pattern, in which a natural phenomenon makes its way into literature — not vice versa. Moreover, the "nature" in which the maid finds the nightingale and the rose itself originates in literature. Landor's parenthetical "we read" (21) makes clear that the maid and her surroundings are as much a product of literary art as is

---

[33] Joseph Kestner proposes that Landor's use of a framed narrative in *Gebir* indicates the poem's affiliation with a particular classical genre, the epyllion; see Kestner, "The Genre of Landor's *Gebir*," *The Wordsworth Circle* 5.1 (1974): 45. However, given the presence in the *1001 Nights* not only of a frame (as in "The Nightingale and Rose") but also of numerous embedded tales (as in *Gebir*), it is more likely that such framing marks instead the works' important relationship with orientalism.

[34] Astrabad (mod. sp. "Asterabad"; now known as Gorgan or Gurgan) is a city in northern Iran.

the story that moves her. Ultimately there is no oriental nature depicted, only layers of oriental literature.[35] Once again, art's dominance is complete.

The precedence of art over nature is reaffirmed in the subsequent section when the maid's versified prayer turns out to be at least as powerful as the original tale of the "song-men." God grants the maid's request to preserve the rose after its lover's death, to "Protect at least the one / From what the other bore" (69–70). Whereas nature would dictate not only the death of the wounded nightingale but also the drooping of the rose, the artful speech of the maid averts this outcome. Art's potency is reinforced further in the poem's final section, in which the speaker implies that only a "deaf man" would favor the "low unvarying voice / Of Cuckoo" over "the Rose's bird" (89–92). These lines suggest a clear choice between oriental literary art and a dull ("unvarying") version of European nature; the nightingale and oriental art are evidently to be preferred.

Landor's presentation here corresponds generally with Gautier's in "Les Souhaits." For both poets, the Orient is fundamentally artful and (therefore) preferable to a staid Europe. By identifying the art(fulness) of the Orient in terms of literature rather than architecture, though, Landor appropriates the Middle East as a model for his own literary efforts in a more direct fashion than Gautier. The heart of Landor's poem is the Persian story of the nightingale and the rose, upon which he layers the story of the "song-men" who tell that story, upon which he layers the story of the maid who hears the story the "song-men" tell, upon which he layers the fact that "we read" the story of the maid. The outermost layer, his poem "The Nightingale and Rose," thus becomes his own rendition of the story we have supposedly read.[36] In a sense, then, Landor is placing himself within his own verse narrative, as an oriental rather than orientalist literary artisan. Landor's insertion of himself in his Middle Eastern model is also a manifestation of his larger effort to experiment at the edges of a mainstream romanticism with which he was never quite comfortable.[37] Joseph Kestner, Pierre Vitoux, and others have seen this effort in terms of a (neo)classical impulse, to which Landor was no doubt vulnerable.[38] However, orientalism gives him a more effective means to this end. In "The Nightingale and Rose," he carefully delineates an aspect of the Arabic/Persian literary tradition and then reproduces it. As he does so, he

---

[35] Landor's instinct to represent the Orient solely in terms of texts is typical of nineteenth-century orientalism, as mentioned above; see for elaboration Mitchell, *Colonising Egypt* 31 and Said, *Orientalism* 23, 177.

[36] This multiple embedding is of course also reminiscent of the narrative techniques of the *1001 Nights*, as Landor himself would almost certainly have recognized.

[37] On Landor's relationship with romanticism, see for instance Robert Pinsky, *Landor's Poetry* (Chicago: U of Chicago P, 1968) esp. 24–32.

[38] See Kestner, "The Genre of Landor's *Gebir*"; and Vitoux, "*Gebir* as an Heroic Poem," *The Wordsworth Circle* 7.1 (1976): 51–7. Landor was, after all, far more accomplished as a Latinist than an orientalist.

devalues one of the key tenets of romanticism, the privileging of nature for aesthetic purposes. More importantly, he proffers in its stead a vision of oriental literary art set free from the constraining relationship with reality assumed in Western poetics.

Nightingales and roses II: Moore and the Orient as an ideal

The Persian story of the nightingale and the rose also provides the basis for Thomas Moore's short poem "Beauty and Song."[39] Like Landor, Moore uses the story as a framework for the development of an aesthetic position. Although his position differs significantly from Landor's, his topic — the correct relationship between art and nature — is the same, and he shares with Landor and the other poets discussed thus far the presumption that there is an integral connection between the East and art.

"Beauty and Song" is structured around an exchange of conversation between the rose and her lover, and concludes with a statement of Moore's poetics. Both the nightingale's opening comments and the rose's reply are introduced with references to a conventionalized version of nature:

> Down in yon summer vale,
>   Where the rill flows,
> Thus said a Nightingale
>   To his loved Rose: —
> "Though rich the pleasures
> "Of song's sweet measures,
> "Vain were its melody,
> "Rose, without thee."
>
> Then from the green recess
>   Of her night-bow'r,
> Beaming with bashfulness,
>   Spoke the bright flow'r:—

---

[39] "Beauty and Song" appeared in Moore's own collection of his *Poetical Works* in 1841 (London: Longman, Orme, Brown, Green, and Longmans, vol. 5). It was not included in an 1829 *Poetical Works* (Paris: Galignani); we may presume that the poem was written at some time during the intervening twelve years, but the exact date of composition is uncertain.

Most critical discussion of Moore's orientalism has centered on his best-known orientalist poem, *Lalla Rookh* (1817; see chapter 3), see for example Wallace Cable Brown, "Thomas Moore and English Interest in the East," *Studies in Philology* 34 (1937): 576–87; Sharafuddin, *Islam and Romantic Orientalism* ch. 3; Smith, *Islam in English Literature* 195–201; Thérèse Tessier, *La Poésie lyrique de Thomas Moore* (Paris: Didier, 1976) pt. 4; and G.M. Wickens, "*Lalla Rookh* and the Romantic Tradition of Islamic Literature in English," *Yearbook of Comparative and General Literature* 20 (1971): 61–6.

My source for Moore's poetry is *The Poetical Works of Thomas Moore* (New York: A.C. Armstrong and Son, 1884).

> "Though morn should lend her
> "Its sunniest splendor,
> "What would the Rose be,
> "Unsung by thee?" (1–16)

The structure of "Beauty and Song" resembles that of Leconte de Lisle's "L'Orient" poems in its use of generic European images of nature to set the scene for the oriental elements. And like Leconte de Lisle's first "L'Orient" and Gautier's "Les Souhaits," Moore's poem then posits the Orient as the origin of beauty and as the force responsible for creating beauty from the natural (European) landscape. In Moore's rendition, however, the emphasis falls more heavily on the interdependence of art and nature, where the rose represents nature (more specifically, natural beauty) and the nightingale stands for art (song). Art, the nightingale says, needs nature as its subject. In turn, the rose responds that nature needs art to achieve its greatest beauty, for the simple enhancement of even the sunniest morning is not enough.

Moore expresses the inadequacy of the morning in the vocabulary of stock romantic nature imagery: the "summer vale," "rill," "green recess," and "nightbow'r." Yet the sentiment is certainly not that of Wordsworthian romanticism, which would instead extol the sunny morning. The strikingly conventional vocabulary seems to emphasize the artful rather than the natural — quite the opposite of its usual romantic function. Indeed, the artful/poetic takes precedence over the natural throughout these lines. This is evident, for instance, in the placement of the rose's defense of art in the second stanza so that it appears to supercede the nightingale's praise of nature in the first. Although Moore does not stress the literariness of the rose as Landor does, the fact remains that this rose is derived from literary tradition; to interpret it as a purely natural phenomenon would be to miss much of its significance. Thus by selecting the rose as nature's standard-bearer, Moore is from the beginning placing nature under the aegis of art.

The relative positions of nature and art become more difficult to ascertain in the poem's final stanza, however:

> Thus still let Song attend
>   Woman's bright way;
> Thus still let woman lend
>   Light to the lay.
> Like stars, through heaven's sea,
> Floating in harmony,
> Beauty shall glide along,
> Circled by Song. (17–24)

"Song" begins and ends the stanza, in a sense "circling" it as the final line prescribes. Its identification with art here appears fairly straightforward, since song has been the figure for art throughout the poem. But nature — whether in the form of conventionalized landscape or in the persona of the rose — is not mentioned in this stanza. Its place is taken first by "Woman" and then by "Beauty," each of which has essentially the same relationship with song/art that nature has in the first two stanzas. If nature were valued mainly for itself (as Wordsworth would value it, for instance), such an exchange would be impossible. Instead, the substitution of woman and beauty for nature suggests that nature is, from the start, esteemed chiefly for its poetic or aesthetic function. The substitution also reflects Moore's continued reliance on his understanding of the original Persian story, in which the rose plays the role of a female beloved.[40] By inserting a woman (albeit a generic one) in the place of the rose, he not only removes the rose even farther from a purely natural status but also implicitly restates the power of the Persian model as art.

However, the final stanza also limits the elevation of art and song over nature (and its substitutes, woman and beauty). Beauty, for instance, is a more active player than song; it is given a real verb ("shall glide") rather than a mere participle ("circled"). More importantly, beauty/woman is the subject of all but the first and last lines of the stanza. In short, while the poem may at one time or another appear to privilege either art/song or nature/woman/beauty, overall it maintains the value of each and posits for them a relatively balanced relationship, skewed perhaps in favor of art but mediated by beauty's alliance with both. Thus where Landor's rendition of the Persian legend dispenses with nature, Moore's holds open a place for nature so long as it is remains "circled" within art's orbit.

Unlike Landor, Moore does not make a point of his poem's orientalism. He neither mentions the East nor acknowledges the oriental source of the love story of the nightingale and the rose. Yet the Middle East remains significant in Moore's exhibition of his poetics in "Beauty and Song." The poem attempts to present an idealized world in which art and nature will coexist in a mutually supportive and clearly defined relationship distinct from the romantic one. By choosing the nightingale and rose as the channel through which to express this relationship, Moore is in effect claiming the Orient as the world in which his ideal is realized. He does not join the other poets so far discussed in this chapter in seeing the Middle East as exclusively the province of art, as a domain in which nature is relegated to a subordinate function, if not banished entirely. Nonetheless, he shares with these other poets the notion that nature's place in the Orient is not the supreme one that it is in romantic Europe. By presenting art and nature as intertwined and interdependent in the Orient, Moore indicates the great extent to which he shares the other poets' attachment

---

[40] The Persian language does not use grammatical gender; this legend does not necessarily specify the sex of either the rose or the nightingale. The story's English interpreters seem to have been most comfortable with a female rose and a male nightingale.

to an artful East, one that offers a point of departure from a romanticism too bound up in nature and from a classicism too narrowly devoted to mimesis.

Hemans's Middle Eastern models

Both Felicia Hemans, writing at the cusp of the Victorian era, and Alfred Tennyson, a true Victorian, join Landor and Moore in turning to the literatures of the East as a venue in which to elaborate their own poetics. To a greater or lesser extent and with varying degrees of enthusiasm, both also model poems on oriental (or orientalist) literature. Although Hemans's characteristic ambivalence makes its mark on both "An Hour of Romance" and "The Mourner for the Barmecides," the two poems I will treat before moving on to Tennyson, her acceptance of an intimate linkage between the Orient and literary art remains solid and unquestioned as the basis for the aesthetic approach evolved in these poems.

"An Hour of Romance" is based not on a Middle Eastern literary tradition, as Landor's and Moore's poems are, but on Walter Scott's 1825 novel *The Talisman*, which is set in the Levant during the time of the Crusades.[41] The poem describes the experience of the speaker, an English reader of Scott's novel.

>There were thick leaves above me and around,
>   And low sweet sighs, like those of childhood's sleep,
>Amidst their dimness, and a fitful sound
>   As of soft showers on water; — dark and deep
>Lay the oak shadows o'er the turf, so still
>They seem'd but pictur'd glooms; a hidden rill,
>Made music, such as haunts us in a dream,
>Under the fern tufts; and a tender gleam
>Of soft green light, as by the glowworm shed,
>   Came pouring through the woven beech-boughs down,
>And steep'd the magic page wherein I read
>   Of royal chivalry and old renown,
>A tale of Palestine. (1–13)

---

[41] Scott's 1832 introduction disavows *The Talisman*'s orientalism. Citing Southey's *Thalaba* and Moore's *Lalla Rookh*, Scott announces that since "the Eastern themes had been already so successfully handled by those who were acknowledged to be masters of their craft," he would not attempt to "enter [...] into competition with them" (Scott, introduction [1832], *The Talisman* [New York: Dodd, Mead, 1929] 8). Be that as it may, *The Talisman* clearly takes advantage of contemporary British interest in orientalism. Hemans, whose poem was written at least six years before the appearance of Scott's introduction, accepts the novel as orientalist without question.

The reader is seated outdoors, in a conventionally natural setting. However, as in Moore's "Beauty and Song," the conventionality of the depiction of nature challenges its naturalness. Hemans's piling of natural features bears some resemblance to Gautier's in "In deserto." Directly or through simile, she includes so many natural elements that they become more symbolically representative — even quintessential — than visually compelling. The process of abstraction from reality is furthered by the scene's association with altered states of consciousness ("childhood's sleep" and "dream") and with the supernatural ("magic"). Thus, while the scene first appears to ground the poem in a concrete reality, that reality turns out instead to be insecure. On the other hand, whereas Gautier builds a composite landscape which ranges beyond the perception of any individual, Hemans describes a scene which could be observed by a single person. This visual accessibility (however diffuse) enables the scene, unlike Gautier's, to remain more or less within the realm of the natural.

The hold of the natural is confirmed in the subsequent section, as the speaker retreats mid-line from "the magic page" to resume a conventionalized depiction of the English scene. In the next six lines, Hemans adds even more elements stereotypical of English nature: bees, flowers, "blue skies, and amber sunshine," a dragon fly, and a "lone wood-pigeon" in a "dell."[42] Yet this quintessential image eventually succumbs to the power of the orientalist tale:

> But ere long,
> All sense of these things faded, as the spell,
> Breathing from that high gorgeous tale, grew strong
> On my chain'd soul — 'twas not the leaves I heard;
> — A Syrian wind the lion-banner stirr'd,
> Through its proud floating folds — 'twas not the brook,
> Singing in secret through its grassy glen —
> A wild shrill trumpet of the Saracen
> Peal'd from the desert's lonely heart, and shook
> The burning air. — Like clouds when winds are high,
> O'er glittering sands flew steeds of Araby,
> And tents rose up, and sudden lance and spear
> Flash'd where a fountain's diamond wave lay clear,
> Shadow'd by graceful palm-trees. (20–33)

---

[42] Hemans's admiration for English nature is virtually inseparable from the domestic patriotism at which she is particularly adept. See for instance "The Homes of England" (1827), one of her best-known poems. For further discussion, see Tricia Lootens, "Hemans and Home: Victorianism, Feminine 'Internal Enemies,' and the Domestication of National Identity," *PMLA* 109.2 (1994): 238–53; Mack et al., "Literary History, Romanticism, and Felicia Hemans" 223–33; and Nanora Sweet, "History, Imperialism, and the Aesthetics of the Beautiful: Hemans and the Post-Napoleonic Moment," *At the Limits of Romanticism: Essays in Cultural, Feminist, and Materialist Criticism*, ed. Mary A. Favret and Nicola J. Watson (Bloomington: Indiana UP, 1994) 170–84.

As the tale overwhelms its reader, images derived from Scott's novel transform and replace the natural landscape of the reader's surroundings. Nature does not exactly disappear, but it undergoes a kind of ontological mutation; for example, the speaker still notices the leaves rustling but hears them not as leaves but as "the lion-banner" stirring in a "Syrian wind." In effect, nature is supplanted through the (re)interpretive framework provided by the orientalist novel.

The novel takes precedence here, but only temporarily. The conclusion of "An Hour of Romance" reveals once again Hemans's ambivalence towards the power of orientalism. A child's laugh — "A voice of happy childhood!" (41), "the shout / Of merry England's joy" (33–4) — breaks through the speaker's literary illusion. Hemans presents this intrusion in virtually the same way that she presented the Orient's infiltration of English nature earlier in the poem. Both English and Eastern scenes are typified by their blue skies (16, 36) and each "fades" (21, 39) as the other threatens it. In neither case, moreover, is the fading immediate; rather, the threatened scene, whether English or oriental, hangs on for a few moments, as if resisting its eviction. In the end, Hemans's speaker also appears unsure of whether to resist, claiming to welcome the English child's laughter but perhaps protesting too much (and with oddly contorted syntax): "Yet might I scarce bewail the vision gone, / My heart so leapt to that sweet laughter's tone" (43–4).

At its most basic, "An Hour of Romance" is about the conflict of nature and present-time reality with an orientalist literary art that acknowledges neither. To a degree, Hemans's exploration of this conflict is independent of the orientalism of the literary art in question. She tells us, for instance, that the page is magic before she tells that the content of the page is orientalist. On the other hand, Hemans frames the poem's fundamental aesthetic conflict (between art and nature) in terms of a struggle for the speaker's attention and imagination, divided here between an explicitly, emphatically English scene and an equally explicitly, emphatically orientalist one. The remarkable impact of *The Talisman*'s story on the speaker has to do with its orientalism specifically, not simply with its appeal as a tale. Moreover, through its orientalism, the world depicted in Scott's novel is distinguished completely and successfully from the English world of nature. As in the poems of Moore, Landor, Gautier, Leconte de Lisle, and Wordsworth already discussed, the Orient in "An Hour of Romance" is an ally of art rather than of nature. Hemans's respect for the power of such art is obvious, but it is tempered by her continuing devotion to England and nature. However strongly attracted she might be to the art of the Orient, she resists adopting it directly as a model for her own poetic production.

This resistance is substantially diminished in "The Mourner for the Barmecides" (1828), another orientalist poem in which Hemans's association of literary art with the Middle East remains firm. This poem is set entirely in the Middle East, eliminating the English component on which the aesthetic statement of "An Hour of Romance" relies. In England's absence, there is no opportunity for the poem to stage a conflict between English nature and orientalist art, as "An Hour of Romance" does so insistently. Instead, the ascendancy of oriental art as a poetic model becomes sharper.

"The Mourner for the Barmecides" tells the story of an old man, raised in the house of the Barmecide vizirs, who takes it upon himself to keep alive the memory of their heroic deeds, "By song or high recital" (26). To an ever-increasing and appreciative audience, he tells "Many a glorious tale" (22). When Haroun, the caliph who had sacked the Barmecides, hears of these performances, he summons the old man and sentences him to death.[43] The aged orator asks for and is granted one last chance to speak, which he uses to welcome the opportunity to join the Barmecides in death. He praises them once again and predicts that their name will never "from earth depart" (60), for it will be taken up and proclaimed by the surroundings, from the wind to the fountains: "The very walls your bounty rear'd [...] / Shall find a murmur to record your tale, my glorious dead!" (73–4).

Haroun is so moved by the old man's last words that he lifts the death sentence:

> while the old man sang, a mist of tears
> O'er Haroun's eyes had gathered, and a thought —
> Oh! many a sudden and remorseful thought —
> Of his youth's once loved friends, the martyr'd race,
> O'erflow'd his softening heart. — "Live! live!" he cried,
> "Thou faithful unto death! live on, and still
> Speak of thy lords — they *were* a princely band!"
> (81–7; emphasis hers)

The narrative of "The Mourner for the Barmecides" announces the broad power of words to move and persuade. Yet even more than in "An Hour of Romance," this message is so thoroughly couched in orientalist tropes and conventions that it assumes a great specificity. To begin with, Hemans establishes the centrality of storytelling to this Middle Eastern social setting; the speaker notes, for instance, that the old man is able quickly to amass a large and eager audience. More important, though, are the less tangible aspects of Middle Eastern storytelling. The old man explains in detail how the surroundings are actively involved in the recitation of the Barmecides' story. Moreover, many elements of these surroundings are depicted as identifiably,

---

[43] Haroun [Hârûn al-Rashîd] ruled the Abbasid empire in Baghdad from 786 to 809; he beheaded the powerful Barmecide vizir Giafar [Ja'far] in 803. Although the immediate basis for Hemans's story is historical, not literary, this Haroun is the same one who figures in the *1001 Nights*, as any informed nineteenth-century reader would probably have recognized.

even exclusively oriental (in connotation if not in origin): "desert sands" (68), "the many gushing founts" (69), and "the grass [...] where lute and cittern rung" (75). Hemans presents an environment in which every feature can be — and is — almost automatically turned to the purpose of art. This is equally true of natural phenomena (air, wind, midnight), of man-made ones (walls), and of natural features that have been marked by human activity (battlefields, springs). Unlike the English nature of "An Hour of Romance," the environmental features of the Middle East seem to have no independent purpose or value. Instead they exist in service to the Barmecides' tale.

This devotion of the environment to art is far from unique to the content of the old man's final speech; in fact, that speech reflects the relationship between his recitation and his surroundings that is established earlier in the poem. Just after explaining that "The songs had ceased / The lights, the perfumes, and the genii tales, / Had ceased" (10–12), the poem's speaker announces that the fountain's "voice" continues to sing. As it turns out, though, that voice is not entirely alone:

> And still another voice! — an aged man,
> Yet with a dark and fervent eye beneath
> His silvery hair, came day by day, and sate
> On a white column's fragment; and drew forth,
> From the forsaken walls and dim arcades,
> A tone that shook them with its answering thrill
> To his deep accents. (16–22)

In a striking example of the presumed unnatural interconnectedness of Middle Eastern people and places discussed in chapter 3, the old man's voice is made to correspond with the fountain's, and his body to stand as a counterpart of his surroundings. His white hair matches the color of the column; indeed as he sits on the column he seems almost an extension of it. Furthermore, his recitation is presented as both originating in and returning to the structures that surround him. While he speaks for himself, they also speak through him. Even if he is executed, the poem predicts, his surroundings will continue to tell the story he now recites.

In establishing perpetuity as the single most important feature of this oriental(ist) tale, Hemans of course relies upon such standard orientalist conventions as the timelessness of the East. For her contemporary readers, furthermore, any such tale with the power to enable its own continuation would inevitably recall what was, for the nineteenth century, the quintessential work of oriental(ist) literary art: the *1001 Nights*. Hemans may not give her old man the exotic sexual appeal of Shahrazad, but she does grant him the ability to sway Haroun, the most powerful ruler of his time. Like Shahrazad, the old man earns his reprieve with his ability to tell. Even more to the point, his stay of execution, like hers, is intended to permit the continuation of the tale: as

Haroun proclaims, "live on, and still / Speak." This circumstantial link between the old man and Shahrazad is further reinforced by Hemans's choice of sovereign; Haroun is the same caliph who plays a great part in Shahrazad's tales, although he is of course not the king who nightly threatens her life.

"The Mourner for the Barmecides" ascribes to oriental literary art a uniquely permanent potency to which, Hemans implies, poetry in general might aspire. This model of poetry in perpetuity derives from the notion that art in the Orient is all-encompassing. The Middle East offers an ideal literary world in that each of its elements, from the convict to his sovereign to the environment (natural or constructed), participates in the production of art. No aspect of Oriental "reality" stands outside art.

Grounding a poetics in the *1001 Nights*: Tennyson

Tennyson's idealization of the Islamic Orient as an aesthetic origin has much in common with those already described, as becomes evident in his 1830 poem "Recollections of the Arabian Nights."[44] The *1001 Nights* is first and foremost a model for "Recollections," but it becomes also Tennyson's standard for an idealized realm in which there are no restraints on the imagination. As the poem's speaker inserts himself into the world of the *1001 Nights*, envisioning himself in Baghdad during "the golden prime / Of good Haroun Alraschid," he provides a rich, elaborate, and stereotypical description of the sights that greet him. The speaker's experience of his travels along the Tigris into Baghdad and finally into the halls of the caliph is framed as a retrospective, a fantasized adventure of youth vividly recalled:

> When the breeze of a joyful dawn blew free
> In the silken sail of infancy,
> The tide of time flowed back with me,
>   The forward-flowing tide of time;
> And many a sheeny summer-morn,
> Adown the Tigris I was borne,
> By Bagdat's shrines of fretted gold,
> High-wallèd gardens green and old;
> True Mussulman was I and sworn,
>   For it was in the golden prime
>   Of good Haroun Alraschid. (1–11)

---

[44] For sources, see Tennyson, *The Poems of Tennyson* 1: 225; and Paden, *Tennyson in Egypt* 130–2, n. 103. "Recollections" has been much noted by critics; Herbert Tucker gives it particular attention in his *Tennyson and the Doom of Romanticism* (Cambridge: Harvard UP, 1988) 78–87. Compare Leconte de Lisle's 1842 poem "Une nuit d'Orient" for a partial French counterpart of "Recollections."

This treatment of the Orient is unexceptional overall. Tennyson's presentation of this journey as a child's fantasy is consistent with the *1001 Nights*'s wide acceptance as children's literature.[45] The characterization of this fantasy as a reversal of the flow of time can scarcely be new when both fantasies generally and the Middle East in particular are conventionally held to be timeless.

Further, "Recollections" closely follows nineteenth-century orientalist poems' tendency to present Middle Eastern nature as artful. The overwhelmingly detailed descriptions of the scenes surrounding the speaker consistently elide distinctions between natural and man-made. The second stanza establishes this mode, juxtaposing natural scenery with ornate interior settings. In the next stanza, the two no longer appear side by side; instead, nature itself is ornamented:

> all
> The sloping of the moon-lit sward
> Was damask-work, and deep inlay
> Of braided blooms unmown, which crept
> Adown to where the water slept (26–30)

The ornamentation of the natural setting is explicitly artful; "damask-work," "inlay," and "braided" all entail human craft — and craft that is, moreover, the particular specialty of the Orient. The term "damask" derives from the name of the Syrian city of Damascus; so too, Middle Eastern artisans are (at this time and still today) famous for their fine inlaid work.[46] Throughout the poem, Tennyson reasserts the ornamentation of Middle Eastern natural phenomena, from "Imbowered vaults of pillared palm" in the fourth stanza to "The hollow-vaulted dark" in the twelfth. Even where his descriptions of natural scenery are relatively straightforward, he piles them up, one conventional image upon another, draped in archaisms and general verbal preciousness, so that they become something of their own ornamentation.[47]

The aesthetic value of the Middle Eastern setting is evident from these artificed descriptions; its source in "Recollections" is the Eastern world's

---

[45] See Ahmed, *Edward W. Lane* 12–14; Beer, "Fragmentations and Ironies" 262; and Richardson, *Literature, Education, and Romanticism* 116–7, 123, 126.

[46] This poem's flowered slope prefigures the slippage between meadows and festoons or a coastal wave and an embroidered scarf in Leconte de Lisle's first "L'Orient." It has, however, little in common with the woven flowers of Wordsworth's "The Haunted Tree," for example, since those flowers always already belong to the domain of artifice rather than to that of nature.

[47] See particularly stanza 10. Gordon's comments on "accumulation and aggregation" as aesthetic strategies are relevant here; see *Ornament, Fantasy, and Desire* 21. Harold Bloom interprets "Recollections" as a "voyage [...] through nature in search of a center transcending nature," and acknowledges that for Tennyson (in his early years) the destination of this voyage was the Orient. Bloom does not comment on Tennyson's imposition of the artful upon the natural, however. See Bloom, ed., *Alfred Lord Tennyson* (New York: Chelsea, 1985) 6–7.

separation from the universe of ordinary experience, as the seventh stanza demonstrates:

> The living airs of middle night
> Died round the bulbul as he sung;[48]
> Not he: but something which possessed
> The darkness of the world, delight,
> Life, anguish, death, immortal love,
> Ceasing not, mingled, unrepressed,
>   Apart from place, withholding time,
>   But flattering the golden prime
>   Of good Haroun Alraschid. (69–77)

Like Landor and Moore, Tennyson characterizes bulbul/nightingale as a singer.[49] However, his nightingale's place is quickly filled by "something" else, an unidentified singer characterized (like the conventionalized Orient itself) by the perpetual coexistence of grand opposites. Most important, though, are the traits mentioned last: "Apart from place, withholding time." By making this stereotypical trait the culminating feature of the unknown singer, and by justifying it as "flattering the golden prime / of good Haroun Alraschid," Tennyson makes this trait also the defining element of Middle Eastern literary art.

Modeling the vision of oriental literature that it expresses, "Recollections" positions itself likewise "apart from place, withholding time." In the first stanza, for instance, the speaker presents his recollections as habitual throughout his youth rather than grounded in any one particular time. So too, he completely omits reference to any place outside of his oriental fantasy. We can deduce from the title and first stanza that this is a poem based on a reading experience, but Tennyson never asserts the position of the reader — unlike Hemans, for example, who so firmly asserts the geographical and cultural position of her reader in "An Hour of Romance." More significant in this context is the complex structural relationship between "Recollections" and the literary work it claims to recollect. Tennyson reinforces the connections between his poem and its inspiration in various ways. The speaker imagines himself in the world of the *1001 Nights*, even positioning himself as a character in a tale. The action of the poem is explicitly described as taking place at night ("anight" [12]), and even more to the point, in a sequence of

---

[48] Tennyson footnotes "bulbul" as "the Persian name for Nightingale"; see Tennyson, *The Poems of Tennyson* 1: 228. The same word is used in Arabic.

[49] Both Bloom and Tucker observe that these lines also recall Keats's "Ode to a Nightingale" (1819); see Bloom, ed., *Alfred Lord Tennyson* 7; and Tucker, *Tennyson and the Doom of Romanticism* 82–3. Bloom and Tucker are among the numerous critics to note the special importance of this section of "Recollections." See also Fletcher, *Gardens and Grim Ravines* 48–9; John Hollander, "Tennyson's Melody," *Alfred Lord Tennyson*, ed. Harold Bloom (New York: Chelsea, 1985) 107–8; and Yohannan, *Persian Poetry in England and America* 87–8.

nights ("another night in night" [37]). While the action of tales embedded in the *1001 Nights* is of course not limited to the nighttime, the essential action of the frame tale (Shahrazad's telling of stories) certainly is.

The structure of "Recollections" also replicates, on a small scale, that of the *1001 Nights*. In both content and syntax, each stanza forms a distinct and separate whole, punctuated by the repetition of the refrain: "the golden prime / Of good Haroun Alraschid." Despite this emphatic separation between stanzas, the continuity between them is strong. Just such a combination of continuity and separation is a dominant feature of the narrative of the *1001 Nights*. In order to preserve her life, Shahrazad breaks up her stories into night-long sections, yet her strategy works because each night's segment continues the previous one. Thus while "Recollections" seems to pose as a tale from the *1001 Nights*, it is clear that it owes as much, if not more, to Shahrazad's part of the *1001 Nights*: the frame tale. Tennyson's interest in the *1001 Nights*'s frame tale is, at bottom, an interest in how such tales as Shahrazad's come about, in the process by which literary art — oriental literary art — is produced.

"Recollections of the Arabian Nights" begins by offering itself as a poem about the experience of reading — specifically, the experience of reading a book excellently suited, as Robert Southey says, "to induce a love of reading."[50] But as my analysis shows, "Recollections" turns out to be also about writing, about the production of literature that will do for a reader what Tennyson and Southey, among many others, recognize that the *1001 Nights* has done for them. The reading experience that Tennyson both recollects for himself and seeks to replicate for his readers is one that frees the imagination to enter a world of fantasy, totally escaping the real-world surroundings with which Hemans and her speaker struggle in "An Hour of Romance." Like Gautier's "Les Souhaits," "Recollections" identifies this freedom of imagination with the Orient, but Tennyson differs from his French contemporary in specifically indicating Middle Eastern literary art — whether the *1001 Nights* or Persian poetry — as a guide and model for this aesthetic stance.

Unlike Landor, who persistently reminds the reader of his oriental model's standing in relation to its domestic counterpart, Tennyson entirely omits any such domestic point of reference, keeping "Recollections" within the bounds of the literary universe of the Middle East. Yet one could easily read "Recollections" as a response to poems such as Coleridge's "To Nature," which mentions with disdain the artful and classically oriental "fretted dome" and "incense," and announces instead its enthusiastic preference for the natural

---

[50] Southey, "To Henry Southey," Aug. 25, 1800, *The Life and Correspondence of Robert Southey* 2: 110.

"blue sky" and "the sweet fragrance that the wild flower yields."[51] Yet by so pointedly eliminating such standard natural, domestic — and romantic — elements from "Recollections," Tennyson effectively declares his independence from them, proclaiming instead the absolute sufficiency of his oriental model of literary art and of the poetics he derives from it. Of the poems discussed in this chapter thus far, "Recollections" exemplifies the most radical and most specific incorporation of orientalism into its poetics.

The Orient and Tennyson's p(a)lace of art

The great depth of Tennyson's reliance on the Orient as a foundation for his poetics can be gauged from his longer poem "The Palace of Art."[52] The position of the Orient in this complicated poem is itself far from straightforward. While the poem contains many references to the East, it is not orientalist as a whole. Critics have generally disregarded the understated orientalism of "The Palace," except perhaps to note the unmistakable similarity between the poem's first lines and the beginning of one of the nineteenth century's most famous orientalist poems, Coleridge's "Kubla Khan."[53] But Tennyson's engagement with the Orient in "The Palace" does not end with "Kubla Khan." Rather, the Middle East becomes the essential grounding element of a much larger poetics, which finally subsumes it to a degree unmatched in "Recollections of the Arabian Nights" or any of the other poems yet discussed.

After stipulating his soul's splendid and absolute isolation from "the world" (13), the poem's speaker describes the glories of the palace he has built for his soul.[54]

---

[51] "To Nature" was first published in 1836 and was probably written in 1820. See *The Poetical Works of Samuel Taylor Coleridge*, ed. Ernest Hartley Coleridge (London: Henry Frowde, 1912) 429.
[52] First published in 1832, two years after "Recollections," "The Palace" was extensively revised for republication in 1842. I will use the 1842 text, with reference to 1832 as needed. See *The Poems of Tennyson* 1: 436–56. For other substantial discussions of this poem, see Armstrong, *Victorian Poetry* 77–83; Brian Goldberg, "'A Sea Reflecting Love': Tennyson, Shelley, and the Aesthetics of the Image in the Marketplace," *Modern Language Quarterly* 59.1 (March 1998): 90–7; Kerry McSweeney, *Tennyson and Swinburne as Romantic Naturalists* (Toronto: U of Toronto P, 1981) 47–50; Ricks, *Tennyson* 86–8; and Tucker, *Tennyson and the Doom of Romanticism* 118–25.
[53] "Kubla Khan" was published in 1816, sixteen years before Tennyson's "The Palace of Art." The poem begins: "In Xanadu did Kubla Khan / A stately pleasure-dome decree / Where Alph, the sacred river, ran." Tennyson renders his version in the first person: "I built my soul a lordly pleasure-house, / Wherein at ease for aye to dwell" (1–2).
[54] Fletcher interprets this isolation in terms of the depiction of the palace's surrounding landscape rather than of the palace itself; see Fletcher, *Gardens and Grim Ravines* 51.

> Full of great rooms and small the palace stood,
> All various, each a perfect whole
> From living Nature, fit for every mood
> And change in my still soul (57–60)

Despite the prominent reference to nature, each room contains a certain kind of art. Although Tennyson does not allude specifically to the Orient, the overwrought language and the wealth of sumptuous detail have much in common with his descriptions of Hârûn al-Rashîd's Baghdad in "Recollections."[55] As Tennyson continues his depiction of the palace its orientalism comes even more clearly into view. The soul asks herself,

> And who shall gaze upon
> My palace with unblinded eyes,
> While this great bow will waver in the sun,
> And that sweet incense rise? (41–4)

The soul's arrogance in attributing the sun's brightness to her own palace recalls that of the stereotypical oriental despot, especially coming as it does directly after Tennyson's orientalized description of the palace and its surroundings.[56] The reference to incense, an Eastern commodity, also enhances the stanza's orientalism.[57]

As the speaker goes on to describe the contents of the soul's palace, the Orient continues to play an important role. The speaker begins with a series of outdoor scenes. The first of these to be granted a full stanza is clearly Middle Eastern, though not identified as such. Not only is this landscape characterized by that essential Middle Eastern feature — sand — but its sole occupant is, as in so many such scenes, a lone and lonely wanderer:

> One seemed all dark and red — a tract of sand,
> And some one pacing there alone,
> Who paced for ever in a glimmering land,
> Lit with a low large moon. (65–8)

Contrasting sharply with the desert scene is the final image in this group:

> And one, an English home — gray twilight poured
> On dewy pastures, dewy trees,
> Softer than sleep — all things in order stored,
> A haunt of ancient Peace. (85–8)

---

[55] In addition, Ricks suggests that some of Tennyson's description may be related to an image from H.J. Weber's *Tales of the East* (1812); see *The Poems of Tennyson* 1: 439.

[56] The soul's granting of the sun's characteristics to her palace echoes Coleridge's mention of "That sunny dome!" in "Kubla Khan" (47); a connection between these two images would confirm the orientalism of Tennyson's.

[57] This reference is repeated from the description of the palace (39); another line two stanzas later (45) mentions incense yet again.

Because of their placement, these two images serve to frame the entire group, as if "every landscape fair" (89) could be contained within the bounds set by these two extremes. In this context, the Middle East, like England, functions as a kind of aesthetic guidepost, a marker at the edge of art's range.

The next group of images focuses on religious belief and includes an explicitly Islamic stanza:

> Or thronging all one porch of Paradise
>   A group of Houris bowed to see
> The dying Islamite, with hands and eyes
>   That said, We wait for thee. (101–4)

In contrast, the third group of images, that of "wise men" (131), makes no mention of any Middle Eastern figures.[58] Yet when he introduces the wise men in the 1832 version of the poem, Tennyson's speaker gives the entire group a Middle Eastern cast:

> And underneath freshcarved in cedarwood,
>   Somewhat alike in form and face,
> The Genii of every climate stood,
>   All brothers of one race. (1832; 137–40)

This stanza unifies the world's wise men under a single oriental umbrella. In a poem where artisanship is so strongly identified as oriental, the mention of carving serves this end, as does the choice of cedarwood, with its Levantine associations. Most importantly, all the wise men (most of whom are artists and men of literature) are designated "Genii," a word that would almost certainly have evoked a strong sense of the oriental in the minds of Tennyson's readers. By casting these men as "Genii," he gives them, and the art they represent, a common Middle Eastern origin.[59]

---

[58] Several biblical figures appear in the 1832 version of the poem as well, but it would be inappropriate to consider such references orientalist in any meaningful way. Christopher Ricks notes that Tennyson considered including Averroes, but the Hispano-Arab philosopher does not appear in either version. See Tennyson, *The Poems of Tennyson* 1: 447.

[59] Even if Tennyson intended "genii" as the plural of "genius" rather than "genie," the oriental resonance would be inescapable. His usage of the word here resonates with Wordsworth's in *The Prelude*; the passage in question also finds larger echoes in "The Palace":

> There was a time when whatsoe'er is feign'd
> Of airy Palaces, and Gardens built
> By Genii of Romance, or hath in grave
> Authentic History been set forth of Rome,
> Alcairo, Babylon, or Persepolis (7.77–81)

(I have quoted from the 1805–06 version of the poem, but this passage remains substantially unchanged in 1850; see also *The Prelude* [1850], 7.456.)

The remainder of "The Palace of Art" describes the soul's enjoyment of the palace and of its contents, and then her descent into anguish as she recognizes her loneliness. In the last two stanzas she exposes this change of heart:

> She threw her royal robes away.
> "Make me a cottage in the vale," she said,
> "Where I may mourn and pray.
>
> "Yet pull not down my palace towers, that are
> So lightly, beautifully built:
> Perchance I may return with others there
> When I have purged my guilt." (290–6)

The soul's new dream of refuge has an unmistakable English flavor to it, especially when amplified by the speaker's earlier description of "an English home" as a place of "all things in order stored, / A haunt of ancient Peace" (85, 87–8). The speaker's tormented soul clearly has in mind just such a place of order and tranquillity in which she might recover. As the final stanza indicates, she does not intend her retreat to be permanent but maintains instead the future possibility of a less narcissistic enjoyment of the pleasures of her palace.

Brian Goldberg argues that in "The Palace of Art," "Tennyson wishes to picture an institutionally unbound utopia through the beautiful pleasures of his moral aesthetic."[60] As my reading of the poem shows, this utopia finds its closest approximation in the East. By the poem's end, the orientalized palace of art has become the aesthetic destination towards which the poem aims in retrospect, and in a far more complex and humble way than when the palace was first presented.[61] Through the palace and its art, orientalism remains an aesthetic model, but the poem's ending suggests that it must be given a fuller life than that of an individual's fantasy, however elaborate. In short, to be a successful aesthetic strategy, orientalism must be integrated into a complete aesthetic approach; if it exists only unto itself, it will be, to recall Hugo's "Novembre," a fantasy destined to fade.

Thus in this era, Tennyson's conception of art is inseparable from his interest in the Orient.[62] The soul, who is both the principal guardian and

---

[60] Goldberg, "'A Sea Reflecting Love,'" 97.

[61] Isobel Armstrong's reading of the poem emphasizes the jumbled coexistence of occidental and oriental cultural artifacts: "All is contemporary, simultaneous, available, and thus all is estranged" (Armstrong, *Victorian Poetry* 79). Although cogent, her interpretation underestimates both the palace's orientalism and the repeated polarization of English and Eastern that places that orientalism in a position of aesthetic significance.

[62] To place Tennyson's orientalism at the center of his poetics during this period is not to deny the imperialist and antioriental, even racist bent of some of his later poems. For further discussion, see Shaw, "Tennyson's Dark Continent"; and John McBratney, "Rebuilding Akbar's 'Fane.'" As McBratney points out, even Tennyson's earlier poems are "part of the

principal admirer of art, is, by extention, an oriental despot. The palace in which she keeps and appreciates art appears as the product of oriental design — even while it is the work of the speaker's own imagination. The speaker's role becomes symbolically equivalent to that of the unmentioned oriental designers, builders, and artisans who would create a despot's palace. In this way, the entire process of the production of art is orientalized, even presented as fundamentally oriental in origin.[63] To the extent that "the poetic act" is to be "reveal[ed] as artifice" in Tennyson's poetry, as Isobel Armstrong charges,[64] it is also to be exposed as essentially (although perhaps not obviously) orientalist in its artifice.

Critics have not usually seen Tennyson as an advocate of art for its own sake, but his use of the Orient in "Recollections" and "The Palace of Art" brings him surprisingly close to such a position.[65] Not only is the Orient exalted in general terms as a place of art, but it becomes a model for poetic art in particular, more directly so in "Recollections" but in more important ways in "The Palace." In choosing this model, Tennyson pulls away from romanticism's assumptions about poetry; these poems neither imitate nature nor express inner emotion with sincerity. Rather, they imitate other art, oriental or orientalized, creating a universe in which there is, in the end, only art, existing unto itself. In "Recollections," the result is recognizably orientalist, since unlike "The Palace," that poem does not explore the larger implications of the poet's aesthetic choices. For Tennyson, orientalism means freedom of imagination, and concomitantly freedom from the literary models provided by his romantic elders. "Recollections" simply delights in this freedom, while "The Palace" demonstrates both its extraordinary potential and its risks if indulged improperly. The soul's "guilt" is not only merely guilt at her own immoral selfishness. It is also guilt at the exaltation of art that exists in isolation: art for art's sake.

That Tennyson rejects the option of art for its own sake does not mean that he rejects orientalism, however. At the end of "The Palace," he posits his oriental palace as an aesthetic goal, symbolic of an unrestricted imagination and of art for its own sake, but he maintains that this goal must not be sought in isolation or as an escape. Instead, orientalism, along with the artifice it represents, must become part of a larger aesthetic program. This program is domestic rather than exotic, as can be deduced from its point of origin in the

---

Orientalist project to master the East" (412); however, this in no way diminishes their significance in the evolution of Tennyson's poetics.

[63] It is worth remembering here the importance ascribed by the European imagination to architecture as an oriental art form; see my discussion of Leconte de Lisle and Gautier above.

[64] Armstrong, *Victorian Poetry* 46. Armstrong does not address orientalism in this context.

[65] McSweeney goes so far as to describe as "embarrassment" Tennyson's reaction to art for art's sake tendencies in his poetry; see McSweeney, *Tennyson and Swinburne as Romantic Naturalists* 46.

"cottage in the vale." By subsuming orientalism within this new cultural and aesthetic framework, while at the same time rejecting its value as pure fantasy, Tennyson not only allows orientalism to retain its position at the center of his poetics but in fact also grants it an influence it does not have when it is held within the limits of its own borders.

Gautier's orientalist poetics and art for art's sake

Tennyson's contemporary Théophile Gautier derives his own robust poetics from a similar assimilation of the Orient. The development of Gautier's avant-garde poetic vision is manifested with particular clarity in *Émaux et camées* [*Enamels and Cameos*], a celebrated collection "often considered the poetic model par excellence of the idea of art for art's sake," as L. Cassandra Hamrick observes.[66] *Émaux et camées* takes its cue from the early nineteenth century's grandest collection of orientalist poems: Hugo's *Les Orientales*. *Les Orientales* revels in the great allure of the East but ultimately discards it in favor of a return to Paris. Gautier's *Émaux et camées* is framed like *Les Orientales*, with an initial "Préface" to signal the collection's orientalism and a final poem that makes a definitive aesthetic statement. However, *Émaux et camées* does not conclude by renouncing orientalism. Instead, like Tennyson, Gautier reveals his orientalism as an integral part of a larger aesthetic strategy, a strategy both farther reaching and more fully articulated than Tennyson's.

The basis of this strategy is spelled out in Gautier's prefatory sonnet.[67] Like Tennyson's "The Palace of Art," Gautier's "Préface" begins with an old assumption about the Orient and oriental(ist) literature: that they offer a retreat from the world. The example Gautier chooses is Johann Wolfgang von Goethe (1749–1832), who was writing his famous orientalist work, the *West-Ostlicher Divan*, during the Napoleonic upheavals of 1811.[68]

---

[66] L. Cassandra Hamrick, "Gautier et l'anarchie de l'art," *Relire Théophile Gautier: Le plaisir du texte*, ed. Freeman G. Henry (Amsterdam: Rodopi, 1998) 110. For a general discussion of Gautier's connection with "l'art pour l'art," see Franck Ruby, "Théophile Gautier et la question de 'l'Art pour l'Art,'" *Bulletin de la Société Théophile Gautier* 20 (1998): 3–13.

Émaux et camées was first published in 1852 and was well received from the start. Gautier added to the collection over his lifetime, more than doubling the number of poems by the time of the final edition in 1872; see Charles de Lovenjoul, *Histoire des oeuvres de Théophile Gautier*, vol. 2 (Paris: Charpentier, 1887) 26–7; and Tennant, *Théophile Gautier* 58–9.

[67] "Préface" was included in the original 1852 edition of *Émaux et camées*. For a brief discussion of sources, see Gautier, *Poésies complètes* 1: xciii.

[68] The *Divan* (the word is Persian for "collection of poetry") did not take its final form until 1827, although portions were published beginning in 1819. For more information, see Alexander Rogers's introduction to the *Divan* in *Goethe's Reineke Fox, West-Eastern Divan, and Achilleid*, trans. Rogers (London: George Bell and Sons, 1890) 197–8. Some sense of the *Divan*'s huge influence in Europe can be gained from Raymond Schwab, *The Oriental Renaissance* 6, 208–9.

> Pendant les guerres de l'empire,
> Goethe, au bruit du canon brutal,
> Fit *le Divan occidental*,
> Fraîche oasis où l'art respire. (1–4; italics his)
>
> [During the wars of the empire, / Goethe, to the sound of the brutal cannon/canon, / Made *The Occidental Divan*, / Cool oasis where art rests.]

From the outset, though, this is more than simple escapism. By naming the sound of the cannon as the sole concrete manifestation of the oppressive imperial wars, Gautier raises the possibility of a double meaning. While "canon" in the sense of "cannon" is a weapon, the line makes no distinction between this meaning and "canon" in the sense of literary "canon." If we incorporate this second meaning into our reading, Goethe's composition of the *West-Ostlicher Divan* becomes, in Gautier's interpretation, a response to literary as well as military events of the time. Gautier's subsequent depiction of Goethe's work as a "Fraîche oasis où l'art respire" [Cool oasis where art rests] confirms such a reading. The stereotypical image of the oasis here acquires an aesthetic function as a place where art too may find relief, whether from the intrusions of worldly troubles or from the constraints of literary tradition.[69]

The following stanza specifies the literary role of the Orient in Goethe's *Divan*:

> Pour Nisami quittant Shakspear,
> Il se parfuma de çantal,
> Et sur un mètre oriental
> Nota le chant qu'Hudhud soupire. (5–8)[70]
>
> [Leaving Shakespeare for Nisami, / He scented himself with sandalwood, / And in an oriental meter / Noted the song that the Hudhud sighs.]

Goethe's models are, Gautier asserts, Eastern ones in both form and content; Goethe follows the example of the Persian poet Nizâmî rather than Shakespeare, and in doing so he not only uses an oriental meter but depicts the song of the Hudhud, a bird whose appearance in the Qur'an gives it an

---

[69] Historically, these particular worldly troubles have everything to do with the nineteenth century's advancing imperialism. That Gautier deflects them suggests a strong desire to maintain the Orient as a place of fantasy, safe from the intrusion of military imperialism but open to exploration and exploitation as an aesthetic site.

[70] Nisami (Nizâmî; 1140–1202) is one of Persia's most eminent and influential poets. Although he has a collection of lyric poems, he is best known for his five epics. The Hudhud, or hoopoe, is a bird with a reputation for piety and a role in several versions of the Solomon legend, including that contained in the Qur'an (Sura 27). See A.J. Wensinck, "Hudhud," *The Encyclopedia of Islam*, 2nd ed.

explicitly Islamic connotation. Gautier's choice of the English Shakespeare instead of a German writer suggests an assumption on his part of a pan-European literary tradition, rather than a national one (e.g. English or German), against which the oriental and Islamic traditions stand in opposition. While Gautier is by no means unique in making such an assumption — we might remember, for instance, the coalescence of French and English in Wordsworth's "Septimi Gades" (chapter 3) — his inclusion here of three of the most prominent European national literatures (Goethe's German, Shakespeare's English, his own French) gives the polarization of European and Eastern an unusual solidity.

Goethe is, in Gautier's rendition, fashioning himself and his work after Islamic Middle Eastern models, having determinedly rejected European ones. In turn, Gautier fashions his own artistic image after Goethe's:

> Comme Goethe sur son divan
> A Weimar s'isolait des choses
> Et d'Hafiz effeuillait les roses,
>
> Sans prendre garde à l'ouragan
> Qui fouettait mes vitres fermées,
> Moi, j'ai fait *Émaux et camées*. (9–14; italics his)[71]
>
> [As Goethe on his divan / At Weimar isolated himself from things / And stripped the roses of Hafiz,
>
> Without paying mind to the storm / That was lashing my closed windows, / Me, I have made *Émaux et camées*.]

With this modeling in mind, it is not difficult to find correspondences between Gautier's collection and Goethe's — from the superficial (both mention Hâfiz in the first poem) to the essential (both show a sustained preoccupation with poetry and poetics). Moreover, by patterning his own work upon that of a poet who patterned his on the oriental, Gautier is, by extension, casting Goethe as oriental. At the end of the stanza, Goethe even appears to outdo his Middle Eastern model, stripping from the great poet Hâfiz the roses that symbolize his poetry. Gautier orientalizes Goethe yet further here, situating him "sur son divan" [on his divan]; Gautier's punning choice of words at once reflects the title of Goethe's text and poses him as a Middle Eastern sultan reclining on a couch. Goethe's isolation from "des choses" [things] is appropriate to such a figure, stereotypically removed from the cares of the world, but it is also an

---

[71] Hafiz (Hâfiz; 1325–1390) is among the most important Persian poets. He devoted himself particularly to the lyric ghazal form and to panegyric. According to G.M. Wickens, Goethe knew Hâfiz's poetry through an 1812-13 German prose translation; see Wickens, "Hâfiz," *The Encyclopedia of Islam*, 2nd ed. (Leiden: E.J. Brill, 1958–).

implicit reference to the antimimetic tendency of orientalism, the freedom that orientalism offers from the representation of things.[72]

Once Goethe is revealed to be at least as oriental as his Middle Eastern models, Gautier can introduce himself as Goethe's own follower. Like Goethe, he takes no notice of things; in the course of his disregard, he produces *Émaux et camées* just as Goethe produces his *Divan*. The particular thing on which he focuses his disregard is not, however, the "bruit du canon brutal" [the sound of the brutal can(n)on] but rather the storm, a natural phenomenon. Yet this storm can be related to the "canon" in both its senses. First, like cannon fire in war, it is an outside force, loud and intrusive, about which the poet can do nothing. More importantly, though, the literary canon traditionally incorporates a certain notion of nature's aesthetic role. By choosing pointedly to ignore a natural phenomenon, a phenomenon that is moreover clearly hostile, Gautier is reinforcing the distinction he has already drawn between his own poetry and the (canonical) literary art that depends upon the representation of things in nature.

A look back at *Les Orientales*'s concluding poem, "Novembre," confirms this reading. For Hugo, the damp, stormy weather of Paris defines that city, and by extension Europe as a whole, in contradistinction to the warm, sunny East. In turn, it is through confronting — through *not* disregarding — this particular climatic trait that Hugo's speaker comes to terms with his aesthetic shift away from the Orient and back to a domestic universe and to the mimetic representation of nature. So while Gautier's storm may at first seem to have little to do with the cannon/canon against which Goethe presents his *Divan*, it is in fact very much part of the same concern with the matter of literature. Mentored by Goethe, Gautier argues for closed windows, muffled ears, and blinkered eyes. Art rests undisturbed in the isolation of an oasis, imitative not of nature but of art itself. This is the vision of art that gives rise to the idea of art for its own sake — the aesthetic philosophy of which *Émaux et camées* is one of the cardinal texts.[73]

Given the prefatory sonnet's great effort to define *Émaux et camées* as profoundly and essentially orientalist, it is at first surprising that so little of the collection deals specifically with oriental material, especially when compared with either Hugo's *Les Orientales* or Goethe's *Divan*. To be sure, there are a

---

[72] For an interesting and relevant analysis of how Gautier's travel writing shows his resistance to mimesis, see Schick, "A Case Study of Descriptive Perversion."

[73] Lowe offers a comparable observation about Flaubert: "The oriental motif is the distinguishing mark of [...] a sentimentalism that longs for a memory of earlier innocence, an impossible union, a lost wholeness in which European culture is faithfully reflected in its oriental Other" (*Critical Terrains* 95). It is interesting that she is later able to make so similar an argument about Roland Barthes, despite the century separating him from Flaubert: "The imagined Orient — as critique of the Occident — becomes an emblem of his 'poetics of escape,' a desire to transcend semiology and the ideology of signifier and signified, to invent a place that exceeds binary structure itself" (154).

few quite characteristically orientalist poems, including "Nostalgies d'obelisques" ["Nostalgia of Obelisks"] and "La Fellah" ["The Fellah"]. In most cases, though, orientalist references appear in poems that are in no other way orientalist.[74] Even these references are not overwhelmingly common. On the other hand, Gautier's indirect, understated approach is very much in keeping with the significance he accords orientalism. As his "Préface" tells us, orientalism comprises much more than subject matter, however rich; rather, it is the original and defining feature of the collection's poetics. Given this, there is no need for him to luxuriate obsessively in the details of a fantastical East. That such a fantastical East underlies *Émaux et camées* is evident from such lines as these from "Le Poème de la femme" ["The Poem of the Woman"]:

> Sur un tapis de Cachemire,
> C'est la sultane du sérail,
> Riant au miroir qui l'admire
> Avec un rire de corail;
>
> La Géorgienne indolente,
> Avec son souple narguilhé,
> Étalant sa hanche opulente,
> Un pied sous l'autre replié. (41–8)
>
> [On a carpet from Cashmere, / It is the sultana of the seraglio, / Smiling at the mirror which admires her / With a coral smile;
>
> The indolent Georgian woman, / With her supple narghile, / Displaying her opulent hip, / One foot folded under the other.]

Conventionalized orientalist images of this sort do not sustain Gautier's interest through the collection, however.

Such details are, moreover, entirely absent from the final poem of *Émaux et camées*, in which Gautier spells out his aesthetic program. Indeed, this last poem, boldly entitled "L'Art," includes nothing identifiably orientalist.[75] "L'Art" begins with an assault on "contraintes fausses" [false constraints] (5),

---

[74] See for example "Contralto" ["Contralto"] (73–6) and "Ce que disent les hirondelles" ["What the Swallows Say"] (41–4).

[75] "L'Art" first appeared in 1857 in the periodical *L'Artiste*; it was entitled "A Monsieur Théodore de Banville; réponse à son Odelette" and was composed in reaction to Banville's 1856 poem "A Th. Gautier"; see *Poésies complètes de Théophile Gautier* 1: cxxviii–cxxix. "L'Art" was included, with some revision, in the 1858 edition of *Émaux et camées*; see de Lovenjoul, *Histoire des oeuvres de Théophile Gautier* 2: 137. Gautier specified that "L'Art" always be printed as the final poem of *Émaux et camées*, although he seems otherwise to have given little attention to the arrangement of the collection. "L'Art" has been much noted by critics; see for example Hamrick, "Gautier et l'anarchie de l'Art" 112–4; Lardoux, "L'Orient dans les poésies de Théophile Gautier" 222; Richardson, *Théophile Gautier* 152–5; Tennant, *Théophile Gautier* 59, 66–7; and Peter Whyte, "'L'Art' de Gautier: genèse et sens," *Relire Théophile Gautier* 119–39.

"rythme commode" [convenient rhythm] (10), and other instruments of poetic tradition. Gautier announces that instead the production of art should be a struggle:

> Statuaire, repousse
> L'argile que pétrit
>   Le pouce,
> Quand flotte ailleurs l'esprit;
>
> Lutte avec le carrare,
> Avec le paros dur
>   Et rare,
> Gardiens du contour pur;
>
> [...]
>
> Peintre, fuis l'aquarelle,
> Et fixe la couleur
>   Trop frêle
> Au four de l'émailleur.
>
> Fais les sirènes bleues,
> Tordant de cent façons
>   Leurs queues,
> Les monstres de blasons (13-20, 29-36)[76]

[Sculptor, reject / The clay that is kneaded by / The thumb, / When the spirit drifts elsewhere;

Vie with the carrara marble, / With the paros marble hard / And rare, / Guardians of the pure contour;

Painter, flee the watercolor, / And fix the too fragile / Color / In the enameler's kiln.

Make blue mermaids, / Twisting in a hundred ways / Their tails, / Monstrous blazons]

The result will be "L'art robuste" [Robust art] (41), art that survives the decline of cities (44), the fall of emperors (48), and even the death of gods (49): "les vers souverains / Demeurent / Plus forts que les airains" [sovereign verses / Remain / Stronger than bronze] (50-2).[77] The final stanza is a command to the artist:

---

[76] As the nonmetallic colors on heraldic coats of arms are termed "émaux" [enamels], there is a technical link between "blasons" [blazons] and the reference to the enameler's kiln.

[77] Gautier's assertion of the permanence of art here echoes Shelley's in "Ozymandias" (1818), a poem whose affiliation with the Middle East (pharaonic Egypt specifically) is much more obvious.

> Sculpte, lime, ciselle;
> Que ton rêve flottant
>   Se scelle
> Dans le bloc résistant! (53–6)

[Sculpt, polish, chisel; / That your drifting dream / Affix itself / To the resistant block!]

When this poem is reconsidered in light of the collection's "Préface," the extent to which orientalism is the foundation for Gautier's aesthetic statement in "L'Art" becomes clear. The primary purpose of both the prefatory sonnet and the concluding "L'Art" is to announce and advocate a departure from contemporary preoccupations, whether geopolitical or aesthetic. As Gautier's introduction to *Émaux et camées*, the "Préface" sets the terms of the discussion; they are the terms of orientalism. The prefatory poem's insistence on Goethe's adoption of Nizâmî and Hâfiz rather than of Shakespeare or of current events — and in turn on Gautier's adoption of Goethe — prefigures the position expressed in "L'Art." Further, the orientalism entailed in the "Préface" provides the means by which the artists (plastic, visual, or literary) scolded in "L'Art" might discard the conventional constraints that Gautier evidently disdains.

Thus if we join generations of critics in taking "L'Art" as an important statement of Gautier's aesthetic philosophy, we must at the same time recognize this philosophy's origins in orientalism. Pierre Lardoux argues that "L'Art" "is truly a text of synthesis, a poetic art where Orient and Occident find themselves associated in a sublime fashion. The true victory of the Orient is undoubtedly connected with the fact that, in a fashion which seems irreversible, arabesque, decoration, and imagination are henceforth tightly associated with art."[78] Lardoux deserves great credit for acknowledging (as few critics have) the presence and importance of orientalism in "L'Art." However, it is crucial also to emphasize that the Orient's "true victory" is achieved in this poem from behind the scenes. The absence of orientalism from the surface level of "L'Art" reflects orientalism's complete absorption into Gautier's aesthetics; orientalism permeates, but invisibly. By allowing orientalism to operate from this point of virtual occlusion in the text, Gautier thereby opens for it a vastly broader aesthetic plane. The orientalism of "L'Art" is entirely abstracted from any empirically verifiable Middle East and liberated from any dependence on the Middle East as a subject; it has become an orientalism belonging solely to the world of the aesthetic, of poetics. "L'art

---

[78] Lardoux, "L'Orient dans les poésies de Théophile Gautier" 222. Hartman also links Gautier's orientalism with "l'art pour l'art," but sees the two as deriving from the same impulse (Hartman, *Three Nineteenth-Century French Writer/Artists* 6). As my readings of both the "Préface" and "L'Art" demonstrate, it is more fruitful to see orientalism as generative of "l'art pour l'art."

pour l'art" evolves as a phenomenon independent from orientalism, but the notion of art for its own sake takes orientalism as its starting point and retains it as its point of reference.

Orientalist poetics, Oscar Wilde: culmination

When at the turn of the nineteenth century Wordsworth calls for a return to nature, he is proposing a remedy that could reinvigorate poetry and restore it to what he presents as its true purpose. His neoclassical predecessors looked to classical texts with much the same goal in mind. In this sense, the nineteenth-century poets who use the Orient as Wordsworth uses nature are following a well-used trajectory. As art for art's sake emerges from orientalism in the second part of the century, the Orient's aesthetic potency appears on a par with nature's or the classics'. Oscar Wilde's poem "Athanasia" (1879) expresses this potency succinctly.[79] The poem's originating incident is one repeated often enough in the nineteenth century, that of an Egyptian mummy being unwrapped in a museum in Britain.[80] The poem begins:

> To that gaunt House of Art which lacks for naught
>   Of all the great things men have saved from Time,
> The withered body of a girl was brought
>   Dead ere the world's glad youth had touched its prime,
> And seen by lonely Arabs lying hid
> In the dim womb of some black pyramid.
>
> But when they had unloosed the linen band
>   Which swathed the Egyptian's body, — lo! was found
> Closed in the wasted hollow of her hand
>   A little seed, which sown in English ground
> Did wondrous snow of starry blossoms bear
> And spread rich odours through our spring-tide air.
>
> With such strange arts this flower did allure
>   That all forgotten was the asphodel,
> And the brown bee, the lily's paramour,
>   Forsook the cup where he was wont to dwell (1–16)[81]

---

[79] For a reading of this poem in relation to imperial decline, see Nick Frankel, "'Ave Imperatrix': Oscar Wilde and the Poetry of Englishness," *Victorian Poetry* 35.2 (1997): 122–3.

[80] Many mummies were transported to England and unwrapped during Wilde's lifetime; the journal *Archaeologia*, for instance, describes numerous unwrappings in painful scientific detail.

[81] Henry David Thoreau alludes to a similar event in *Walden* (1854), observing that "we will not forget that some Egyptian wheat was handed down to us by a mummy" (Thoreau, *Walden; or, Life in the Woods* [New York: Anchor, 1973] 26).

The (stereotypically) "lonely" Arabs' responsibility for retrieving the mummy assimilates pharaonic Egypt to the Islamic Orient; the mummy and her flower carry the exotic force of both. The mummy's flower is a "wondrous" one that has an effect unlike that of any flower in nature. Its "rich odours" code it as oriental; they pervade the English atmosphere. The flower's "strange arts" make it capable of outdoing nature within nature's own sphere. The flower disrupts the usual workings of the natural environment; the bee loses interest in the lily (stanza 3), the dragonfly in the narcissus (stanza 4), the nightingale in the hills, and the dove in the woods (stanza 5). Yet the flower is disruptive to art as well; virtually all of the apparently natural phenomena disturbed by the flower are laden with classical or conventional poetic connotations that make them as significant to art as to nature.

The mummified girl herself assumes a similarly subversive function. She penetrates the "House of Art," the domain of "all the great things men have saved from Time," even though it is not clear that she is either a "great thing" or really "saved from Time." Indeed, such categories are hardly relevant to her. Already dead "ere the world's glad youth had touched its prime," she has escaped the bonds of time by preceding them; she is without time, timeless in the true sense. By implication, then, she stands outside history and therefore, despite her physical location within the museum, outside the history of art and culture that the museum represents. Her flower shares her dissociation from history:

> to this bright flower a thousand years
>   Seemed but the lingering of a summer's day,
> It never knew the tide of cankering fears
>   Which turn a boy's gold hair to withered grey,
> The dread desire of death it never knew,
> Or how all folk that they were born must rue. (43–8)

Both the flower and the dead girl are, then, ontologically other in relation to their naturally derived and historically bound European counterparts.

With the metaphor of the mummy and her seed, "Athanasia" captures the aesthetic essence of the Islamic Orient for later-nineteenth-century poets. The Orient is an exotic other, but it flourishes when "sown in English ground." Once rooted, it has the power to destroy Western assumptions about art that have been circulating for centuries; the culturally overdetermined asphodel ceases to appeal. As Wilde's later essay "The Decay of Lying" (chapter 3) shows, this destruction presents a strongly attractive opportunity for the development of a new aesthetic, generated on "English ground" but grounded in orientalism. Like Gautier, to whose young girl/fairy ("Les Souhaits") Wilde's Egyptian girl has a certain resemblance, Wilde formulates the new aesthetic as one of art for its own sake, unrestricted by either nature or the classical artistic tradition.

Throughout the nineteenth century, there is a striking consistency in the characteristics that French and British poets, including Wilde, ascribe to the Orient, ranging from the grand (the Orient as a place of art) to the mundane (Arabs as lonely wanderers in a sandy desert). The Orient's single most important trait is its ontological unnaturalness, which guides orientalist poetry in a movement away from the representation of nature in any strict sense. The unnaturalness of nature in the Middle East is manifested particularly in human beings' relationship with the environment and in the absence of a sharp distinction between the natural and the unnatural, whether supernatural or artificial. The incorporation of the artificial into Middle Eastern nature violates the division between the concepts of nature and art that is otherwise assumed through the beginning of the nineteenth century. The notion that art imitates and represents nature depends upon this assumed separation, upon the ideal of a pure nature, unadulterated by human design. The integral linkage of the Orient and art in nineteenth-century aesthetics undermines the position of nature and raises the possibility of alternatives to mimesis, whether in emulation of oriental art forms or not.

Given the relative consistency of orientalist depictions of the Islamic Middle East, the Orient's versatility in nineteenth-century poetics is remarkable. While the Orient offers Gautier and Wilde a route towards a defined aesthetic ideal, it gives other poets (Arnold, Hemans, Landor, Leconte de Lisle, Moore, Musset, and Tennyson) a means by which to establish their positions vis-à-vis major contemporary and recent trends in poetry and poetics. For still other poets (Hugo, Shelley, Southey, Wordsworth), the Orient is a space of experimentation as they work to articulate attitudes towards certain poetic concepts. Yet all thirteen of these poets seem to assume without question that the Orient is an appropriate and productive site for the exploration of aesthetic problems, including the crucial relationship between nature and art. Each poet's work confirms that the Orient constitutes a greater gift than exotic subject matter. Orientalism offers a standard against which to react, a guide to follow, an example to imitate or to exceed. At times, as in Gautier's "Les Souhaits" or Tennyson's "Recollections of the Arabian Nights," orientalism's trace is heavily laid. At other times, as in Gautier's "L'Art" or Tennyson's "The Palace of Art," the trace is obscured or drops away. Yet it is there that we must look for the culmination of orientalist poetics, for there it has become an invisible center of gravity, holding the poem in a secure orbit around it. For the last half of the nineteenth century, from Gautier's "L'Art" in 1857 to Wilde's "The Decay of Lying" in 1891, it is this version of orientalist poetics that underpins the crucial idea of art for art's sake and thereby is able to structure, often from a point of virtual invisibility, the aesthetic developments of these decades.

Bibliography

Abrams, M.H. *The Correspondent Breeze: Essays on English Romanticism*. New York: Norton, 1984.
———. *The Mirror and the Lamp: Romantic Theory and the Critical Tradition*. Oxford: Oxford UP, 1953.
Ahmed, Leila. *Edward W. Lane*. London: Longman, 1978.
Aktulum, Kubilay. "Les Stéréotypes dans *Constantinople*." *Bulletin de la Société Théophile Gautier* 20 (1998): 33–53.
Ali, Muhsin Jassim. *Scheherazade in England: A Study of Nineteenth-Century English Criticism of the* Arabian Nights. Washington: Three Continents P, 1981.
Allott, Kenneth, ed. *Matthew Arnold*. Athens: Ohio UP, 1976.
Alloula, Malek. *The Colonial Harem*. 1981. Trans. Myrna Godzich and Wlad Godzich. Minneapolis: U of Minnesota P, 1986.
Arac, Jonathan and Harriet Ritvo, eds. *Macropolitics of Nineteenth-Century Literature: Nationalism, Exoticism, Imperialism*. Philadelphia: U of Pennsylvania P, 1991.
Aristotle, *Poetics*. Trans. Leon Golden. Tallahassee: UP of Florida, 1981.
Armstrong, Isobel. *Victorian Poetry: Poetry, Poetics and Politics*. London: Routledge, 1993.
Arnold, Matthew. *Essays in Criticism: First Series*. Ed. Thomas Marion Hoctor, S.S.J. Chicago: U of Chicago P, 1968.
———. *The Poems of Matthew Arnold*. Ed. Kenneth Allott and Miriam Allott. London: Longman, 1979.
Asad, Talal. "Two European Images of Non-European Rule." *Anthropology and the Colonial Encounter*. Ed. Talal Asad. London: Ithaca P, 1973.
Bate, W.J., ed. *Criticism: The Major Texts*. New York: Harcourt Brace Jovanovich, 1970.
Baudelaire, Charles. *Oeuvres complètes*. Ed. Marcel A. Ruff. Paris: Éditions du Seuil, 1968.
Beach, Joseph. *The Concept of Nature in Nineteenth-Century English Poetry*. New York: Pageant Book Company, 1956.
Beer, John. "Fragmentations and Ironies." *Questioning Romanticism*. Ed. John Beer. Baltimore: Johns Hopkins UP, 1995.
Behdad, Ali. *Belated Travelers: Orientalism in the Age of Colonial Dissolution*. Durham: Duke UP, 1994.
Behrendt, Stephen C. *Shelley and His Audiences*. Lincoln: U of Nebraska P, 1989.

Bewell, Alan. *Wordsworth and the Enlightenment: Nature, Man, and Society in the Experimental Poetry.* New Haven: Yale UP, 1989.
Beyer, Werner. *The Enchanted Forest.* Oxford: Basil Blackwell, 1963.
Bhabha, Homi. *The Location of Culture.* London: Routledge, 1994.
Bloom, Harold, ed. *Alfred Lord Tennyson.* New York: Chelsea, 1985.
Bongie, Chris. *Exotic Memories: Literature, Colonialism, and the Fin de Siècle.* Stanford: Stanford UP, 1991.
Bony, Jacques. "Musset et les formes poétiques." *Revue d'histoire littéraire de la France* 96.3 (1996): 483–93.
Bosworth, C. Edmund. "Arabic Influences in the Literature of Nineteenth and Early Twentieth Century Britain." *Tradition and Modernity in Arabic Language and Literature.* Ed. J.R. Smart. Richmond, UK: Curzon P, 1996. 155–64.
Boyd, John D., S.J. *The Function of Mimesis and Its Decline.* Cambridge: Harvard UP, 1968.
Brahimi, Denise. *Théophile et Judith vont en Orient.* Paris: La Boîte à Documents, 1990.
Brantlinger, Patrick. *Rule of Darkness: British Literature and Imperialism, 1830–1914.* Ithaca: Cornell UP, 1988.
Brown, Nathaniel. *Sexuality and Feminism in Shelley.* Cambridge: Harvard UP, 1979.
Brown, Wallace Cable. "Thomas Moore and the English Interest in the East." *Studies in Philology* 34 (1937): 576–87.
Bruce, James. *Travels to Discover the Source of the Nile, In the Years 1768, 1769, 1770, 1771, 1772 & 1773.* London: G.G.J. and J. Robinson, 1790.
Bruneau, Jean. *Le "Conte Oriental" de Flaubert.* Paris: Denoël, 1973.
Brunon, Jean-Claude. "Arabesque, baroque, caprice: essai sur la portée des *Grotesques* dans l'esthétique de Gautier." *L'Art et l'artiste.* Vol. 2. Proc. of International Colloquium, Sept. 1982, Montpellier. 369–79.
Buckler, William E. *On the Poetry of Matthew Arnold: Essays in Critical Reconstruction.* New York: New York UP, 1982.
Buisine, Alain. *L'Orient voilé.* Paris: Zulma, 1993.
Bulgin, Kathleen. "L'Appel de l'Orient au voyageur en Espagne." *L'Orient de Théophile Gautier.* Vol. 1. Proc. of International Colloquium, May 1990, Monte Cristo. 153–60.
Burwick, Frederick. "The Romantic Concept of Mimesis: *Idem et Alter.*" *Questioning Romanticism.* Ed. John Beer. Baltimore: Johns Hopkins UP, 1995. 179–208.
Butler, Marilyn. "Byron and the Empire in the East." *Byron: Augustan and Romantic.* Ed. Andrew Rutherford. London: Macmillan, 1990. 63–81.
———. "The Orientalism of Byron's *Giaour.*" *Byron and the Limits of Fiction.* Ed. Bernard Beatty and Vincent Newey. Liverpool: Liverpool UP, 1988. 78–96.

———. "Plotting the Revolution: The Political Narratives of Romantic Poetry and Criticism." *Romantic Revolutions: Criticism and Theory*. Ed. Kenneth R. Johnston et al. Bloomington: Indiana UP, 1990. 133–57.

———. "Repossessing the Past: The Case for an Open Literary History." *Rethinking Historicism: Critical Readings in Romantic History*. Ed. Marjorie Levinson, Marilyn Butler, Jerome McGann, Paul Hamilton. Oxford: Basil Blackwell, 1989. 64–84.

———. "Romanticism in England." *Romanticism in National Context*. Ed. Roy Porter and Mikulas Teich. Cambridge: Cambridge UP, 1988. 37–67.

Byron, George Gordon. *The Complete Poetical Works*. Ed. Jerome McGann. Vols. 3, 5. Oxford: Clarendon, 1981, 1986.

———. *Don Juan*. Ed. T.G. Steffan, E. Steffan, and W.W. Pratt. Rev. ed. Harmondsworth, UK: Penguin, 1977.

Cameron, Kenneth N. "A Major Source of *The Revolt of Islam*." *PMLA* 56 (1941): 175–206.

Cannon, Garland. "The Construction of the European Image of the Orient: A Bicentenary Reappraisal of Sir William Jones as Poet and Translator." *Comparative Criticism* 8 (1986): 167–88.

———. "Sir William Jones and Literary Orientalism." *Oriental Prospects: Western Literature and the Lure of the East*. Ed. C.C. Barfoot and Theo D'haen. Amsterdam: Rodopi, 1998. 27–41.

Caracciolo, Peter L., ed. *The* Arabian Nights *in English Literature: Studies in the Reception of* The Thousand and One Nights *into British Culture*. London: Macmillan, 1988.

Catani, Magda Campanini. "Le *Don Juan* d'Alfred de Musset." *Don Giovanni a più voci*. Ed. Anna Maria Finoli. Bologna: Cisalpino, 1996. 195–210.

Çelik, Zeynep. *Displaying the Orient: Architecture of Islam at Nineteenth-Century World's Fairs*. Berkeley: U of California P, 1992.

Chételat, E.J., ed. *Les Occidentales, ou lettres critiques sur les Orientales*. Paris: Hautecoeur-Martinet, 1829; rpt. 1970.

Chotard, Loïc. "A propos du Byronisme de Musset: la réception de Lord Byron à l'Académie Française." *Revue de littérature comparée* 2 (1990): 347–54.

[Coleridge, John Taylor]. "*Laon and Cythna, or the Revolution of the Golden City*." *Quarterly Review* 42 (April 1819): 460–71.

Coleridge, Samuel Taylor. *The Poetical Works of Samuel Taylor Coleridge*. Ed. Ernest Hartley Coleridge. London: Henry Frowde, 1912.

Conant, Martha Pike. *The Oriental Tale in England in the Eighteenth Century*. New York: Columbia UP, 1908; rpt. 1966.

Cooper, Barbara. "Parodying Hugo." *European Romantic Review* 2.1 (1991): 23–38.

Cotsell, Michael, ed. *Creditable Warriors, 1830–1876*. Atlantic Highlands, NJ: Ashfield, 1990.

Crichfield, Grant. "Decamps, Orientalist Intertext, and Counter-Discourse in Gautier's *Constantinople*." *Nineteenth-Century French Studies* 21.3–4 (1993): 305–21.
Culler, A. Dwight. *Imaginative Reason: The Poetry of Matthew Arnold*. New Haven: Yale UP, 1966.
Daniel, Norman. *Islam and the West: The Making of an Image*. Edinburgh: Edinburgh UP, 1960.
———. *Islam, Europe and Empire*. Edinburgh: Edinburgh UP, 1966.
de Lovenjoul, Charles. *Histoire des oeuvres de Théophile Gautier*. Vol. 2. Paris: Charpentier, 1887.
de Meester, Marie E. *Oriental Influences in the English Literature of the Nineteenth Century*. Heidelberg: Carl Winters, 1915.
Derrida, Jacques. *The Truth in Painting*. 1978. Trans. Geoff Bennington and Ian McLeod. Chicago: U of Chicago P, 1987.
Djaït, Hichem. *L'Europe et l'Islam*. Paris: Éditions du Seuil, 1978.
Edgeworth, Maria. "Murad the Unlucky." *Oriental Tales*. Ed. Robert L. Mack. Oxford: Oxford UP, 1992. 213–77.
El Nouty, Hassan. *Le Proche-Orient dans la littérature française, de Nerval à Barrès*. Paris: Nizet, 1958.
The Encyclopedia of Islam. 1st ed. Leiden: E.J. Brill, 1913–1936; rpt. 1987.
The Encyclopedia of Religion. New York: Macmillan, 1987.
Fairlie, Alison. *Leconte de Lisle's Poems on the Barbarian Races*. Cambridge: Cambridge UP, 1947.
Favret, Mary A. and Nicola J. Watson. *At the Limits of Romanticism: Essays in Cultural, Feminist, and Materialist Criticism*. Bloomington: Indiana UP, 1994.
Ferriss, Suzanne. "Romantic Carnivalesque: Byron's *The Tale of Calil, Beppo*, and *Don Juan*." *Rereading Byron: Essays Selected from Hofstra University's Byron Bicentennial Conference*. Ed. Alice Levine and Robert N. Keane. New York: Garland, 1993. 133–49.
Fertel, Randy J. "Antipastoral and the Attack on Naturalism in Tennyson's *Idylls of the King*." *Victorian Poetry* 19.4 (1981): 337–50.
Fetzer, John Francis. "Romantic Irony." *European Romanticism: Literary Cross-Currents, Modes, and Models*. Ed. Gerhart Hoffmeister. Detroit: Wayne State UP, 1990. 19–36.
Fischer, Hermann. *Romantic Verse Narrative: The History of a Genre*. 1964. Trans. Sue Bollans. Cambridge: Cambridge UP, 1991.
Fletcher, Pauline. *Gardens and Grim Ravines: The Language of Landscape in Victorian Poetry*. Princeton: Princeton UP, 1983.
Forman, H. Buxton. *The Shelley Library: An Essay in Bibliography*. London: Reeves and Turner, 1886.
Frankel, Nick. "'Ave Imperatrix': Oscar Wilde and the Poetry of Englishness." *Victorian Poetry* 35.2 (1997): 117–37.

Franklin, Caroline. "Haidée and Neuha: Byron's Heroines of the South." *Byron Journal*. 18 (1990): 37–49.

Fry, Paul H. "Green to the Very Door? The Natural Wordsworth." *Studies in Romanticism*. 35.4 (1996): 535–51.

Galland, Antoine. *Les Milles et une nuits: contes arabes traduits par Galland*. Vol. 1. Paris: Garnier, 1960.

Garber, Frederick. *Self, Text, and Romantic Irony: The Example of Byron*. Princeteon: Princeton UP, 1988.

Gastinel, Pierre. *Le Romantisme d'Alfred de Musset*. Paris: Hachette, [1933].

Gautier, Théophile. *L'Orient*. 2 vols. Paris: Charpentier, 1877.

———. *Poésies complètes de Théophile Gautier*. Ed. René Jasinski. 3 vols. Paris: Nizet, 1970.

———. *Voyage en Egypte*. Ed. Paolo Tortonese. Paris: La Boîte à Documents, 1991.

Gebauer, Gunter and Christoph Wulf, *Mimesis: Culture, Art, Society*. Trans. Don Reneau. Berkeley: U of California P, 1995.

Goethe, Johann Wolfgang von. *Goethe's Reineke Fox, West-Eastern Divan, and Achilleid*. Trans. Alexander Rogers. London: George Bell and Sons, 1890.

Goldberg, Brian. "'A Sea Reflecting Love': Tennyson, Shelley, and the Aesthetics of the Image in the Marketplace." *Modern Language Quarterly*. 59.1 (1998): 71–97.

Goldberg, Jeffrey. "The Education of a Holy Warrior." *New York Times Magazine*. 25 June 2000: 32+.

Gordon, Rae Beth. *Ornament, Fantasy, and Desire in Nineteenth-Century French Literature*. Princeton: Princeton UP, 1992.

Grimes, Kyle. "Censorship, Violence, and Political Rhetoric: *The Revolt of Islam* in Its Time." *Keats-Shelley Journal* 43 (1994): 98–116.

Grossir, Claudine. *L'Islam des Romantiques*. Vol. 1. Paris: Maisonneuve et Larose, 1984.

Gutschera, Deborah A. "The Drama of Reenactment in Shelley's *The Revolt of Islam*." *Keats-Shelley Journal* 35 (1986): 111–25.

Haddad, Emily. "Florence Nightingale, Felicia Hemans, and James Bruce's 'Fountains of the Nile.'" *Journal of African Travel-Writing* 5 (1998): 53–69.

Haddawy, Husain, trans. *The Arabian Nights*. New York: W.W. Norton, 1990.

Hamrick, L. Cassandra. "Gautier et l'anarchie de l'art." *Relire Théophile Gautier: le plaisir du texte*. Ed. Freeman G. Henry. Amsterdam: Rodopi, 1998. 91–117.

Harper, Mary J. "Recovering the Other: Women and the Orient in Writings of Early Nineteenth-Century France." *Critical Matrix: Princeton Working Papers in Women's Studies* 1.3 (1985).

Hartman, Elwood. *Three Nineteenth-Century French Writer/Artists and the Maghreb: The Literary and Artistic Depictions of North Africa by Théophile Gautier, Eugène Fromentin, and Pierre Loti*. Tübingen: Narr, 1994.

Haslett, Moyra. *Byron's* Don Juan *and the Don Juan Legend*. Oxford: Clarendon, 1997.

Haswell, Richard H. "Shelley's *The Revolt of Islam*: 'The Connexion of Its Parts.'" *Keats-Shelley Journal* 25 (1976): 81–102.

Haxell, Nichola. "Hugo, Gautier and the Obelisk of Luxor (Place de la Concorde) During the Second Republic." *Nineteenth-Century French Studies* 18.1–2 (1989–90): 65–77.

Heffernan, James A.W. "Wordsworth's London: The Imperial Monster." *Studies in Romanticism* 37.3 (1998): 421–43.

Hemans, Felicia. *The Poetical Works of Felicia Dorothea Hemans*. Oxford: Oxford UP, 1914.

Hentsch, Thierry. *Imagining the Middle East*. Trans. Fred. A. Reed. Montreal: Black Rose Books, 1992.

Hickey, Alison. "Coleridge, Southey, 'and Co.': Collaboration and Authority." *Studies in Romanticism* 37.3 (1998): 305–49.

Hoffpauir, Richard. "The Thematic Structure of Southey's Epic Poetry." *The Wordsworth Circle* 6.4 (1975): 240–8.

Hollander, John. "Tennyson's Melody." *Alfred Lord Tennyson*. Ed. Harold Bloom. New York: Chelsea, 1985. 103–26.

Honan, Part. *Matthew Arnold: A Life*. New York: McGraw-Hill,1981.

———. "Matthew Arnold: Europeanism and England." *Creditable Warriors, 1830–1876*. Ed. Michael Cotsell. Atlantic Highlands, NJ: Ashfield, 1990. 143–57.

Hourani, Albert. *Europe and the Middle East*. Berkeley: U of California P, 1980.

———. *Islam in European Thought*. Cambridge: Cambridge UP, 1991.

Hughes, Robert. "Envoy to Two Cultures." *Time*. June 21, 1992: 60–2.

Hugo, Victor. *Odes et Ballades, Les Orientales*. Paris: Flammarion, 1968.

———. *Les Orientales*. Ed. Élisabeth Barineau. 2 vols. Paris: Marcel Didier, 1952, 1954.

Irwin, Robert. *The Arabian Nights: A Companion*. London: Allen Lane, 1994.

[Jeffrey, Francis]. "*Thalaba the Destroyer*." *Edinburgh Review* 1 (Oct. 1802): 63–83.

Jones, Mark. "Double Economics: Ambivalence in Wordsworth's Pastoral." *PMLA* 108.5 (1993): 1098–113.

Jones, William. *Works*. Vols. 10, 12. London: Stockdale and Walker, 1807.

Jourda, Pierre. *L'Exotisme dans la littérature depuis Chateaubriand*. 2 vols. Paris: Boivin, 1938, 1956.

Kabbani, Rana. *Imperial Fictions: Europe's Myths of Orient*. London: Pandora, 1994.

Kabitoglou, E. Douka. "Shelley's (Feminist) Discourse on the Female: *The Revolt of Islam*." *Arbeiten aus Anglistik und Amerikanistik* 15.2 (1990): 139–50.
Keach, William. "Cythna's Subtler Language." *Studies in Romanticism* 37.1 (1998): 7–16.
Kelsall, Malcolm. "Byron and the Women of the Harem." *Rereading Byron: Essays Selected from Hofstra University's Byron Bicentennial Conference.* Ed. Alice Levine and Robert N. Keane. New York: Garland, 1993. 165–73.
Kestner, Joseph. "The Genre of Landor's *Gebir*." *The Wordsworth Circle* 5.1 (1974): 41–9.
Kühnel, Ernst. *The Arabesque: Meaning and Transformation of an Ornament*. 1949. Trans. Richard Ettinghausen. Graz, Austria: Verlag für Sammler, 1976.
Landor, Walter Savage. *The Poetical Works of Walter Savage Landor*. Ed. Stephen Wheeler. 3 vols. Oxford: Clarendon, 1937.
Laplace-Sinatra, Michael. "'I *Will* Live Beyond This Life': Shelley, Prefaces and Reviewers." *Keats-Shelley Review* 13 (1999): 88–104.
Lardoux, Jacques. "L'Orient dans les poésies de Théophile Gautier." *L'Orient de Théophile Gautier*. Vol. 1. Proc. of International Colloquium, May 1990, Monte Cristo. 213–31.
Latimer, Dan. "Real Culture and Unreal Nature: Wordsworth's Kingdom of Dissimilitude." *New Orleans Review* 14.1 (1987): 45–54.
Laubriet, Pierre. "Théophile Gautier, un annonciateur de l'esprit 'fin de siècle'?" *Bulletin de la Société Théophile Gautier* 13 (1991): 7–34.
Leask, Nigel. *British Romantic Writers and the East: Anxieties of Empire*. Cambridge: Cambridge UP, 1992.
Leconte de Lisle. *Oeuvres de Leconte de Lisle*. Ed. Edgard Pich. 4 vols. Paris: Société d'édition "Les belles lettres," 1976.
Levinson, Marjorie. *The Romantic Fragment Poem: A Critique of a Form*. Chapel Hill: U of North Carolina P, 1986.
Lindner, Larry. "Tunisia: Where the sands of time are still vibrant." *The Boston Globe*. 23 Oct. 1994. Special Section: "Adventures in Travel": 10+.
Lootens, Tricia. "Hemans and Home: Victorianism, Feminine 'Internal Enemies,' and the Domestication of National Identity." *PMLA* 109.2 (1994): 238–53.
Lovejoy, Arthur O. "On the Discrimination of Romanticisms." *English Romantic Poets: Modern Essays in Criticism*. Ed. M.H. Abrams. New York: Oxford UP, 1960. 3–24.
Lowe, Lisa. *Critical Terrains: French and British Orientalisms*. Ithaca: Cornell UP, 1991.
Mack, Anne, J.J. Rome, and Georg Mannejc. "Literary History, Romanticism, and Felicia Hemans." *Modern Language Quarterly* 54.2 (1993): 215–35.

MacKenzie, John M. *Orientalism: History, Theory, and the Arts*. Manchester: Manchester UP, 1995.
Magri, Véronique. *Le Discours sur l'autre: à travers quatre récits de voyage en Orient*. Paris: Honoré Champion, 1995.
Makdisi, Saree. *Romantic Imperialism: Universal Empire and the Culture of Modernity*. Cambridge: Cambridge UP, 1998.
Mannsåker, Frances. "Elegancy and Wilderness: Reflections of the East in the Eighteenth-Century Imagination." *Exoticism in the Enlightenment*. Ed. G.S. Rousseau and Roy Porter. Manchester: Manchester UP, 1990. 175–95.
Marez, Curtis. "The Other Addict: Reflections on Colonialism and Oscar Wilde's Opium Smoke Screen." *ELH* 64.1 (1997): 257–87.
McBratney, John. "Rebuilding Akbar's 'Fane': Tennyson's Reclamation of the East." *Victorian Poetry* 31.4 (1993): 411–7.
McFarland, Thomas. "Green Savannahs: Wordsworth and the Moral Bonding with Nature." *European Romantic Review* 3.1 (1992): 41–64.
———. *Romanticism and the Forms of Ruin: Wordsworth, Coleridge, and the Modalities of Fragmentation*. Princeton: Princeton UP, 1981.
McGann, Jerome J. "*Don Juan*: Form." *Lord Byron's* Don Juan. Ed. Harold Bloom. New York: Chelsea House, 1987.
McLuhan, Marshall. "Tennyson and Picturesque Poetry." *Alfred Lord Tennyson*. Ed. Harold Bloom. New York: Chelsea, 1985. 41–56.
McNiece, Gerald. *Shelley and the Revolutionary Idea*. Cambridge: Harvard UP, 1969.
McSweeney, Kerry. *Tennyson and Swinburne as Romantic Naturalists*. Toronto: U of Toronto P, 1981.
Melberg, Arne. *Theories of Mimesis*. Cambridge: Cambridge UP, 1995.
Mellor, Anne K. "Immortality or Monstrosity? Reflections on the Sublime in Romantic Literature and Art." *The Romantic Imagination: Literature and Art in England and Germany*. Ed. Frederick Burwick and Jürgen Klein. Amsterdam: Rodopi, 1996.
Metlitzki, Dorothee. *The Matter of Araby in Medieval England*. New Haven: Yale UP, 1977.
Milligan, Barry. *Pleasures and Pains: Opium and the Orient in Nineteenth-Century British Culture*. Charlottesville: UP of Virginia, 1995.
Mitchell, Timothy. *Colonising Egypt*. Cambridge: Cambridge UP, 1988.
Moore, Thomas. *Lalla Rookh, An Oriental Romance*. London: Longman, Orme, Brown, Green, and Longmans; and Philadelphia: Lea and Blanchard, 1839.
———. *Poetical Works*. Paris: Galignani, 1829.
———. *Poetical Works*. London: Longman, Orme, Brown, Green, and Longmans, 1841.
———. *The Poetical Works of Thomas Moore*. New York: A.C. Armstrong and Son, 1884.

Mordell, Albert, ed. *Notorious Literary Attacks*. New York: Boni and Liveright, 1926.
Morgan, Peter. "Southey on Poetry." *Tennessee Studies in Literature*. 26 (1971): 77–89.
Morgan, Thaïs E. "Rereading Nature: Wordsworth between Swinburne and Arnold." *Victorian Poetry* 24.4 (1986): 427–39.
Murray, E.B. "'Elective Affinity' in *The Revolt of Islam*." *Journal of English and Germanic Philology* 67 (1968): 570–85.
Musset, Alfred de. *Poésies complètes*. Ed. Maurice Allem. Paris: Gallimard, 1957.
———. *Premières Poésies, Poésies nouvelles*. Ed. Patrick Berthier. Paris: Gallimard, 1976.
Mutman, Mahmut and Meyda Yegenoglu, eds. *Orientalism and Cultural Differences*. Inscriptions 6. Santa Cruz: Center for Cultural Studies, University of California at Santa Cruz, 1992.
Naddaff, Sandra. *Arabesque: Narrative Structure and the Aesthetics of Repetition in 1001 Nights*. Evanston, IL: Northwestern UP, 1991.
Najarian, James. "'Curled minion, dancer, coiner of sweet words': Keats, Dandyism, and Sexual Indeterminacy in *Sohrab and Rustum*." *Victorian Poetry* 35.1 (1997): 23–42.
Nasir, Sari J. *The Arabs and the English*. London: Longman, 1976; 2nd ed. 1979.
Nunokawa, Jeff. "Oscar Wilde in Japan: Aestheticism, Orientalism and the Derealization of the Homosexual." *Oscar Wilde: A Collection of Critical Essays*. Ed. Jonathan Freedman. Upper Saddle River, NJ: Prentice Hall, 1996. 149–57.
Orel, Harold. "Shelley's *The Revolt of Islam*: The Last Great Poem of the English Enlightenment?" *Studies on Voltaire and the Eighteenth Century* 89 (1972): 1187–207.
Osborne, Edna. *Oriental Diction and Theme in English Verse, 1740–1840*. Bulletin of the University of Kansas Humanistic Studies 2.1 (1916).
Paden, W.D. *Tennyson in Egypt: A Study of the Imagery in His Earlier Work*. Lawrence, KS: U of Kansas Publications, 1942.
Paret, R. "Al-Burâk." *The Encyclopedia of Islam*. 2nd ed. Leiden: E.J. Brill, 1958–.
Peacock, Thomas Love. *Memoirs of Shelley and Other Essays and Reviews*. Ed. Howard Mills. London: Rupert Hart-Davis, 1970.
Peltason, Timothy. "Tennyson, Nature, and Romantic Nature Poetry." *Philological Quarterly* 63.1 (1984): 75–93.
Pich, Edgard. *Leconte de Lisle et sa création poétique: Poèmes antiques et Poèmes barbares, 1852–1874*. Paris: Chirat, 1975.
Pinsky, Robert. *Landor's Poetry*. Chicago: U of Chicago P, 1968.
Porter, Dennis. *Haunted Journeys: Desire and Transgression in European Travel Writing*. Princeton: Princeton UP, 1991.

———. "Orientalism and Its Problems." *The Politics of Theory*. Ed. Francis Barker et al. Colchester, UK: University of Essex, 1983. 179–211.
Proudfit, Charles L. "Southey and Landor: A Literary Friendship." *The Wordsworth Circle* 5.2 (1974): 105–12.
Rajan, Balachandra. "Monstrous Mythologies: Southey and *The Curse of Kehama*." *European Romantic Review* 9.2 (1998): 201–16.
Rees, Margaret. *Alfred de Musset*. New York: Twayne, 1971.
Reiman, Donald H., ed. *Shelley and his Circle, 1773–1822*. Vol. 5. Cambridge: Harvard UP, 1973.
Richardson, Alan. "Escape from the Seraglio: Cultural Transvestism in *Don Juan*." *Rereading Byron: Essays Selected from Hofstra University's Byron Bicentennial Conference*. Ed. Alice Levine and Robert N. Keane. New York: Garland, 1993. 175–85.
———. *Literature, Education, and Romanticism: Reading as Social Practice, 1780–1832*. Cambridge: Cambridge UP, 1994.
Richardson, Joanna. *Théophile Gautier: His Life and Times*. London: Max Reinhardt, 1958.
Ricks, Christopher. *Tennyson*. 2nd ed. London: Macmillan, 1989.
Rieben, Pierre-André. *Délires Romantiques: Musset, Nodier, Gautier, Hugo*. Paris: José Corti, 1989.
Rieder, John. "Wordsworth and Romanticism in the Academy." *At the Limits of Romanticism: Essays in Cultural, Feminist, and Materialist Criticism*. Ed. Mary A. Favret and Nicola J. Watson. Bloomington: Indiana UP, 1994. 21–39.
Riffaterre, Michael. *Semiotics of Poetry*. Bloomington: Indiana UP, 1978.
Robinson, Charles E. "Percy Bysshe Shelley, Charles Ollier, and William Blackwood: The Contexts of Early Nineteenth-Century Publishing." *Shelley Revalued: Essays from the Gregynog Conference*. Ed. Kelvin Everest. Leicester: Leicester UP, 1983. 183–226.
Rodinson, Maxime. *Europe and the Mystique of Islam*. 1980. Trans. Roger Veinus. Seattle: U of Washington P, 1991.
Roper, Alan. *Arnold's Poetic Landscapes*. Baltimore: Johns Hopkins UP, 1969.
Rossington, Michael. "Shelley and the Orient." *The Keats-Shelley Review* 6 (1991): 18–36.
Rousseau, G.S. and Roy Porter, eds. *Exoticism in the Enlightenment*. Manchester: Manchester UP, 1990.
Ruby, Franck. "Théophile Gautier et la question de 'l'art pour l'art.'" *Bulletin de la Société Théophile Gautier* 20 (1998): 3–13.
Ruff, James Lynn. *Shelley's* The Revolt of Islam. Salzburg: Institut für Englishe Sprache und Literatur, Universität Salzburg, 1972.
Saglia, Diego. "Epic or Domestic?: Felicia Hemans's Heroic Poetry and the Myth of the Victorian Poetess." *Rivista di Studi Vittoriani* 2.4 (1997): 125–47.

———. "Nationalist Texts and Counter-Texts: Southey's *Roderick* and the Dissensions of the Annotated Romance. *Nineteenth-Century Literature* 53.4 (1999): 421–51.
———. "Spain and Byron's Construction of Place." *Byron Journal*. 22 (1994): 31–42.
Said, Edward W. *Orientalism*. New York: Random House, 1978.
Sammells, Neil. "Wilde Nature." *Writing the Environment: Ecocriticism and Literature*. Ed. Richard Kerridge and Neil Sammells. London: Zed, 1998. 124–33.
Schick, Constance Gosselin. "A Case Study of Descriptive Perversion: Théophile Gautier's Travel Literature." *Romanic Review* 78.3 (1987): 359–67.
Schimmel, Annemarie. *Mystical Dimensions of Islam*. Chapel Hill: U of North Carolina P, 1975.
Schlegel, Friedrich. *Dialogue on Poetry and Literary Aphorisms*. Trans. Ernst Behler and Roman Struc. University Park: Pennsylvania State UP, 1968.
Schrieke, B., J. Horovitz, and J.E. Bencheikh. "Mi'rādj." *The Encyclopedia of Islam*. 2nd ed. Leiden: E.J. Brill, 1958–.
Schwab, Raymond. *The Oriental Renaissance: Europe's Rediscovery of India and the East, 1680–1880*. 1950. Trans. Gene Patterson-Black and Victor Reinking. New York: Columbia UP, 1984.
[Scott, Walter]. "The Curse of Kehama." *Quarterly Review* 9 (Feb. 1811): 40–61.
———. *The Talisman*. 1825. New York: Dodd, Mead, 1929.
Sedgwick, Henry Dwight. *Alfred de Musset: 1810–1857*. Indianapolis: Bobbs-Merrill, 1931.
Seyhan, Azade. *Representation and Its Discontents: The Critical Legacy of German Romanticism*. Berkeley: U of California P, 1992.
Sharafuddin, Mohammed. *Islam and Romantic Orientalism: Literary Encounters with the Orient*. London: I.B. Tauris, 1994.
Shatto, Susan. "The Strange Charm of 'Far, Far Away': Tennyson, the Continent, and the Empire." *Creditable Warriors, 1830–1876*. Ed. Michael Cotsell. Atlantic Highlands, NJ: Ashfield, 1990. 113–29.
Shaw, Marion. "Tennyson's Dark Continent." *Victorian Poetry* 32.2 (1994): 157–69.
Shelley, Percy Bysshe. *The Complete Poetical Works of Percy Bysshe Shelley*. Ed. Roger Ingpen and Walter E. Peck. Vol. 1. New York: Charles Scribner's Sons, 1927.
———. *The Complete Poetical Works of Percy Bysshe Shelley*. Ed. Thomas Hutchinson. New York: Oxford UP, 1933.
———. *The Complete Poetical Works of Percy Bysshe Shelley*. Ed. Neville Rogers. Vols. 1, 2. Oxford: Oxford UP, 1975.

———. *The Letters of Percy Bysshe Shelley.* Ed. Roger Ingpen. Vol. 2. London: Sir Isaac Pitman & Sons, 1909.
———. *The Poetical Works of Percy Bysshe Shelley.* Ed. W.M. Rossetti. Vol. 1. London: E. Moxon, Son, & Co., 1870.
Shurbutt, Sylvia Bailey. "Matthew Arnold's Concept of Nature: A Synthesist's View." *Victorian Poetry* 23.1 (1985): 97–104.
———. "The Poetry of Matthew Arnold: Nature and the Oriental Wisdom." *University of Dayton Review* 17.3 (1985–86): 41–8.
Singh, Jyotsna G. *Colonial Narratives/Cultural Dialogues: "Discoveries" of India in the Language of Colonialism.* London: Routledge, 1996.
Smith, Byron Porter. *Islam in English Literature.* Delmar, NY: Caravan, 1939; 2nd ed. 1977.
Southern, R.W. *Western Views of Islam in the Middle Ages.* Cambridge: Harvard UP, 1962.
Southey, Robert. *The Complete Poetical Works of Robert Southey.* New York: D. Appleton; and Philadelphia: George S. Appleton, 1846.
———. "Gebir; a Poem." *Critical Review* 27 (Sept. 1799): 29–39.
———. *The Life and Correspondence of Robert Southey.* Ed. Charles Cuthbert Southey. Vols. 1, 2. London: Longman, Brown, Green, and Longmans, 1849, 1850.
Sperry, Stuart. "The Sexual Theme in Shelley's *The Revolt of Islam.*" *Journal of English and Germanic Philology* 82.1 (1983): 32–49.
———. *Shelley's Major Verse: The Narrative and Dramatic Poetry.* Cambridge: Harvard UP, 1988.
Steele, Robert O. "The Avant-gardism of Leconte de Lisle." *Nineteenth-Century French Studies* 17.3–4 (1989): 318–25.
Stones, Graeme. "'Upon a dromedary mounted high.'" *Charles Lamb Bulletin* 104 (1998): 145–58.
Super, R.H. *Walter Savage Landor: A Biography.* New York: New York UP, 1954.
Sweet, Nanora. "History, Imperialism, and the Aesthetics of the Beautiful: Hemans and the Post-Napoleonic Moment." *At the Limits of Romanticism: Essays in Cultural, Feminist, and Materialist Criticism.* Ed. Mary A. Favret and Nicola J. Watson. Bloomington: Indiana UP, 1994. 170–84.
Taussig, Michael. *Mimesis and Alterity: A Particular History of the Senses.* New York: Routledge, 1993.
[Taylor, William]. "*Thalaba the Destroyer.*" *The Critical Review* 39 (Sept. 1803): 369–79.
Tennant, P.E. *Théophile Gautier.* London: Athlone, 1975.
Tennyson, Alfred. *The Poems of Tennyson.* Ed. Christopher Ricks. 2nd ed. 3 vols. Berkeley: U of California P, 1987.
Tessier, Thérèse. *La Poésie lyrique de Thomas Moore.* Paris: Didier, 1976.
Thacker, Christopher. *The Wildness Pleases: The Origins of Romanticism.* New York: St. Martin's, 1983.

"*Thalaba the Destroyer*." *Monthly Review* 39 (Sept. 1802): 240–51.
Thesing, William B. "Matthew Arnold and the Possibilities of the Nineteenth-Century City." *CLA Journal* 24.3 (1981): 287–303.
Thoreau, Henry David. *Walden: or, Life in the Woods*. 1854. New York: Anchor, 1973.
Thorpe, Douglas. "Shelley's Golden Verbal City." *Journal of English and German Philology* 86.2 (1987): 215–27.
Tidrick, Kathryn. *Heart-beguiling Araby: The English Romance with Arabia*. Cambridge: Cambridge UP, 1981; rev. ed.1989.
Tucker, Herbert. *Tennyson and the Doom of Romanticism*. Cambridge: Harvard UP, 1988.
Turner, Bryan S. *Orientalism, Postmodernism and Globalism*. London: Routledge, 1994.
Vianey, Joseph. *Les Poèmes barbares de Leconte de Lisle*. Paris: Nizet, 1955.
Vitoux, Pierre. "*Gebir* as an Heroic Poem." *The Wordsworth Circle* 7.1 (1976): 51–7.
Vives, Luc. "Les Poèmes de la momie: influence de l'imaginaire orientaliste et égyptisant de Théophile Gautier dans l'oeuvre de Charles Baudelaire." *Bulletin de la Société Théophile Gautier* 21 (1999): 53-70.
Voisin, Marcel. "La Pensée de Théophile Gautier." *Relire Théophile Gautier: le plaisir du texte*. Ed. Freeman G. Henry. Amsterdam: Rodopi, 1998. 73–89.
Waardenburg, Jean-Jacques. *L'Islam dans le miroir de l'occident*. Paris: Mouton, 1963.
Watt, W. Montgomery. *Muhammad: Prophet and Statesman*. Oxford: Oxford UP, 1961.
Wensinck, A. J. "Hudhud." *The Encyclopedia of Islam*. 2nd ed. Leiden: E.J. Brill, 1958–.
Wesling, Donald. *Wordsworth and the Adequacy of Landscape*. London: Routledge and Kegan Paul, 1970.
Whitton, David. *Molière: Don Juan*. Cambridge: Cambridge UP, 1995.
Whyte, Peter. "'L'Art' de Gautier: genèse et sens." *Relire Théophile Gautier: le plaisir du texte*. Ed. Freeman G. Henry. Amsterdam: Rodopi, 1998. 119–39.
Wickens, G. M. "Hāfiz." *The Encyclopedia of Islam*. 2nd. ed. Leiden: E.J. Brill, 1958–.
———. "*Lalla Rookh* and the Romantic Tradition of Islamic Literature in English." *Yearbook of Comparative and General Literature* 20 (1971): 61–6.
Wilde, Oscar. *Complete Works of Oscar Wilde*. Ed. J.B. Foreman. London: Collins, 1966; rpt. 1983.
Wolfson, Susan J. "'Domestic Affections' and 'the spear of Minerva': Felicia Hemans and the Dilemma of Gender." *Re-Visioning Romanticism: British*

Women Writers, 1776–1837. Ed. Carol Shiner Wilson and Joel Haefner. Philadelphia: U of Pennsylvania P, 1994. 128–66.

———. "'Their she Condition': Cross-Dressing and the Politics of Gender in Don Juan." *ELH* 54.3 (1987): 585–617.

Wollstonecraft, *A Vindication of the Rights of Woman*. 1792. Ed. Carol H. Poston. New York: Norton, 1975.

Woodring, Carl. "Wordsworth and the Victorians." *The Age of William Wordsworth: Critical Essays on the Romantic Tradition*. Ed. Kenneth R. Johnston and Gene W. Ruoff. New Brunswick: Rutgers UP, 1987. 261–75.

Woolford, "The Sick King in Bokhara: Arnold and the Sublime of Suffering." *Matthew Arnold: Between Two Worlds*. Ed. Robert Giddings. London: Vision , 1986. 100–20.

Wordsworth, William. *Early Poems and Fragments, 1785–1797*. Ed. Carol Landon and Jared Curtis. Ithaca: Cornell UP, 1997.

———. *Poems*. Ed. John O. Hayden. 2 vols. London: Penguin, 1977.

———. *The Prelude, or Growth of a Poet's Mind*. Ed. Ernest de Selincourt. 2nd ed. rev. by Helen Darbishire. Oxford: Clarendon, 1959.

"The Works of the English Poets, from Chaucer to Cowper." *Quarterly Review* 23 (Oct. 1814): 60–90.

Worringer, Wilhelm. *Abstraction and Empathy: A Contribution to the Psychology of Style*. 1908. Trans. Michael Bullock. New York: International Universities P, 1967.

Xiaoyi, Zhou. "Oscar Wilde's Orientalism and Late Nineteenth-Century European Consumer Culture." *ARIEL: A Review of International English Literature* 28.4 (1997): 49–71.

Yee, Jennifer. "La Tahoser de Gautier et la Salammbô de Flaubert: l'orientale et le voyage au-delà de l'histoire." *Australian Journal of French Studies* 36.2 (1999): 188–99.

Yegenoglu, Meyda. *Colonial Fantasies: Towards a Feminist Reading of Orientalism*. Cambridge: Cambridge UP, 1998.

Yohannan, John D. *Persian Poetry in England and America: A 200-Year History*. Delmar, NY: Caravan, 1977.

Index

Abrams, M.H. 2, 101–2, 106, 157n.3
Addison, Joseph 48
aestheticism 6, 155
Africa 40, 81, 85, 110, 118
Algeria 7n.21, 59n.13, 126n.62
allegory 14, 35, 52–3, 54, 82
annotation 41–5, 141
arabesque 6, 50–53, 60, 64, 65, 82, 83n.81, 89n.98, 97, 160n.10, 170, 198
Arabia 33–8, 42, 62, 84, 104, 105, 107, 115, 123, 165
Arabian Nights; see *Thousand and One Nights*
"Arabian Tale;" see "oriental tale"
archetype, character or setting as 35–6, 38, 58, 93–4, 107, 125, 167
architecture 7, 40n.83, 43n.91, 121n.53, 140, 146, 151, 155, 160–61, 165, 167, 169–71, 173, 174, 191
Aristotle 11, 48, 55, 101
Armstrong, Isobel 2, 142n.89, 190n.61,191
Arnold, Matthew 136, 142, 152, 201
  and nature 9, 101, 141, 151, 153
  Works:
    "In Harmony with Nature" 142–7, 148, 149
    "A Persian Passion Play" 142n.89
    "The Sick King in Bokhara" 142, 144–7, 148, 149, 161n.12
art 3, 10, 59, 73, 153, 155, 167, 176–7, 180, 186, 197, 200
  as affiliated with Orient 156–7, 160–61, 163, 168–71, 173–5, 177–8, 181–4, 189–91, 201
art for art's sake 2, 6, 10, 69, 119, 155, 170–71, 191, 195, 199, 201
Asia 56, 65–7, 128
Austen, Jane 109
avant-garde, literary 2, 6, 8–9, 154, 169

Baghdad 5, 151, 166, 181n.43, 183, 188
Barthes, Roland 51n.126, 89, 195n.73

Basra 150–51
Baudelaire, Charles 66n.29, 85n.87, 95n.101, 129n.68
Beer, John 83, 84, 104n.15
Behdad, Ali 8
Bewell, Alan 105–6, 108n.28
Bhabha, Homi 65
Bibliothèque orientale; see Barthélemy d'Herbelot
Bongie, Chris 7
Brantlinger, Patrick 7
Bruce, James 110–12, 113, 138, 139
Bukhara 145–6
Butler, Marilyn 15, 29n.61, 35, 43n.94, 52n.131, 103, 107
Byron, George Gordon 55, 89, 96, 104, 152, 171n.29
  and nature 9, 142, 146, 151
  Works:
    The Bride of Abydos 136–8, 140, 157n.4
    The Corsair 136, 138–40
    Don Juan 9, 55, 74–9, 81, 82, 84, 85, 86–7, 89n.97, 90–92, 94, 100
    The Giaour 84n.84, 136, 138–41
    "Turkish Tales" 76, 136, 139, 140, 141, 146

Çelik, Zeynep 7, 169n.24
Chénier, Louis de 37, 43
Chételat, E.J. 70–75, 101, 102, 154
China 56
Christianity 22–4, 25n.51, 92, 142n.89, 161n.14
Coleridge, Samuel Taylor 58n.12, 84, 95n.101, 104, 186, 187, 188n.56
colonialism 6, 17n.26, 29, 43n.91, 54, 63n.24
Constantinople 14, 15, 18, 24, 76, 140
Cooper, Barbara 70, 79
Critical Review 45

Daniel, Norman 6, 25n.49, 109
decoration; *see* ornament
Derrida, Jacques 44, 49n.120, 51n.126, 160
desert 9, 26, 31, 33–6, 42–3, 68, 84, 103n.10, 104–6, 108, 110, 111–12, 113n.43, 115, 119–20, 122–4, 126–37, 140, 146, 157n.6, 182, 188, 193, 201
de Quincey, Thomas 55n.2, 95n.101
didacticism 9, 12, 13, 25–32, 35, 38, 46, 53
digression, narrative 77–8, 81, 84, 86, 90
disorder, as stereotype of Orient 43, 63–4, 76–8
dream 25, 26, 60, 63, 65–8, 93–5, 96, 121–5, 179, 198; *see also* fantasy

Edgeworth, Maria 27
Edinburgh Review 45, 46
Egypt 56, 110, 115, 117, 126n.62, 128, 168n.22, 197n.77, 199–200
exoticism 2, 3, 16, 26n.55, 33, 35, 42, 53, 62, 76, 88, 104, 105, 107, 115n.45, 118, 119, 126, 191, 200, 201
experimentation, poetic 2, 10, 13, 27, 52, 59, 60, 65, 74, 85, 100, 101, 121, 152, 154, 201

fantasy 1, 5, 9, 49, 58–60, 62, 64–6, 68–9, 87, 92, 94–6, 99–100, 164–7, 169, 183–6, 190, 192, 193n.69, 196
Ferriss, Suzanne 75, 77, 78, 82n.75
Flaubert, Gustave 42n.90, 126, 168n.23, 195n.73
Fletcher, Pauline 151–2, 187n.54
Foucault, Michel 6
fragment, as literary device 82–4, 87, 88, 141, 168n.23
French Revolution 13–15
Fry, Paul 103, 112

Galland, Antoine 4, 95
Gautier, Théophile 137, 147, 152, 201
  and art 2, 10, 155, 180, 197
  and nature 9, 101, 142, 153
  Works:
    "L'Art" 6, 196–8, 201
    "La Caravane" 126–30, 131, 132
    "Ce que disent les hirondelles" 1
    Émaux et camées 192, 195, 196

"La Fellah" 1, 196
"In deserto" 130–6, 140, 179
"Nostalgies d'obélisques" 196
"Le Poème de la femme" 196
"Préface" 192–6, 198
Roman de la momie 128
"Les Souhaits" 161n.12, 164–71, 173, 174, 176, 186, 200, 201
Goethe, Johann Wolfgang von 192–5, 198
Gordon, Rae Beth 46, 52, 83n.81, 121n.53, 170, 184n.47
Greece 14, 18, 19n.35, 20, 40, 58, 72, 73, 81, 85

Hâfiz 83, 194, 198
Hârûn al-Rashîd 181, 182–3, 185, 186, 188
Hazlitt, William 12, 48
Heffernan, James 102, 105n.16, 105n.18
hellenism 56
Hemans, Felicia 10, 113, 125, 152, 155, 178, 201
  and nature 9, 101, 124, 127, 136, 137, 138, 142
  Works:
    "An Hour of Romance" 6, 178–81, 185, 186
    Lays of Many Lands 109
    "The Mourner for the Barmecides" 178, 180–83
    Records of Woman 109
    "The Traveller at the Source of the Nile" 110–12, 127, 138, 139, 151
Herbelot, Barthélemy d' 88, 99
Horace 11, 12, 27, 32
Hugo, Victor 2, 55, 80, 84, 86, 89, 91, 99, 100, 118, 124–5, 127, 135, 201
  and mimesis 6, 55, 84, 87, 98, 101
  Works:
    "Adieux de l'hôtesse arabe" 60, 62–5, 69, 71, 73, 78, 82
    "La Douleur du pacha" 59–62, 63, 64, 65, 69, 119, 132n.72
    Hernani 70, 79
    "Novembre" 6, 59–60, 65–9, 79, 112, 163, 190, 195
    Les Orientales 9, 55–9, 61, 65, 70, 71, 73, 74, 75, 76, 79, 85, 92, 99, 102, 118, 125, 192, 195

"Les Têtes du sérail" 1
illustrations 114–8
imagination 48, 56, 59, 61, 64, 69, 75, 83, 84, 92–3, 99, 125, 141n.88, 164, 167, 168, 171, 180, 183, 191, 198
imperialism 3, 8, 17, 111, 142n.89, 165, 190n.62, 193n.69, 199n.79
India 4, 40, 99n.105, 108n.29, 109, 115n.46, 166
Iran 144n.93, 151n.105, 173n.34; *see also* Persia
Islam 3, 17n.28, 18, 22–5, 33n.74, 39, 58n.11, 88, 121, 123–5, 144, 146, 169, 172, 189, 194
Italy 40, 72, 165

Jeffrey, Francis 43n.94, 46, 47, 51
Jerusalem 121, 123
Johnson, Samuel 11, 12, 27, 48
Jones, William 3, 83, 154n.114, 172n.32

Koran; *see* Qur'an

Landor, Walter Savage 6, 10, 155, 178, 180, 186, 201
    Works:
        Gebir 17n.28, 31, 173n.33
        "The Nightingale and Rose" 171–5, 177, 185
Lane, Edward 4n.11, 36n.78, 172n.32
Leask, Nigel 8, 17
Leconte de Lisle, Charles 118, 147, 152, 201
    and art 10, 155, 157–8, 180
    and nature 9, 101, 135, 142, 153
    Works:
        "Le Désert" 119–25, 126, 127, 129, 131, 132, 163
        "L'Orient" 6, 158–64, 176, 184n.46
        "Le Palmier" 160n.11
        Poèmes barbares 118
Levant 40n.84, 123, 158, 161n.14, 163n.15, 178, 189
literary convention 2, 6, 9, 10, 59, 61, 76, 79, 85, 93, 97–100, 176, 179, 184, 191, 198, 200
local color, as literary device 34, 58, 59, 86, 89, 99, 119
Lowe, Lisa 8, 21n.39, 25, 44n.100, 51n.126, 54, 61, 63n.24, 168n.23, 195n.73

McFarland, Thomas 83n.79, 84, 93, 102n.5, 105, 106, 120
MacKenzie, John 7
Makdisi, Saree 8, 17n.26, 64, 101, 108n.29, 113, 140, 141n.88, 157, 160
Mecca 123
meter, poetic 45, 50–52, 97, 193
mimesis 5, 10, 47–9, 53, 55, 59–61, 69, 72, 75–6, 79, 84, 87, 91–2, 95, 96, 102, 115, 149, 152, 201; *see also* representation, literary
    destabilization of 6, 9, 12, 51–3, 64–5, 74, 78, 81–2, 83, 85, 89–90, 93, 94, 100, 125, 128, 130–31, 133, 136, 141, 154, 155, 169, 170–71, 178, 201
    and Orient 3, 4, 58, 66, 70, 118, 125, 141, 152, 153, 154n.114, 155, 191, 195
Mitchell, Timothy 7, 76, 174n.35
modernity 8, 101, 112, 125, 135
Mohammed; *see* Muḥammad
Monthly Review 45, 46, 47
Moore, Thomas 10, 104, 155, 180, 128n.67, 178, 201
    Works:
        "Beauty and Song" 6, 171, 175–7, 185
        Lalla Rookh 115, 117, 118, 175n.39, 1778n.41
        illustration for 115, 116–18
Moses 133–4, 135
Muʻallaqât 30n.69, 83, 147n.99
Muḥammad 67, 121, 123
Musset, Alfred de 6, 9, 55, 84, 201
    Works:
        A quoi rêvent les jeunes filles 80
        Lorenzaccio 79
        "Namouna" 9, 55, 70, 76, 79–100

Naddaff, Sandra 51
nature 3, 8, 9, 52, 71, 72, 74, 75, 80, 102–5, 115, 145, 152, 168, 175–8, 186–7
    displacement of 101, 124, 129–30, 132, 134, 135, 136, 141, 152, 157, 160, 173–4, 176–7, 179,

180, 184, 188, 195, 199, 200–201
imitation of; *see* mimesis
Orient as unnatural 10, 21, 101, 103, 106–8, 111–13, 117–21, 123–4, 128, 132, 135–8, 140–41, 146, 147, 151, 152, 154, 155–6, 169–70, 184, 201
  relation with humans 106–9, 111–12, 120–21, 123, 127, 129, 135, 136, 137–44, 146–8, 150–52, 182, 201
  and supernatural 42, 48, 49, 72
neoclassicism 9, 48, 50, 51, 55, 59, 65, 69, 70, 72–5, 79, 85, 154n.114, 174, 199
Nerval, Gerard de 126
Nizâmî 193, 198
Norway 165, 168
Nubia 60, 61, 165, 168

Ollier, Charles 23
order, as stereotype 79, 90, 190; *see also* disorder
"oriental tale" 26, 28, 30, 46–7, 50, 52, 53, 76, 85, 86, 98
orientalist poetics 2, 8, 10, 12, 60, 69, 152, 169, 201
ornament, as orientalist motif 40, 41, 50–53, 64, 83n.81, 153, 157, 160–61, 170–71, 184, 198

Palestine 178
Paris 65–8, 192, 195
Parnassianism 6, 118, 119, 125, 155
Peacock, Thomas Love 103, 154
Persia 4, 40, 42, 51, 58, 142n.89, 154n.114, 171, 172, 174, 175, 177, 186, 193
Plato 101
plot, literary 10, 46, 47, 86
Pococke, Edward 37
Poland 40, 42
Portugal 30, 40, 42

Qur'an 28, 33, 57, 123n.56, 193

Racine, Jean 70–71, 73
repetition, textual 26, 41, 43, 51–2, 82, 87, 94, 186
representation, literary 3, 5, 9, 47–55, 58–61, 64–6, 68–9, 74–6, 78–9, 81–5, 87–9, 91–100, 128, 141, 152, 154, 155, 195, 201; *see also* mimesis
Reynolds, Joshua 11–12
Richardson, Alan 27, 28, 76
Riffaterre, Michael 130, 131, 133, 136
Rodinson, Maxime 7
romanticism 6, 8, 16, 17n.28, 55, 58n.11, 70, 72, 81–2, 83, 84, 88, 89, 99n.105, 101, 106–7, 108, 112, 113, 118, 119, 121, 125, 129–30, 132, 135, 136, 137, 138, 140, 143, 146, 147, 149, 151, 152, 153, 155, 174–5, 176, 177, 178, 187, 191
Rossetti, William Michael 26–7
rural environment 9, 102, 106–7, 120, 136, 139–40, 147, 159

Saglia, Diego 41n.87, 44, 51, 52n.130, 76n.55, 141
Said, Edward 2, 5n.17, 6–8, 16, 18n.30, 28n.59, 36n.78, 42n.90, 50, 54, 65, 83n.76, 87, 100, 174n.35
Schlegel, Friedrich 50
Schwab, Raymond 2, 6, 56n.4, 63n.24, 113, 119n.50, 192n.68
Scotland 110–11, 138, 139, 151
Scott, Walter 12, 104, 178, 180
sexism 21, 24–5
Seyhan, Azade 16, 35, 52, 81–2, 83, 87, 88, 89, 96, 99n.105
Shakespeare, William 193–4, 198
Sharafuddin, Mohammed 8, 17n.28, 33n.74, 36n.78, 42n.88, 113n.43, 141n.88
Shelley, Percy Bysshe 2, 13, 21, 25, 28, 55, 100, 105, 201
  Works:
    A Defence of Poetry 12, 32, 49
    Hellas 18, 19n.35, 23n.42, 26n.55
    "The Lady of the South" 1
    Laon and Cythna 23–4; *see The Revolt of Islam*
    "Ozymandias" 17, 105n.19, 197n.77
    The Revolt of Islam 9, 12–30, 32, 52–4, 63, 100, 105, 146
Sidney, Philip 11, 12, 48
slavery 17–21, 24–5, 76, 81
Southey, Robert 55, 75, 80n.65, 92, 104,

113, 172n.32, 186, 201
and poetry as information 2, 29–30, 32, 33, 42, 61; *see also* didacticism
Works:
The Curse of Kehama 12, 50
Roderick, the Last of the Goths 44, 141
Thalaba the Destroyer 6, 9, 12, 28–54, 61, 64, 82, 93, 97, 104, 113, 115, 117, 118, 178n.41
illustration for 114, 115, 117–8
Spain 57–9, 73, 74, 76, 81, 85, 126n.62, 130n.69, 134, 153
stereotype 16, 26, 35, 34n.75, 43, 62–3, 65, 66n.29, 68, 100, 120, 135, 153n.110, 155, 159, 165, 179, 183, 185, 188, 194, 200
supernatural, the 46, 49, 61, 72, 104, 113, 121, 123, 135, 157, 168, 170, 179, 201; *see also* nature
Syria 119, 123, 124, 179, 180, 184

Taylor, William 45, 47
Tennyson, Alfred 136, 152, 171n.29, 178, 201
and art 2, 6, 10, 155, 186, 188
and nature 9, 101, 147, 153, 188
Works:
Idylls of the King 152
"On a Mourner" 148–50
"The Palace of Art" 187–92, 201
"Persia" 1, 151n.105
"Recollections of the Arabian Nights" 183–7, 188, 191, 201
"Written by an Exile of Bassorah, while sailing down the Euphrates" 147, 149–52
Thackeray, William 169
Thousand and One Nights 3, 4–5, 26–7, 30, 32–3, 42n.89, 44, 60, 83, 85, 86, 95, 96, 98, 151, 173n.33, 174n.36, 181n.43, 182, 183–6
timelessness, as stereotype of Orient 16–17, 26, 62–5, 172, 182, 184, 185, 200

Turkey 14, 16, 18, 19n.35, 20, 21, 25n.49, 51, 58, 73, 76, 78, 126n.62, 128, 154n.114, 166
Turner, Brian S. 7
tyranny 17–26, 29
religion as 21–2, 24–5

urban environment 136, 146–7, 151

verisimilitude 5, 26, 130
Volney, Constantin-François 37, 39, 105n.19

Wilde, Oscar 2, 153–5, 171n.29, 173, 201
and art 6, 10, 153–4
Works:
"Athanasia" 199–200
"The Decay of Lying" 2, 153, 200, 201
Wollstonecraft, Mary 25, 30n.69
Wordsworth, William 104–6, 113, 125, 152, 201
and art 10, 149, 155, 157, 180
and nature 2, 6, 9, 101, 102–9, 112, 120–21, 124, 127, 129, 135, 136, 137, 138, 140–42, 149, 158, 159–60, 169n.25, 176, 177, 199
Works:
"The Haunted Tree" 155–7, 160–61, 184n.46
"I wandered lonely as a cloud" 132
"Mary Barker's Lines Addressed to a Noble Lord" 1
"*A Poet!* He hath put his heart to school" 157n.3
Preface, *Lyrical Ballads* 9n.25
The Prelude 84, 104, 105, 157n.6, 189n.59
"Ruth" 105, 107
"Septimi Gades" 6, 104, 105, 107–9, 111, 112, 120, 124, 127, 131, 139, 147, 149, 151, 194
"The Solitary Reaper" 104, 105

Yegenoglu, Meyda 7